Child Care: Sense and Fable

Patricia Morgan
CHILD CARE
Sense and Fable

Temple Smith · London

First published in Great Britain 1975
by Maurice Temple Smith Ltd
37 Great Russell Street, London WC1
© 1974 Patricia Morgan
ISBN 0 8511 7059 5
Printed in Great Britain by
Billing & Sons Ltd, Guildford and London

Contents

For Jim Miller

*It is one of the characteristic prejudices of the
reaction of the nineteenth century against the
eighteenth, to accord to the unreasoning elements
in human nature the infallibility which the
eighteenth century is supposed to have ascribed to
the reasoning elements. For the apotheosis of
Reason we have substituted that of Instinct; and
we call everything instinct which we find in
ourselves and for which we cannot trace any
rational foundation. This idolatry, infinitely more
degrading than the other, and the most pernicious
of the false worships of the present day, of all of
which it is now the main support, will probably
hold its ground until it gives way before a sound
psychology laying bare the real root of much that
is bowed down to as the intention of Nature and
the ordinance of God.*

*John Stuart Mill,
The Subjection of Women, 1869*

Foreword

This book deals with one of the best-known psychological theories of our time; one, moreover, which has many important social consequences, and which, if true, might be crucial to our estimation of certain social institutions and customs. The Maternal Deprivation Theory is concerned with environmental influences which make for a healthy mental and emotional development of the child; it centres on the role and function of the mother, and thus, again if true, has far-reaching consequences for the development of more egalitarian sexual *mores* in our society, and for the elimination of taboos on working mothers. Most people who are familiar with the theory are probably under the confident impression that there is ample experimental and observational evidence to demonstrate that the theory is in fact, if not 'true' in any absolute sense, yet at least along the right lines, and supported by the evidence which is available. There is also a widespread belief that this evidence is based on properly controlled and designed studies; that the results of these studies are relevant to the theory; and that they bear out the theory in important aspects.

Unfortunately, as the author of this important critical review of the evidence makes clear, none of these beliefs can be supported. The studies on which the theory of maternal deprivation is based are badly designed, poorly controlled and executed, and often irrelevant to the theory they are supposed to support. The theory itself is internally contradictory, and derives from principles which themselves are at best doubtful, and at worst discredited. Furthermore, there is now good evidence, deriving from proper experimental studies, which emphatically goes counter to the tenets of the theory. If the theory itself is as important as its proponents believe, and as many psychiatrists, psychologists, social workers, teachers and medical men would seem to think, then clearly this excellent review of the literature, which for the first time exposes it to a proper scrutiny, also is of very great importance. I believe that the destruction of this myth will have a wonderfully liberating influence on many people who have felt fearful or constrained in going counter to its teachings. The general tenor of Freudian teaching has always been anti-feminist; it is always the mother who is blamed for whatever neurotic or psychotic disasters overwhelm the growing child. Yet there has always been a complete absence of any evidence supporting these beliefs; it is good to see the facts spelled out in detail in connection with at least one of the many theories relating to the mother—child relationship.

It is perhaps rather sad that the major contribution which psychology has made to our knowledge of important social phenomena has been the creation of myths, from the Oedipus complex to maternal deprivation. Fortunately, psychology has also given us a methodology which enables us to disprove these myths, and put them in their place. Possibly, also, we may not be able to absolve society completely from blame; many educated people have in the past only been too happy to embrace these myths with considerable eagerness, without looking at the evidence on which they were so tenuously based. It is this combination of myth-makers and myth-consumers which has proved to be such a barrier to the desirable goal of making psychology more scientific; as bad money drives out good, according to Gresham's Law, so bad but popular theories drive out good theories, which may not be so easy to understand, and appreciation of which necessitates looking at the details of complex experimental studies. But where truth is complex, we have no real choice; purely verbal solutions to our problems are inadequate, however much they may please the novelist and the poet. Hard, experimental, quantitive evidence is the only medium of exchange which science recognises; facile semantics is the prerogative of politics. We are indebted to the author of this book for introducing respect for facts into an area in which for too long speculation has been rampant; mothers in particular should read and ponder the conclusions which are of the utmost importance for the sort of decisions which they have to make more and more about the kind of life they wish to lead.

H.J. EYSENCK

Introduction

This book is about the Maternal Deprivation Theory, simply because that theory has played a remarkably influential role in a whole system of social attitudes and beliefs in Western countries since the war. Briefly stated, the theory is that the *unbroken care of one mother* is vital to every infant, not just for its immediate welfare and contentment, but for its future mental and emotional health. It has been a definite scientific discovery, we are told, that deprivation of this indivisible mother-love in infancy leads to irreversible personality damage of a more or less serious kind, having a wide range of ill-effects both on the individual and society.

The theory is representative of a network of ideas which have become established in the last couple of decades or so. One could call this network an ideology, since it combines fact with value judgements, theory with practice, explanation with emotive reassurance, in a way that provides maximum insulation from rational criticism at any given point. It extends to such diverse matters as education, anthropology, criminology, social policy, ethics; and at its centre is a profoundly new view of childhood.

The ideology can best be identified through a number of leading beliefs which are almost universally shared, at least in their broad form. Early childhood is held to be by far the most crucial period in forming the adult's personality, abilities and future mental condition. For good or ill, the basis for these is laid by about five years of age, after which room for change, even given the most favourable of circumstances, is limited. The vital process taking place during these five years is explained in an environmentalist way, in the sense that important differences between individuals must ultimately be traceable to different patterns of early experience. But the account is not environmentalist in the older sense of supposing the child a *tabula rasa* at birth, a piece of clay which can be moulded in almost any direction by the appropriate training and teaching. On the contrary, the newborn infant has a distinctly human nature, consisting of basic psychological drives, needs and fears, whose growth must go through certain stages, which can be nourished and satisfied or repressed and thwarted, but cannot be eradicated or fundamentally altered. Experiences are manifested as extremely powerful, total impressions, having profound effects on the child which are quite unlike their discriminate, assimilable character in an adult. Thus the optimum environment for a child is not one of active interference and imposition, but a more passive one of protection, of insulation from potentially damaging frustrations and stresses: of satisfying the child's basic 'needs', and allowing its natural propensities to unfold in their own way in an atmosphere of trusting security. The pattern should not be dictated by the demands of an adult's values and culture, but by the given, spontaneous 'needs' of the child itself, to which the adult should sympathetically respond. Indeed, attempts to mould the child in accordance with cultural expectations are seen as dangerous and productive of later mental disturbance.

The last idea is most important, since it implies that there is a natural, universal course of development for the human personality, which is prior to any particular human culture. Once this course is discovered, child-rearing practices cease to be culturally relative and like medicine, become scientifically based on the most effective techniques for furthering this underlying potential. Indeed, cultures themselves, it is suggested, acquire their characteristics from the personalities of their individual members, which in turn are formed in early parent–child interaction. (The ideology is better described as naturalist rather than environmentalist.) The really effective factors in the environment which create the adult person, and thus transmit a certain social distribution of character types, attributes, handicaps and inequalities to the next generation, are those which operate in the years before a child enters the wider community – in a pre-cultural, private realm of individual relationships. These factors are not, as was once believed, the inculcation of explicit norms, values and habits, the rational learning of a culture through the conscious efforts of the parents: they are the primitive and vastly more powerful unconscious influences of acceptance or rejection, fear, guilt, love and hatred, operating through the infant psyche.[1]

Crucial to this whole process of adult-creation, and having the most momentous consequences, is the presence (or absence) of a secure, unimpaired 'love' relationship with one mother. Or, if not this, at least the uninterrupted presence of one mother which, like living in a 'family' (a unit of biological parents and offspring), is in itself intrinsically good and, often in spite of its members, diffuses a benefical influence.

It is fairly easy to see how the Maternal Deprivation Theory comes to occupy a strategic place in the picture, representing and encapsulating so many of the ideas which form what I have loosely termed an ideology. But it has also come to occupy this position because it is widely believed that the Theory (unlike others) has been strikingly confirmed by experimental studies of children. Today there is hardly a person who is not familiar with the Theory in one version or another, thanks to the powerful support it enjoys among doctors, child-care experts, journalists and broadcasters. There are differences in emphasis and detail among the experts, and some greatly over-simplified accounts of the Theory going about. But the main proposition is not in dispute.

Needless to say, the implications have been profound. Motherhood has been raised to a position of unprecedented importance: 'A mother's job is inevitably exacting, especially when her children are small. It is a craftsman's job and perhaps the most skilled in the world.'[2] It has become an awe-inspiring responsibility, requiring skill, dedication and psychological insight. The well-meaning advice of a previous generation is found to be not only unreliable, but in many instances positively harmful: through new understanding of the infant psyche it is seen how secondary the effects of training and explicit education are when compared with the unconscious processes triggered by the earliest experiences. The mother today may well feel that she cannot rely to any great extent on the school, peer-group, friends or relatives to help in providing her child's elementary lessons about the

world; she may be convinced that it is she who largely
constitutes the environment that ultimately decides whether
he will grow up intelligent or dull, emotionally free or
immature and repressed, loving and cooperative or
'affectionless' and hating the world.

The movement for female liberation, to be taken at all
seriously, could not afford to dispute that mothers must
somehow reconcile their emancipation with giving priority to
their young children. Before the days of widely-available
contraception it was said that woman's social disadvantages
stemmed from the 'biological tragedy' of her profuse
reproduction — the tyranny of the womb. Now this has been
broken, she might be inclined to feel that it has been neatly
replaced by a new, equally implacable Fact of Nature: her
child's need for her uninterrupted, undivided and devoted
attention.

Although most husbands spend far more time at home
than they did a generation ago, they have not generally
extended, or even exercised, their traditional role as the
children's trainers and mentors. Rather, their principal task is
defined as earning enough to provide the (extremely
expensive) child-centred environment in which their own
child's potential can blossom. In emergencies they may play
the role of 'Spare Mum',[3] but it is not advocated that they
compete with the mother—infant tie. It is seen as preferable
that their relationship with their children, at least when the
latter are very young, be via the mother: through making her
secure, content and free from outside worries. Home and
family are where the modern male's emotional commitments
are usually located — or where they should be encouraged to
be located. Women may not have become emancipated but
men have become domesticated, and the necessity for links
with relatives, friends or any communal group outside the
family has diminished. The 'new' family of the postwar
world, with both partners deeply devoted to their offspring
has been widely acclaimed (particularly by sociologists) as
the great social success of the century.[4]

The policies of social welfare agencies have also had to be
revised in the light of the radical discovery that a person's
important human qualities are largely formed in the years
before he goes to school. Even the class structure of society,

which was previously seen as being based on the ownership and control of wealth and the relationships of production these generate, is now felt by many to be sustained primarily by unequal infant environments. The way to improve the opportunities in life of the unskilled working class, for example, is to improve the 'mothering' and attention which the children receive in the family. Deprivation, illiteracy, deliquency and even cruelty to children have been dealt with, not by replacing or supplementing parental by other influences, but by supporting and investing in the home, no matter how inadequate it seems. However intolerable the child's home conditions, complete separation is thought to have effects yet more intolerable. And to support this hard contention, the hapless, abandoned inmates of austere and inhuman institutions are pointed to, the assumption frequently being that these child-rearing arrangements are the only possible alternative to the nuclear family.

The corrective and rehabilitating effects of school, community or extra-familial environment for the child have been pushed far into the background. Where they are resorted to, it is with a bad conscience and a sense of calculated risk, as being at best very inadequate substitutes for parental love, and at worst, possible agencies of even further warping and alienation. Delinquency and marked anti-social tendencies are nearly always traced to lack of love somewhere in the past — usually early childhood. The only real way to prevent crime is to ensure that all children have truly loving homes: if this is successful, the rest will surely follow, and most of the need for clumsy, quasi-punitive measures later on will be mercifully avoided.

The changes in ideas and motive forces have been considerable. But so, too, has been the underlying revolution in child psychology. Given what is known about the crucial effects of maternal deprivation on later personality development, these changes are surely reasonable, and represent an unqualified advance.

The main criticism of them, however, is that we have no particular reason to believe that the Maternal Deprivation Theory is true. Contrary to the impression of social workers, doctors, educationists, teachers, welfare agencies — almost everyone except academic departments and certain hospitals — the Theory is not grounded in well-controlled experiments and investigations in psychology but stems from psychoanalysis, which has never been a scientifically grounded discipline, but always a speculative enquiry, endlessly fertile and fascinating, but quite resistant to any clear, empirical testing.

Nor, contrary to the general impression, has later analytical psychology been made more scientific by modified formulations which abandon the wilder mythologies of Freud. In some hands the myths have been watered down, or more usually, changed to suit the sentiments of the times (for example, Freud's fierce patriarchal authoritarianism is replaced by an emphasis on love and unrepressed libidinal expression). But the clinical insight of the analyst is paramount, and the theories are in no way publicly testable. The stark fact is — and there is no point in being pussyfooted about it — that the theories of psychoanalysis, whether in the new or the old packaging, have no more empirical support than mesmerism or palmistry.

In spite of this, psychoanalysis has so shaped our intellectual beliefs in this century that many of its classic ideas about human personality and motivation, however unsupported by evidence, have become part of 'commonsense' wisdom. Its popularity, by contrast with experimental psychology, has been in part due to the exaggerated hopes which have been placed on it, of finding explanations for all important aspects of human mentality, and thereby a key to much else. More has been demanded, and promised, than a scientific psychology could reasonably undertake to give, and the influence of psychoanalysis on intellectual and artistic thought has been incalculable. Theories that attempt to explain the sum total of human experience and that, furthermore, can be mastered in a very short time, are infinitely more exciting than fragmentary data which, after years of cautious, repetitious experiments, still only illuminate the surface of human psychology.

The interests of psychoanalysis have been further advanced by the rapid expansion of education, particularly adult education, since the Second World War. To satisfy the demand for psychology courses for doctors, teachers, social workers, nurses and interested laymen of all kinds, course planners and teachers have been recruited from other disciplines. They have assumed psychology to be psychoanalysis, and duly taught the same. For these and other reasons, the content of what passes for psychology has been largely determined by a lay public that has imbibed the theories of psychoanalysis and will often defend them fervently.

It has consequently not been difficult for the professional psychoanalysts (or 'dynamic psychologists' or 'clinicians') to popularise great quantities of 'reasearch studies' which have employed questionable methods and taken entirely for granted certain unproven principles in the psychoanalytic tradition—for example, that an infant has quite definite and discoverable thoughts and concepts about the world, which employ a different 'logic' from that of adults; or that any stress in childhood is alien and potentially traumatising, and that any momentary unhappiness can be construed as stress. When cornered about methodological issues, psychologists of the 'dynamic' or analytical school will often drop the garb of science and argue that human beings cannot be studied by experimental methods like laboratory objects. Where such arguments reach the public — as they are now increasingly. doing — a common result is either woolly confusion, or a completely relativist 'Oh-well-there's-two-schools-of-thought-take-your-pick' attitude.

However, my central criticism of the Maternal Deprivation Theory does not even depend on one's views of psychoanalysis, but on the fact that, for about twenty years, the public, including the most influential bodies responsible for social policy-making, has been persuaded that the connection between maternal deprivation and personality damage has been scientifically established, and that it enjoys the same kind of authoritative standing as other medical discoveries — such as the connection between German measles in pregnancy and congenital defects in the offspring. Indeed, proponents of the Theory have openly compared its standing with our discoveries about the after-effects of rubella in foetal life, and of Vitamin D deficiency in infancy. But the true position is not remotely like this. By experimental standards as strict and coherent as those applied in the case of rubella, for example, the Maternal Deprivation

Theory has no significant scientific support, and there is sufficient counter-evidence to make it decidedly improbable.

Very recently there has appeared the only detailed critical examination of the Maternal Deprivation Theory outside academic journals. Michael Rutter's *Maternal Deprivation Reassessed*[5] does not engage in methodological controversies, but simply assesses the best experimental evidence available for the theory. He shows much deference to its adherents, and goes to great lengths to suggest what connections they might have discovered but misinterpreted. But in the end, after twenty years of research, he can only conclude that there is no proper evidence (except perhaps in an extremely extended sense in which both the terms 'maternal' and 'deprivation' are inapplicable). In fact, the most telling criticisms of maternal deprivation studies — of their experimental methods, their findings and the conclusions drawn from them — were made years ago in the professional journals by psychologists such as Pinneau, O'Connor, Casler and others.

The main body of this book will consist of a search for the figure termed 'the affectionless thief' — the inadequate, love-craving delinquent, incapable of forming deep relationships with anyone, and expressing his inadequacy in criminality. Is this kind of warped personality the result of being deprived of a mother's love in the early years? I shall examine in detail the original research which led to this supposition, and then look at many further attempts to confirm it, while, at the same time, trying to discover connections between the distinct variables of capacity to love, delinquency, personality defects, a happy and loving childhood, and an unbroken connection with one mother. I will examine what we know about personality and its methods of assessment, its genetic, organic and environmental components, and in particular their connection with psychopathy, a disability closely associated with violent criminality and frequently attributed to maternal deprivation. In trying to find evidence that early experiences have irreversible consequences, I will look closely at the classic studies on institutionally-reared children, which have been used as evidence of the damage which an upbringing outside the home can cause.

The concept of the affectionless thief and his otherwise inadequate brothers can be traced back to the theories of Kleinian psychoanalysis. Later chapters examine the standing of Klein's theories and the whole claim of psychoanalysis to provide knowledge about people. More recently, the theoretical basis of the Maternal Deprivation Theory has shifted away from Kleinian theory, and advocates of the theory have looked hopefully at the studies of non-human primates instead (using principally the famous work of the Harlows on Rhesus monkeys — see below). The attempt to make instinct theory do what was previously done by libido theory is part of a widespread popularisation of ethological ideas. They are being eagerly seized on as yielding profound discoveries about the inherent and eternal nature of man. The primate studies, for example, valid and important in themselves, are relevant to the Maternal Deprivation Theory ultimately only as they seem to offer more security in the long run for psychoanalytically-derived doctrines. But the real question is surely the desirability of saving those doctrines at all. Why should we, as serious and responsible people, faced with the very real and widespread problems of our society, still allow ourselves to be influenced by a radically misleading view of child psychology?

This is far from being a theoretical question, for the whole a-cultural, psychoanalytically inspired view of childhood has had some disturbing consequences. It has caused appalling misery in children forced to remain, on the direct advice of Maternal Deprivation Theorists, in the control of violent, cruel or hopelessly negligent parents when they could very probably have had a happier childhood and a better future away from such homes. It is estimated that between four and six hundred children die each year from parental violence and neglect and that many thousands more suffer serious injuries, some (such as brain damage) likely to handicap them permanently.

It has also been used to enforce an unnecessary social seclusion on women with consequent wastage of their abilities and impoverishment of their lives. Over the last few decades there is hardly an ill that flesh is heir to that has not been laid at the door of a lack of maternal care and devotion.

The weight of guilt and fear pressing on woman has been, and continues to be, enormous.

But above all, there has been an abdication by society of responsibility for educating the young in any social skills, norms and values. The isolating effects of rehousing, geographical and social mobility, combined with the belief that compulsory learning is thwarting to the child and that social adequacy and competence have their source in the emotions of early familial interaction, have created a situation in which, gradually, human culture is failing to be handed on. Delinquency, violence, illiteracy, truancy and other indices of social breakdown rise phenomenally, despite a record expenditure on education and family welfare, a higher absolute standard of material life and far greater priority accorded to children, both popularly and officially.

My final chapter attempts to trace in detail the postwar social background within which these profoundly mistaken theories have come to be so widely accepted, and to examine what other attitudes will have to change if they are abandoned. I argue that a rejection, for scientific reasons, of the erroneous view of childhood must involve us in very wide reappraisals of our assumptions about society, ones which transcend most of the current controversies in education and welfare. And those reappraisals need to be faced soon.

1 In Search of
the Affectionless Thief

1 Maternal Deprivation

Among the most important developments of psychiatry during the past quarter of a century has been the steady growth of evidence that the quality of the parental care that a child receives in his earliest years is of vital importance for his future mental health.[1]

John Bowlby, the most eminent of maternal deprivation theorists, begins his monograph, *Maternal Care and Mental Health,* in this way. The work was prepared for the World Health Organisation, in response to its request for advice on the mental health problems of homeless children. The monograph appeared in popular form in 1953, as *Child Care and the Growth of Love.* Two new chapters by Mary D. Salter-Ainsworth, bringing the material up to date, were added in the 1965 edition.[2] The work has been tremendously popular, rarely being absent from any book-counter offering even the most limited range of serious paperback literature, during the past two decades. It is still essential reading for students in most branches of the social sciences, for intending teachers, for all those connected with welfare work, for people attending courses of Liberal or Social Studies, for the well-informed, up-to-date doctor or nurse and, of course, for conscientious, educated parents concerned with their child's future development.

Bowlby's particular contribution to early experience theories is one which has rightly caused much concern among those responsible for the welfare of the young — particularly mothers. It is summed up in his assertion that 'For the moment it is sufficient to say that what is believed to be essential for mental health is that an infant and young child should experience a warm, intimate, and continuous relationship with his mother (or permanent mother substitute — one person who steadily "mothers" him) in which both find satisfaction and enjoyment.' And, 'A state of affairs in which a child does not have this relationship is termed "maternal deprivation" '.[3]

Maternal deprivation, it appears, has harmful effects, varying in seriousness with the degree of separation. Partial separation, for example, removal for a short while from the mother's care to that of someone else gives rise to deprivation that '. . . will be relatively mild if he [the child] is then looked after by someone whom he has already learned to know and trust, but may be considerable if the foster-mother even though loving is a stranger. All these arrangements however, give a child some satisfaction and are therefore examples of *partial deprivation*.'[4] The result of partial deprivation may be expressed by: 'anxiety, excessive need for love, powerful feelings of revenge, and, arising from these last, guilt and depression. A young child, still immature in mind and body, cannot cope with all these emotions and drives. The way in which he responds to these disturbances of his inner life may in the end bring about nervous disorders and instability of character.'[5]

Complete deprivation, where a child 'has no *one* person who cares for him in a personal way and with whom he can feel secure'[6] which appears to be 'not uncommon in institutions, residential nurseries and hospitals',[7] leads to 'far-reaching effects on character development, and may entirely cripple the capacity to make relationships with other people'.[8] It is found that 'A child's development is almost always retarded — physically, intellectually, and socially — and symptoms of physical and mental illness may appear'.[9]

Is this likely to be permanent? In Bowlby's view '. . . some children are grossly damaged for life. This is a sombre conclusion, which must now be regarded as established'.[10] At what age is damage most likely to be done? 'All children', according to Bowlby, 'under about seven years of age seem to be in danger of injury, and some of the effects are clearly discernible within the first few weeks of life'.[11] Continuing research into the problem seems to reveal an increasingly bleak prospect: 'Some observers, however, are now definitely of the opinion that damage is frequently done by changes even as early as three months.'[12] How long does this 'deprivation' have to go on to produce such a state? Would it be produced by total removal from the original mother at an early age to somewhere and someone else? In answer Bowlby says, 'Some observers believe that after three months of deprivation there is a qualitative change, after which recovery is rarely if ever complete.'[13] In other statements by Bowlby it is intimated that this change is capable of occurring after a few weeks' separation. The distinction between partial and total deprivation is rather vague:

> No observation is more common than that of a child separated for a few weeks or months during the second, third or fourth years failing to recognise his mother on reunion. It is probable that this is sometimes a true failure to recognise, based on a loss of the capacity to abstract and identify . . . So far from idolising their parents and wishing to become like them, one side of their nature hates them and wishes to avoid having anything to do with them. This is what brings about aggressively bad or delinquent behaviour; it may also lead ultimately to suicide which is an alternative to murdering his parents.[14]

Burlington and Anna Freud, respected authorities in the field, favour *one day* as the length of time after which the effects of total deprivation become operative.[15]

Is there any way of helping those afflicted with the consequences of maternal deprivation? Cannot modern medicine, which has made such remarkable advances elsewhere in the last century or so, offer any sort of cure, or at least alleviate the more distressing symptoms? Here, I am afraid, Bowlby is driven to endorse the bleak conclusions of Goldfarb, another dedicated worker and expert on the subject of maternal deprivation and its consequences: 'What Dr Goldfarb's work demonstrates without any doubt is that such mothering is almost useless if delayed until after the age of two and a half years. In actual fact this upper age limit for most babies is probably before twelve months.'[16]

With all his experience in the field, Dr Goldfarb himself has to conclude that he has never seen even *one* recovery after psychiatric treatment.[17]

The hope of finding a cure in the near future would seem dim indeed. For if the prerequisite for mental normality, that is, the establishment of a relationship with one particular person, is not accomplished satisfactorily during the first twelve months or so of life, there is the greatest difficulty in making it good, as '. . . the character of the psychic tissue has become fixed. (The limit for many children may well be a good deal earlier.)'[18] This appears even more alarming as the shortcomings and iniquities of the mother are visited on the children, and for many generations:

> The maladjusted and unstable parent met as the cause of child neglect is clearly as often as not the grown-up affectionless, maladjusted child, described earlier as one of the most unhappy products of maternal deprivation. Here again are the fickleness and irresponsibility, the inaccessibility to help, the superficial relationships, the promiscuous sexual behaviour, with all of which the reader will have already become familiar.[19]

Having established the cause of undesirable behaviour, the outcome of future investigation is predicted: 'It is, therefore, probably safe to predict that when a study of parents guilty of physical cruelty to their children is made, personality disturbances will prove the rule and that these will be found often to be the result of deprivation or rejection in childhood.'[20] Deprivation also seems to be the cause of breaches of the moral code by individuals: '. . . the girl who has a socially unacceptable illegitimate baby often comes from an unsatisfactory family background and has developed a neurotic character, the illegitimate baby being in the nature of a symptom of her psychological ill-health.'[21] Unhappy marriage, desertion, separation and divorce are added to the formidable list of ills following in the wake of deprivation. What is more, according to Dr Spock, the deprived infant not only rejects his fellow mortals, but the Deity Himself: 'If there is no one to love a baby (as was true in certain cold, understaffed orphanages in the olden days) he grows up with a shallow, irresponsible personality and with little or no capacity to love anybody, including God.'[22]

The isolation of such an important factor in the causation of mental ill-health, anti-social conduct and mental retardation has had important repercussions on preventive medicine (the possibilities of cure being virtually non-existent with our present limited techniques).

Beginning with the person who is best placed to avoid the disastrous consequences of deprivation, the mother herself, Bowlby gives the following advice: 'I do not think that a week's holiday away from your child is worth the inevitable upset.' And a particular point: 'Leaving a child in a residential nursery is usually a bad idea. The strange surroundings and strange people are bound to upset him and, however kind the people who run it may be, not many nurseries are so planned that each child has only one person to care for him.'[23] The warnings would seem to apply not only to separation for weeks or days at a time, but where they are directed principally to the working mother suggest that separation for a number of hours is to be avoided also — for example, when Bowlby urges that incentives be provided to keep mothers at home: 'Since the mother of young children is not free, or at least should not be free, to earn, there is a strong argument for increased family allowances for children in their early years.'[24]

Those who dispute that a woman should be 'devoting herself entirely to her child' are, Bowlby suggests, themselves victims of maternal deprivation: they are unable to enjoy devotion to their children, because 'many of them may have had poor mothers themselves.'[25]

It has been almost universally agreed that, ideally, early intellectual development should take place in the home and that any nursery education that might have to be provided should concentrate on helping the child from the deprived home.[26] It is therefore not surprising that the only concession some are prepared to make towards extra-familial experience for the young child, is not the nursery school, but the play group attended by both mother and child.[27] Here the mother attends to involve herself in her child's play, instead of using the free time as an opportunity to follow interests of her own. Indeed doing this is still widely regarded with such disapproval that any claim for time for it would be likely to sabotage a campaign for nursery education. Recently a Minister for Education (Margaret Thatcher), assured us that Government plans for an expansion of nursery education intend this to be for three hours a day only, so that mothers cannot avoid their full-time task of child-care.[28]

The dangers of maternal deprivation have been recognised in other developed, but culturally different societies, such as Israel and Czechoslovakia, who have experimented with shared child-care arrangements. The insecurities and doubts, already present in such circumstances, were all greatly intensified by Bowlby's publication and others based upon his work, particularly as they appeared under the auspices of the World Health Organisation. (One prominent publication of the WHO cited creches and day nurseries as causes of permanent mental damage.)[29]

Hardly a week has gone by for many years now without even the most casual reader or listener being reminded somewhere by the media of the ills inherent in separation. The hospitalisation of children is cited as the most common reason for partial deprivation,[30] and it has formed the basis for arguments in favour of home nursing, home confinements, the admission of the mother to hospital or convalescent unit on the illness of the child, and so on. Every possible attempt is made to avoid putting a child in either short- or long-term institutional care, even where the child in question is being physically assaulted at home, or neglected to the point of being grossly malnourished, or denied medical treatment for illness or accident, or is quite delinquent and uncontrolled. For, in the words of Bowlby himself,

> He may be ill-fed and ill-sheltered, he may be very dirty and suffering from disease, he may be ill-treated, but, unless his parents have wholly rejected him, he is secure in the knowledge that there is someone to whom he is of value and will strive, even though inadequately, to provide for him until such time as he can fend for himself.[31]

Thus:

> Efforts made to 'save' a child from his bad surroundings and to give him new standards are commonly of no avail since it is his own parents who, for good or ill, he values and with whom he is identified. (This is a fact of critical

importance when considering how best to help children who are living in intolerable conditions).[32]

Advocates of the Maternal Deprivation Theory still feel that some social workers commit children to care too easily, ignoring the work that has been done in this area:

Although it is a proposition exactly similar in form to those regarding the evil after-effects of rubella in foetal life or deprivation of vitamin A in infancy, there is still a curious resistance to accepting it. Indeed, there are still psychiatrists in all countries who challenge these conclusions, though it is to be remarked that few of them have had training in child psychiatry or experience of work in a child guidance clinic.[33]

It is regrettable that they make their challenge, if Bowlby is correct when he says that 'We suggest that the evidence is now such that it leaves no room for doubt regarding the general proposition — that the prolonged deprivation of the young child of maternal care may have grave and far-reaching effects on his character and on the whole of his future life.'[34]

The claims made about the effects of maternal deprivation are, as we have seen, diverse and far-reaching. There is, for example, bad parental and marital behaviour — a particularly unpleasant manifestation of general social irresponsibility, as it has repercussions over the generations. The reason given for this conduct, as for other defects, is that the person is incapable of forming proper personal relationships or, putting it in the accepted term of Bowlby, is affectionless. Whether the manifestation of persistent delinquency is always part and parcel of this affectionless personality appears to be a matter of dispute, but most theorists either claim or insinuate that it is. This is because the capacity to build and sustain personal relationships (primarily family ones), is held to generalise to socially responsible behaviour. Morally good conduct, respect for law and the rights of others, are considered to be extensions of the feeling of 'love' or 'affection' that binds the individual in a special way to one (or a few) others in his personal, private relationships. Thus failure in the latter automatically disqualifies the person from achieving the former. He steals for the same reason that he cannot build relationships: he cannot love — hence the Affectionless Thief. This constitutes the most important and influential of the claims of the theorists, because of its wide applicability to personal and social inadequacy, and because of the special nature of the causal explanation (inability to love) linking these. The belief that anti-social tendencies result from an insufficient capacity for love and affection, which in turn originates from not having received enough love and affection when young, is very widespread today, whether or not the people who hold it adhere to a particular underlying theory.

Other common claims about the effects of maternal deprivation are that it causes intellectual retardation and stunting of physical growth (dwarfism). These ideas are particularly associated with the researcher René Spitz, who also claimed that actual death resulted from maternal deprivation. Just as Bowlby's work has helped to make the notion that criminality is due to lack of love an accepted idea, so Spitz's work has been enormously important in putting forward the assumption that infants need love for physical survival as urgently as they need food.

But before we can examine the evidence we need to look more closely at the actual concept of maternal deprivation. A great deal of confusion has resulted from loose and inadequate definitions. The one used by Mary D. Salter-Ainsworth in 1965 is as follows:

> Three diverse conditions are known to lead to severe defects: (1) when an infant or young child is separated from his mother or permanent mother-substitute and cared for in an institution where he receives insufficient maternal care; (2) when an infant or young child in his own home is given grossly insufficient maternal care by his mother or permanent mother-substitute and has no adequate mothering from other people to mitigate the insufficiency of the interaction; and (3) when a young child undergoes a series of separations from his mother and/or substitute mother-figures to each of which he has formed attachments.[35]

It would appear from this that for 'deprivation' to be avoided, the child must not merely have an unbroken relationship with one person to which all other contacts are subordinate: it must furthermore be 'mothered', as it is commonly termed. The latter is rather difficult to define. For the moment we could accept it as meaning that the child enjoys a great deal of protective affection (particularly physical), from a mother who makes it the centre of her concerns for a sizeable amount of her time. Clearly there could be situations where the child does not receive this 'mothering', and indeed, could be exposed to continual ill-treatment, yet have an unbroken relationship with one 'mother-figure'. Alternatively, a child could have plentiful 'mothering' from several persons (males as well as females), yet lack a principal 'mother-figure'. Which would constitute the greater deprivation? If it is the former, then when we speak generally of deprivation we must principally mean lack of a certain method of child care, whether in his home or in an institution. If we hold that it is the latter (that is, actual physical separation from the single mother-figure, not necessarily maternal care), which is principally depriving, then we must regard as deprivation *any* severance from the mother, quite independently of the way in which she treats the child. Because such definitions of maternal deprivation as Mary Salter-Ainsworth uses can be broken down on the basis of these two distinct and independent sets of criteria, it is continually necessary to ask which of these definitions a researcher is using. The most frequent interpretation of maternal deprivation used for purpose of research, the way in which the spokesmen for the theory usually argue their case, and the recommendations that are made following the findings, all imply that the term is being used to denote primarily physical separation from the mother. Bowlby nearly always employs such a definition in his research, and has concluded that

> The evidence suggests that three somewhat different experiences can each produce the 'affectionless' and delinquent character in some children:
>> (a) Lack of any opportunity for forming an attachment to a mother-figure during the first three years.

(b) Deprivation for a limited period — at least three months and probably more than six — during the first three or four years.

(c) Changes from one mother-figure to another during the same period.[36]

And elsewhere in the same publication: 'It must never be forgotten that even a bad parent who neglects her child is nonetheless providing much for him.' Thus 'young children thrive better in bad homes than in good institutions.'[37] Ainsworth gives paramount importance to the same definition, as she makes clear when she says:

> There is much evidence that the discontinuity of relations brought about by separation from mother or permanent substitute mother (after an attachment has been established and before the child is old enough to maintain his attachment securely throughout a period of absence) is in itself disturbing to a child, regardless of the extent to which separation ushers in a period of insufficiency. [Poor mothering]. [38]

If the Maternal Deprivation Theory were concerned solely with poor parental behaviour towards children, it would hardly have added anything new to child psychiatry. What has caused the stir has been the new supposition that mere physical separation from the mother is a pathogenic factor in its own right, outweighing other disadvantageous influences to which the child is exposed. Reformulations of the definition (for example by Ainsworth) give more emphasis to the demand that the mother must also 'mother' the child to avoid deprivation; they are perhaps reactions to criticism that the child needs more than just the physical presence of the mother for healthy development. They point to the fact that we are dealing with a tangle of child-rearing concepts when we talk of maternal deprivation, rather than with a specific, carefully delineated theory.

There are, of course, advantages to be gained from employing a theory which straddles different concepts. In the minds of the lay public and, sometimes, the specialists also, two or more of these will be conflated. Because the mother is permanently present, it is assumed that one also fulfils the role prescribed for her by modern child-care experts. Less particularised and more widespread is the notion that, quite simply and automatically, mother equals love and love equals mother. The need for a single mother and the need for 'mothering' (however this is broken down), are, of course, empirically distinct, yet in the minds of many they have often become inseparably united.

The next definitional problem we must contend with is, what length of separation from the mother constitutes deprivation? Some researchers draw a distinction between partial and total deprivation: usually the latter is a separation over three months, as is the case in Bowlby's definition quoted above, although some workers use six months. Partial deprivation seems to refer to circumstances where the child is left for weeks or days at a time, and this presumably is the type of deprivation that occurs when the mother goes out to work. Burlington and Freud,[39] as we have already seen, do not use this distinction, and would appear to consider all separation longer than one day as total. Extreme though this criterion is, it is none the less true that most researchers, having in mind a picture of the acute, episodic trauma of separation, seem to hold that separation of a day or more causes small but measurable damage, that is, implying that if children who have been separated for days at a time are compared with those who have not, the latter will be noticeably healthier mentally. After all, what is it in a separation that is posited as causing the damage, if it is not to a considerable extent the initial shock of separation? Even so, many researchers take the view that the longer the separation, the worse the damage done, because the likelihood of a complete break or severe disruption of the mother—child tie is progressively increased.

The actual ages during which separation is most depriving are generally agreed to be the famous 'first five years of life' (because of what is claimed to be their critical place in human development) with the most delicate area being between six months and three years.

With these considerations in mind I turn now to the findings on the effects of maternal deprivation: findings that render it

the height of social irresponsibility, for example, for mothers
to go out to work; findings that claim that more damage will
be done to a child by removing him from violent and cruel
parents than by leaving him a victim to their vices; findings
that claim that society will suffer less if the child is taught by
parents a way of life antagomistic to all civilised, law-abiding
mores than if he is removed to an institution or alternative
home where a more positive upbringing could be given.

In the following chapters I am going to examine carefully
the quality of this evidence.

2 Original Findings

The research work that was influential in launching the theory of maternal deprivation as a viable explanation of the origins of irreversible damage to an individual's personal and social functioning, was Bowlby's *Forty-Four Juvenile Thieves*. It has had a remarkable and widespread impact. It is often referred to as the original and major study in the field, and from it is drawn the classic picture of typical development damage. Its repercussions have been great indeed, considering its humble origins:

> This research was unplanned; it grew out of the practical problems confronting workers in a busy clinic and has all the defects inherent in such conditions. The number of cases is small, the constitution of the sample chancy, the recording of data unsystematic, the amount of data on different cases uneven. Conclusions drawn in such circumstances are clearly liable to all sorts of errors.[1]

Bowlby says that the study did not test a hypothesis, but merely framed one for later testing:

> Normally scientific research into a problem goes through at least three major phases — the correct formulation of the problem and the bright idea, the further exploration of the problem and the framing of an hypothesis, and finally the planned research designed to test the hypothesis.

So that: 'The research described here can be described as falling into phase two.'[2] It is only a 'preliminary reconnaissance'.

Bowlby divided all the cases he had seen at a child guidance clinic into those who had been reported as stealing and those who had not. The resulting group of forty-four thieves was compared with a control group equal in number, taken from the others. The latter were emotionally disturbed, but did not steal. Bowlby found that the thieves were distinguished from the controls in the following two distinct ways.

First, there were among the thieves fourteen 'affectionless' characters, but none among the controls. Secondly, seventeen of the thieves had suffered complete and prolonged separation from their mothers (six months or more) during the first five years of life; whereas only two of the controls had suffered similar experiences. Also, there was substantial overlap of those thieves who were affectionless and those thieves who had suffered separation. Of the fourteen affectionless characters, twelve were from the group of seventeen who had also suffered separation. Both the two controls who had suffered separation were schizophrenic.

Incidence of mother—child separation.[3]

Type of case	Number in which mother—child separation		Total (%)
	occurred	did not occur	
Affectionless thieves	12	2	14
Other thieves	5	25	30
All thieves	17	27	44
Control cases	2	42	44

Having obtained these figures, Bowlby seems to have moved beyond formulating a hypothesis, and concluded from them that: '...*prolonged separation of a child from his mother (or mother substitute) during the first five years of life stands foremost among the causes of delinquent character* development and persistent misbehaviour.'[4]

Elsewhere he says: 'The foregoing statistical analysis has demonstrated that the prolonged separation of a child from his mother (or mother figure) in the early years commonly leads to his becoming a persistent thief and an Affectionless Character.'[5]

If this is to be taken seriously, the research techniques he employed are indeed open to several serious criticisms. The children referred to the clinic for stealing and chosen for investigation were listed as follows, according to the seriousness of their crimes: Twenty-two whose stealing was defined as chronic and serious; ten whose stealing was defined as persistent, but consisted mainly of irregular pilferings over a longish period; eight who had carried out a few thefts; and four who had stolen on only one occasion. The bodies that had referred the children to the clinic for stealing were not the courts, as eleven of the children were under the age of criminal responsibility, and of those over the age, very few were charged. The sources[6] from which the children were referred for stealing were:

School	22
School at parents' request	2
Parents direct	8
Court at parents' request	3
Probation Officers	9
	44

The children are admitted by Bowlby to be by no means typical of delinquents who come before the courts. With this in mind, he mentions at the beginning of the study that the conclusions drawn from the material provided by the group do 'not permit of conclusions regarding the problem of delinquency as a whole'.[7] In addition, neither the thieves nor the controls were typical of the general child population, being patients at a psychiatric clinic. (Leaving aside the stealing, a third of the members of both groups showed exceptionally high intelligence.)

There is no mention of the control group having been checked for unreported stealing. This is important, since some of the reported stealing which Bowlby does mention in connection with the thief group included 'crimes' such as that of David J. (No. 16), 9.7 years, who had ' . . . together with another boy, pinched an ice-cream from a barrow when the man was not looking. Apart from this he was regarded as absolutely honest.'[8] This somewhat undermines the claim that 'The fact that we are studying mostly chronic delinquents has many advantages, the principal one being that our findings will not be diluted by the inclusion of material derived from casual and stray offenders.'[9]

What we really need is a more stable, public criterion of anti-social activity, rather than the somewhat personal assessments of parents and teachers of the seriousness of the reprehensible acts, even if this be simply court reports or convictions, which in themselves can leave a lot to be desired.

The lack of information on whether or not there was an overlap between the test and control groups on unreported stealing, is disturbingly typical of the obscurity surrounding the whole selection of the two groups. We hear that 'I have compared them [the thieves] with forty-four other children whom I have seen at the London Child Guidance Clinic. These children are an unselected series of cases who did not steal and whose age and intelligence fell between the upper and lower limits of the delinquents.'[10]

From what number of clinic cases were these children 'unselected'? Unless the clinic had only forty-four patients in these age and intelligence brackets, some form of selection must have been employed — even if only that of pulling names out of a hat. Indeed, we are told that neither the *thief* nor the *control* group is typical of the clinic intake. Why not?

> There were thirty-one boys and thirteen girls in the group, whilst in the controls the balance was even more heavily tipped towards boys, of whom there were thirty-four against ten girls. Neither of these figures is quite characteristic of the clinic intake as a whole, which is in the region of sixty per cent boys, and forty per cent girls.[11]

Correct selection of controls is a most important part of any survey investigation; but it is particularly vital to this one, since we are told that the researcher in question personally treated these children at the clinic, and was therefore likely to be familiar with their backgrounds and personalities. He could have been aware which child had been separated from its mother and which had not, *prior* to the investigation. To allow a researcher, naturally having an interest in verifying his hypothesis, such scope for unchecked selection of his research groups, does not accord at all well with standards normally expected of empirical research.

As his mention of affectionless characters indicates, Bowlby is interested in the connections of maternal deprivation with personality, as well as with stealing. He therefore sets himself the task of alotting the two groups of children to six personality categories. He says[12] (this was in 1946): 'An adequate classification of character and neurotic problems in childhood has yet to be constructed.' Therefore, 'Failing an adequate classification, I have used a relatively rough and ready division of the patients into six main groups.'[13]

One of his six categories is Normal. The five others are:

1. The Depressed — children who have been unstable and are now in a more or less depressed frame of mind.
2. The Circular — unstable children who show alternating depression and over-activity.
3. The Hyperthymic — children who tend to constant over-activity.
4. The Affectionless — children characterised by lack of normal affection, shame or sense of responsibility.
5. The Schizoid — children who show marked schizophrenic tendencies.

They were alloted to these categories after a 'careful examination of the child's personality both in its present state and in its past states.'[14]

The use of all these categories is unsatisfactory. The criticism is not that they are Bowlby's (or anybody else's), invention — after all, any new research must begin by assigning definitions to the factors whose relations it proposes to study — but that no explicit criteria are offered for membership in any of these categories. Beyond the vague explanation of terms given above ('unstable', 'over-active', etc.), Bowlby just does not specify by what methods he selected members of these groups. He simply 'carefully examined their personalities'. The result is that it is very difficult for any other researchers to attempt to repeat these findings, since they have no procedures for applying the categories and cannot know whether their assessments of, say, Circular and Hyperthymic types, coincide with Bowlby's or not.

(The results of the only public test used, the IQ test, tend to refute the claim — not specifically associated with

Bowlby — that maternal deprivation leads to mental retardation. The IQ of children in both groups was above the average for the population as a whole. Indeed, exceptionally high IQs were recorded for some individuals in the thief group, for example, a girl with 159 and a boy with 151.)

It is only fair to say that these last-mentioned methodological defects spring not from carelessness on Bowlby's part, but reflect the poor quality of the tools available for personality assessment in Britain in the 1940s. Perhaps no field of empirical psychology in this country has suffered more confusion, both in its concepts and its methods, than personality testing.

There are public, objective personality tests now in use which permit any number of researchers working separately to follow identical procedures and come up with similar findings, no matter what their own attitudes are to the hypothesis under test. These are *Actuarial* tests which use precise and impersonal scoring according to explicit scales, and which involve either the subject (Self-Report Tests),[15] or an observer (Observer-Rated Tests),[16] ticking one of a number of alternative replies to a long series of questions (such as Yes, No, Uncertain, or a larger number of choices). The number of possible replies is fixed and the actual replies obtained coded according to standardised criteria which are defined as recording the occurrence and extent in the person of certain personality attributes. The Actuarial method thus prevents the questioner interpreting the answers himself, since the meaning of any combination of replies has been laid down beforehand.

The *Clinical* approach, towards which Bowlby inclines, is intimately associated with the doctrines and practice of psychoanalysis, but may be more appropriate in individual therapeutic situations, which are independent of any research. But even here there is some doubt that the interview and life-history techniques this employs afford any better information about a subject than could be gained informally by a perceptive and sympathetic layman — everything finally depends on the validity of the theories on which these tests are based. It is now generally held that for research purposes proper, which demand a more precise and reliable result, that can be repeated over a number of subjects and a number of different testers, the Actuarial approach is superior.

Now any test which grades people according to degree and category of *abnormality*, must base its indices, finally, on some comparison of those who are, and are not, suffering from personality tendencies that are damaging – to others much as to themselves. In other words, *what is to count* as abnormality is not something that can be wholly decided by a psychologist claiming to study personality. He must start with the brute facts of real malfunctioning, just as medical science started with the brute facts of illness, and refine these into a clear and systematic form suitable for study. He is not at liberty to apply entirely *a priori* notions of abnormality, while claiming to be using the term in its standard sense.

Secondly, tests for abnormalities make no claim to assess a person's 'whole' personality, any more than tests for diabetes or TB claim to be a general examination of medical and physical type. If a person fails to show any of the trait patterns which the tests are interested in detecting, he is no longer of interest to the investigator and is consigned to 'normality' – which, being the complementary class, covers an enormous combination of personality attributes possessed by him in varying strengths.

Any researcher who consciously claims to be analysising people's *whole* personality, must be implying that his categories describe the full range of personality differences to be found in the general population – a very different proposition from the identification of abnormalities. Most approaches to this task assume that 'personality' consists fundamentally of internal dispositions, or causal factors within the individual which account for his behaviour. Whatever the dispositions or traits which underlie the particular acts of the individual, most psychologists of any sophistication would now think of these as both bipolar and normally distributed: that is, the whole population ranges from one extreme to the other, most people falling near the middle. The well-known model for this is, of course, intelligence as measured by IQ, which is not something one has or has not, but which everybody has to a degree somewhere between retardation and genius, with most people falling around the mid-point of the continuum, for the simple reason that this mid-point (100) has been defined by normal intellectual performance. In just the same way, while there are hermits and life-and-soul-of-the-party people, most would fall near the centre of any envisaged sociability dimension, and the same applies to aggressiveness, persistence, excitability and so on.

Although the present position of personality assessment is, of course, nowhere near adequate, there have been very considerable improvements in the theory, methodology and techniques in this country in recent decades. These have been substantial enough to make the proper appraisal of some earlier research difficult, and perhaps sometimes only dubiously worthwhile. Still, depending on how explicit the researcher was in describing his techniques and stating his assumptions, it is often possible to interpret work usefully in terms of later methodological developments. And it is within this perspective that we must view what Bowlby says about the personalities of his children.

I have already mentioned that Bowlby gives no clear or formal account of the indices he used to place a child in one of his six catagories (Normal, Depressed, Circular, Hyperthymic, Affectionless and Schizoid). He gives so much circumstantial detail of his complex procedures, without mention of his criteria, that it is genuinely difficult to avoid the impression that, given such scope for subjective factors to operate, it would be very suprising if a partisan did *not* somehow find his hypothesis verified — whether guided by an antecedent body of theory or not.

Thus:

> . . . a large number of these children, perhaps half, at their first interview appeared fairly normal. This impression is grossly misleading in a majority of cases and if taken seriously results in a disastrously erroneous diagnosis. For this reason I habitually ignore my psychiatric interviews when no positive signs of disorder have been found, and base my diagnosis on the reports of the mother and teacher. It has often been on a consideration of these reports, whose veracity I am naturally at pains to check both by comparing one against the other and also by their internal consistency, that I have formed the opinion that

the characters of the thieves in this series were abnormal.'

What is being checked for is unclear and so, too, are the reliable symptoms shown by the reports, which the interviews concealed. We are simply assured that '. . . only two of the forty-four thieves were diagnosed as normal characters, and even these two had a few characteristics which showed instability.'[17]

We cannot be certain that the five abnormal personality categories would have emerged as groups of deviant reaction tendencies if they had been based on statistically observed differences between children actually demonstrating marked maladjustment and those who did not.[18] It must be conceded that many of the symptoms for which anxious or perfectionist parents might refer children to a child guidance clinic may not be statistically abnormal in the least. An active child may be a nuisance to some, but unless the nuisance is very pronounced, is hardly abnormal; and unexplained moodiness is common in both adults and children. Unless other disturbing symptoms are present, it is safer to regard this type of behaviour as well within the range of normality. For example, Ronald, 7.0 years

> . . . enjoyed a good fight, a joke and so on. At times he would be lost in his thoughts, day-dreaming, and so on that account he was very absent-minded. But he usually wore a 'cocksure' manner. He had a great tendency to collect things, sometimes bringing home all sorts of old papers for his sisters to play with . . . He was idle over his lessons, but always obedient and well-behaved.

And 'He was friendly, appearing to his mother too affectionate at times. On the whole he had a good relationship with other children.'[19]

Such a typical denizen of many a primary school classroom is diagnosed not as 'Normal' but as 'Hyperthymic'. From what Bowlby says it is difficult to see who would qualify as 'normal', as he holds that his 'conception of abnormality is naturally not confined to obviously anxious or hysterical characters.'[20]

There are, he says, the 'obsessive and perfectionist children who are regarded with admiration by their parents and teachers', whom there would be 'no hesitation in regarding as abnormal'. This can apparently be done 'if only because of their great susceptibility to develop somatic symptoms such as stammer or headache and also depression of every degree of intensity'[21] One might reply that the majority of people have headaches or depressions of *some* degree of intensity.

(Those of a psychoanalytical background still tend to make a habit of conflating their notion of an *ideal*, super-adjusted, perfectly functioning individual with that of the normal personality. No doubt we would all like children not to be fidgety, adults not to be moody, and so forth, but it cannot be over-emphasised how essential it is to base concepts of normality on a proper knowledge of the distribution of attributes in the general population, no matter how far these may depart from our ideals; just as it is essential to base tests for particular defects or difficulties on an analysis of the differences between those who suffer from them and those who do not.)

It is with the category of the affectionless that we are chiefly concerned, and it is therefore here that the absence of any consistent criteria for allocation gives most cause for complaint. The affectionless that Bowlby discovered were the 'fourteen children in this group who had apparently never since infancy shown normal affection to anyone and were, consequently, conspicuously solitary, undemonstrative and unresponsive.'[22] But this classification is transgressed in some cases. For example, Kenneth W. (No. 32), 10.6 years, is affectionless: 'He showed no affection for his mother, but much for his grandfather.'[23] Betty I. (No. 27), 5.7 years, is affectionless: 'She was extremely fond of the baby and liked mothering him. She played well and happily and was popular and sociable with the neighbouring children'. But 'The mother found her an undemonstrative child who was inclined to keep things to herself.'[24] Norman K. (No. 30), 7.8 years, is affectionless: '[He] was said to be a very affectionate child who liked helping his mother in the home — "more like a little girl". But his mother also found him secretive which made it difficult for her to understand him.' However, 'he was fond of his sister and played happily with her.'[25]

What emerges in each of the cases quoted is the suspicion

that the term affectionless is being used not simply to denote lack of affection for anyone, *but rather lack of affection for one's mother*. Grandfathers, babies, sisters, other children, appear to be disqualified as objects of 'normal' affection. This amounts to arbitrary redefinition of the term 'affectionate', which naturally biases the assessments.

Among the cases Bowlby classifies as affectionless there are indeed many who are not reported as showing affection for anyone. But the over-all collection of characteristics which these fourteen children are mentioned as showing, yields little in the way of a pattern of resemblances such as would permit us to recognise a new case as affectionless or not. For instance we know that Bowlby stated that all fourteen were 'undemonstrative and unresponsive'. Yet this does not match what we are told elsewhere. A few of the children were 'unsociable and apathetic, but quite a number are energetic and active.'

Finally, Bowlby makes some predictions for his affectionless group: 'Oddly enough none of the Affectionless thieves appear as sexual offenders. It is strongly my impression, however, that many of them will become promiscuous and in some cases probably sadistic.'[26]

Bearing these things in mind, what might the future hold for the child described in the following quotation?

> As a very young child she had an obsession that she was not like other people. She was a monster. That was her secret which might at any moment be found out. She worked herself into an agony at the prospect of seeing a new face, and to be looked at was torture . . . She did not attach herself to her mother. The companion of her childhood was W.E.N.'[27]

On Bowlby's implicit criteria Florence Nightingale could have been designated an affectionless child, who would grow up with tendencies towards persistent stealing, probably promiscuous, and perhaps sadistic.

3 Some Tests of the Hypothesis

We have already seen how, in his study of forty-four juvenile thieves, Bowlby vacillates between regarding his study merely as the formulation of a hypothesis, to be subsequently tested, and as substantially confirming the hypothesis itself. The latter claim can hardly be sustained, owing to the considerable methodological defects in the study, some of which Bowlby himself at one point virtually admits. We can therefore fall back on the earlier claim, and proceed to ask whether the hypothesis which Bowlby formulated has been empirically tested, and with what result. This has been done on numerous occasions, and includes a study by Bowlby published in 1956.

Many of the studies done in the 1940s and 1950s, with findings both favourable and unfavourable to the theory, were of a very poor standard and are not worth considering here. This includes many of those cited in Bowlby's *Child Care and the Growth of Love* (*Maternal Care and Mental Health*). Here Bowlby rather peremptorily dismisses research which fails to substantiate his case, employing exacting standards which, as O'Connor points out in a critical article, would also demolish his own case if applied to the research he cites in its support.[1] In this and following chapters (which deal with different aspects and interpretations of the theory), I will try to concentrate on research of a reasonable empirical standard, much of which dates from the late fifties onwards. It is important to bear this in mind when we come to consider Bowlby's second study of 1956, for then, of course, he would not have been aware of many of the well-controlled studies that have been undertaken relatively recently. It is merely convenient to place the consideration of Bowlby's second study near the end of this section since so much of it is vitally relevant to the discussion of the importance of 'direct' observation and the psychoanalytic basis of the theory which immediately follow. It is therefore necessary to deal with the material on follow-up studies first.

A consequence which Bowlby explicitly claims for his hypothesis[2] is that approximately one-third of young offenders who appear before the courts will be found to be thieves with affectionless personalities; and that, moreover, this third will constitute the portion which later becomes habitually criminal (recidivists). The direct cause of the affectionless condition of these offenders will be found to be early separation from their mothers.

Attempting to test Bowlby's claim, Siri Naess in Norway[3] in 1959 took a group of delinquent boys and matched them for controls, afterwards investigating the amount of maternal deprivation each group had been exposed to. In outline this is what Bowlby did originally.

Naess selected delinquency cases from the files of the Oslo Child Protection Council, an official body responsible for the treatment of all juvenile offenders in Norway, through whose hands all reported offenders pass. The cases selected were boys between ten and eighteen, and the criteria of selection was an explicit index based, as far as possible, on Bowlby's notion of delinquent character development. Naess decided that for a boy to have such a character development he must show at least two of the following: stealing, truancy, violent behaviour, unruliness, running away, or staying out at night. One of the two symptoms must be stealing, and there must be at least one police case directly related to one or other of these symptoms.

Forty-two boys were chosen, using these criteria. All of the boys had non-delinquent brothers. The brothers constituted the control group. The non-delinquent nature of the controls was established by checking (a) if they had ever been referred to the Child Protection Council; (b) if they had been described as difficult in the files relating to the delinquent brother; and (c) checking their schools for unreported delinquencies. In ten cases no school information was available; of the remaining thirty-two, twenty-eight were described as having shown no misconduct, and four as having shown minor misconduct, such as occasional truancy, but no stealing was reported in any. All forty-two controls satisfied conditions (a) and (b).

Naess deliberately chose pairs of brothers because, as she says, a more reliable result could be obtained if the homes of the delinquent and the control were identical. It was important to isolate the factor of maternal separation as far as possible; for, even if persistent delinquency were shown to be significantly associated with separation from the mother, this need not itself support the deprivation thesis, since both separation from the mother and delinquency might be the product of general parental neglect, where the child is abandoned by a mother who has no interest in its social training. Thus, holding the general home environment constant for both delinquents and controls permits an investigator more confidence in believing that she is observing the effect of the particular variable of maternal deprivation.

The extent of maternal deprivation was measured by twice interviewing the mother of each sibling pair about all possible placing during the children's lives; the two interviews were conducted independently by different people, one of whom had no knowledge of which boys had been classified as delinquent and which as non-delinquent. As a secondary check all the main provincial children's homes and orphanages in Oslo were circulated for any records of placement away from the mother for any of the boys.

If Bowlby's hypothesis is true, of two boys brought up in the same family, one staying with his mother uninterruptedly throughout childhood, and the other cared for in an institution during some of his early years (say, between one and a half and three and a half), the latter should turn out to be the offender in a significant number of instances. As Naess says, the results should show that: *'Prolonged physical separations (that is, lasting at least three months, probably more than six) of a child from his mother during the first five years of life are more frequent among a group of delinquent boys, registered with the police authorities in Oslo, than among their non-delinquent brothers.'*

Her findings can be summarised as follows:[4]

Mother-child separation	controls (mean age 14.53)	delinquents (mean age 14.58)
At least 6 months before age 5	20%	10%
At least 3 months before age 5	27%	15%
At least 1 month before age 5	34%	34%
At least 3 months before age 10	34%	29%

(Statistical source of error lies in both directions.)

This result, on a sample much the same size as Bowlby's, flatly conflicts with the predictions entailed by Bowlby's hypothesis. Indeed, separation from the mother is higher in the non-delinquent group, even for separation of six months and longer. Naess might be entitled to claim that prolonged separation of a child from his mother (or permanent mother-substitute) during the first five years of life stands foremost among the *causes of law-abiding character development.* But, she concludes that her study neither supports Bowlby's hypothesis, nor any other and that his 'unreserved generalisation' in regard to the problem of delinquency is too wide.

In 1968 Cowie, Cowie and Slater[5] investigated in detail all the delinquent girls at the Magdalen Approved School. This was not so much a test of any one hypothesis, as a systematic statistical study of all the factors associated with female delinquents. But they were concerned to test, among many other things, Bowlby's assertion that it is the intransigent third of delinquents (the recidivists) who are caused by maternal deprivation – which suggests, by exclusion, that other environmental influences, generally speaking, cause more minor, remediable forms of delinquent misconduct and are overshadowed in their effect by the one central causal agent. According to Bowlby's hypothesis, maternal deprivation should appear as the principal factor associated with the hard core of persistent thieves. The girls at the approved school came from very disadvantageous circumstances. Compared with delinquent boys, the girls, the researchers found, came from homes where there was more poverty, and mental illness; from homes more likely to be broken or show greater conflict and low standards of behaviour.

The authors used two scales to measure the amount of maternal deprivation that had occurred in the sample of three hundred and eighteen girls. One of these, involving some interpretation, they called 'subjective' and the other, 'objective', being closer to Bowlby's in simply recording periods of physical separation from the mother. Using the subjective criterion, the girl was held to have been maternally deprived if she had been grossly neglected by her mother; if her mother had been away from home for a considerable period, perhaps on account of illness; if her mother had handed the girl over to relatives or parted from her in other ways. Adopted girls were not deemed to have been maternally deprived. The percentage of the sample having suffered deprivation using this definition was thirty-eight.

To satisfy the conditions of the objective criterion, the girl had to have been separated from her mother for at least six months, no period less than this being included. Where more than one period of separation had occurred, the periods were summed and girls who were later adopted were included.

It appeared that forty-three per cent of girls had been separated from their mothers for a period of six months or longer at some time or times in their lives. With fifty-seven girls (or eighteen per cent) separation was from the earliest weeks of infancy, occurring later in eighty-one other girls. Some of the girls had been reunited with their mothers after periods of separation, but as a rule, once separation had occurred it was not made good, and in some cases the girl and her mother were reunited only to be separated again. The permanence of separation shows in the fact that, the higher the age group, the more girls there were in the separated state. Duration of separation ranged from six months to seventeen years, with a mean value of 9.6 years.

The relevant points to emerge from the study were, first, that larceny was no higher in the deprived girls than in the non-deprived, and that there was no difference between the two groups in the type of delinquency committed. Secondly, there was no suggestion that separation at any particular age (for example, the first year of life) was any more destructive of normal personality development than at any other. Separation from the mother was common among these delinquent girls, as were all aspects of parental neglect and abandonment. Only twenty per cent of the girls at the Magdalen came from even superficially normal home backgrounds: gross neglect and ill-treatment were usual, as were incestuous assults by a male relative — a common reason why the girl ran away from home, after which she supported herself by criminal or immoral activities. Separation from the mother in itself showed no sign of exercising any particular influence, over and above all other aspects of parental abdication from the welfare and training of the girl. Bowlby's prediction that separation from the mother should appear as the principal factor among other environmental influences associated with persistent stealing is not corroborated. In particular, if separation is the crucial factor, this suggests that separated children who are later put into the normal care of satisfactory and loving foster parents will still have delinquent, larcenous propensities. Such girls did not appear in the Magdalen.

As can be seen, the findings perhaps tend to support a hypothesis about the connection between general neglect and subsequent delinquency. However, the authors warn us that the material is not entirely adequate for providing a good test of this hypothesis. The study by no means dealt with a cross-section of girls guilty of breaking the law, so that it cannot really give us the full picture of the extent of maternal deprivation in the whole population of female offenders. One reason for girls to be sent to the Magdalen, or to any approved school, is that their homes were grossly inadequate and they lacked the most elementary parental care in the here and now — adolescence, not in infancy. And although minor offences were often involved, a substantial proportion of the girls was admitted to the home under care or protection orders rather than for actual offences. Other girls who broke the law but who had intact homes were, generally speaking, less likely to find themselves placed in approved schools for offences of the same severity. In other words, we have good reason to suspect, as regards minor offences, that children from intact and loving homes will be less likely to appear in approved schools — if only for the reason that the juvenile courts are more reluctant to remove them from their homes for petty crime.

But since, according to Bowlby, those who suffered

maternal deprivation will be found to constitute the hard
core of the recidivist criminal population; and since, however
intact and loving their homes, persistent and serious juvenile
criminals are likely to be placed in approved schools sooner
or later, the Cowie and Slater study seems quite justified in
remarking on the absence of separated and subsequently
fostered or adopted children among the Magdalen inmates.

(The mean IQ of the maternally deprived Magdalen girls
was 98·8, compared with 94·7 for the sample as a whole. This
favours the deprived girls and is significant at the 0·05 level.)

Cockburn and Maclay (1965)[6] studied samples of boys and
girls admitted to two London remand homes by order of a
juvenile court in the first four months of 1961. Every girl
admitted to the remand home between 8 February and 4
May 1961, and on whom a psychiatric report had been
requested, was included. Owing to the greater number of
boys admitted between these dates, every third boy on whom
a psychiatric report had been requested was included. Data
concerning the family and social history of the subjects was
obtained from the probation officer's and psychiatric social
worker's reports and the psychiatric interviews. In neither the
boys nor the girls was there a particularly high rate of
separation from the mother in the first five years of life.
Separation from the father was higher in both the samples,
and particularly among the girls, ten having never known
their fathers and a further fourteen, who were separated at
the time of remand, not having seen him for periods ranging
from two to thirteen years.

These high rates of paternal separation in both the boys
and the girls are just one aspect of a broad condition which is
generally associated with delinquency: the inadequate home,
inadequate   in   the   sense   of   parental   fecklessness,
irresponsibility and the absence of supervision or consistent
teaching of elementary social behaviour. From what we have
observed earlier, and from other studies, we would further
expect this broad condition of neglect to be more
pronounced in the girls, since it is usually only in such
extreme environments that girls will tend to have much
opportunity of indulging in criminal behaviour. This tends to
be confirmed by the high rates of broken homes among the
girls (a further index of general neglect which overlaps that of

paternal separation) compared with the boys. The figures agree well with the findings of other criminologists such as Nye[7] in 1958 and Bagot[8] in 1934-6, which show the rate of broken homes among female delinquents fluctuating fairly closely around fifty per cent, while that of the boys is closer to the population norm (estimated as between eleven and eighteen per cent).

Another study was carried out by Field[9] in 1962 of the relationship between crime and maternal deprivation. It was similar to the Cowie and Slater study, in that it took already apprehended criminals and looked at type and severity of offence and degree of previous maternal deprivation, rather than comparing the criminals with a non-criminal control group in the manner of Naess. But although Field does not use such a control group, he starts with Bowlby's estimation of the extent of maternal deprivation in the general – and the criminal – populations. His aim is to test this estimation for an actual group of criminals. Bowlby has said that, 'If you take a bunch of recidivists you would find at least thirty per cent, very likely fifty per cent, whose delinquent character had been caused that way (that is, by separation from mother), against perhaps ten per cent to fifteen per cent of the general population who would have been maternally deprived.'[10]

Field's intention was:

> ... to test Bowlby's hypothesis on the two types of recidivist who differed in the degree of recidivism exhibited, on the assumption that the number and kind of charges on which a man is convicted are related to the severity of his anti-social conduct and of his delinquent character. The group containing men of more severe delinquent character can then be predicted, on Bowlby's hypothesis, as having a higher incidence of maternal deprivation.[11]

The subjects consisted of forty-two men serving rehabilitative prison sentences (corrective training), and another group of fifty-one men serving the severer sentence of preventive detention (P.D.). The men in the second group had slightly more than twice as many previous convictions as those in the first group, with eight times more convictions for sex offences and six times more for fraud and false pretences. As one would expect, the most frequent type of conviction in both groups was against property. The greater frequency of sex and fradulent offences in the P.D. group, as well as their higher age at first conviction, suggest that different types of men were recruited into the two groups. Offences against the person and larceny are typically committed by younger people and diminish with age, whereas the type of offence that was more common among the P.D. group is comparatively rare in the young, having older devotees.

Field obtained for both groups the percentage of cases where there had been maternal deprivation before the age of five. This information was obtained by searching the case notes for mention of mother—child separation. This was not a satisfactory method, since the notes merely recorded occurrence or non-occurrence of separation, without stating the durations. One must therefore assume that the separations worthy of mention, and likely to be discovered, were of more than a fleeting nature; but whether they match Bowlby's threshold of magnitude — three to six months — we cannot say for certain.

The amount of separation recorded for the two groups was as follows: in the corrective training (mildly criminal) group, 17·14 per cent had been maternally deprived; in the preventive detention (recidivist) group, 17·64 per cent had been maternally deprived. As we can see, the extent of maternal deprivation in each group hardly differs at all, and differs little from what Bowlby estimated for the general population. It falls far below what Bowlby estimated as a minimum extent of maternal deprivation among recidivists. Even allowing that the sample is a very small one, these figures are above the level of statistical significance — that is, the probability is small that this is a merely chance result. If Bowlby's estimate for maternal deprivation in the general population is correct, results such as these could be obtained from any randomly chosen group of people. However, there is no strong reason to suppose that his estimate *is* correct, since he was not basing it on a population sample taken to ascertain the frequency of this variable.

The Douglas and Bromfield study of 5,386 young children,

revealed that fifty-two per cent had been separated from their mothers by the age of six (only the longest separation was recorded for each child).[12] Fourteen per cent had been separated for four weeks or longer. Douglas later found that one in three had been separated for at least a week before the age of four and a half.[13] If anything, surveys of separation reveal just how common is this factor in the lives of young children.

A larger study along the same lines as the Field one was undertaken by Little (1965).[14] Out of 3,047 receptions to Borstal in 1958, 500 were selected to take part in this study. Because of the way in which the records are kept at the Central After-Care Association, Boys Section, a random sample was not possible, and so the sample was selected by using the receptions whose surnames began with letters A, C, D, H, K, M, P, Q, S or W. Borstal records were chosen because most receptions have lengthy criminal records, few being first or occasional offenders; a high proportion, sixty per cent or more, are reconvicted, often for more than one further crime, so that it is possible to distinguish between the offender who continues committing crime after a long period of Borstal training and one who does not. The typical Borstal record is extensive: from the probation officer before committal to Borstal, from the psychologist, psychiatrist and/or social worker at the Borstal Allocation Centre, from the housemaster during Borstal training (part of which involves discussion of family relationships) and from the after-care worker in touch with the inmate during training and after discharge.

Little found separation from one or both parents in eighty per cent of the sample; wartime service is a major factor in this high figure. The most frequent reasons for separation apart from military service during the war, were death, followed by divorce, desertion and parental rejection of the child, all lumped together as a group. Paternal separation was twice as high as maternal.[15]

See table on the following page.

Age at first separation

Separation from	up to 6 mths	6—18 mths	18 mths —5 yrs	5—7 years	7 years and over	Total
Mother	3	8	27	11	50	99
Father	106	26	35	9	38	214
Both parents	25	11	12	8	39	95

A concentration of maternal separation occurs after seven years. The author maintains that it is difficult to compare these figures with the amount of separation to be found in the general population as the latter was not known for the period in question. When the differences within the sample are analysed, the following observations emerge.

A comparison is made between the three groups: non-deprived, separated, and those separated on multiple occasions (a most dire state of affairs according to Bowlby)[16] regardless of whether it was from the mother, father or both parents. No large or consistent differences could be found in the age at the first conviction, the numbers of previous convictions, or the frequency of recidivism after discharge from Borstal. Nor does parental separation appear to influence the type of crime committed, although there was some slight evidence that sex crimes and malicious damage were higher amongst those who were *not* parentally deprived which does not confirm Bowlby's assertion in *Forty-four Juvenile Thieves* that sexual offences are likely to be caused by maternal deprivation.

A comparison is then made between the amounts of recidivism to be found in those separated from their mothers, fathers or both: little difference appears. No differences emerge either when comparisons are made between those separated at different times in their lives. A monotonous similarity between those deprived and those not deprived pervades the study.

No large clear-cut, or consistent relationships could be found, and therefore it must be concluded that the notion of parental separation as a means of differentiating between delinquents, is not a useful one... A general theory of crime ought to be able not merely to distinguish criminals (delinquents) from non-criminals (non-delinquents) but also to differentiate between types of delinquents, charges of recidivism, etc. The separation hypothesis was not able to do this on this sample of offenders.[17]

We can briefly sum up the position reached so far. It is largely negative. The hypothesis was threefold: that separation of a young child from its mother produces an irreversible 'affectionless' personality; that such personalities have a strong propensity to steal; this in turn constitutes the main causal factor in juvenile and later recidivist delinquency. We have seen that, whether treated as substantive research in itself or as merely suggesting a hypothesis for later research, Bowlby's original work is not supported by the later investigations I have considered.

These were generally of a more rigorous standard, and in each case the results were incompatible with what should have been found if the maternal deprivation hypothesis were true. However, many of these investigations were on a small scale. In Chapter 6 I shall look at the results of some larger and wider criminological studies to see what kinds of background condition, if any, can reasonably be identified as causes of crime.

First, however, in the next chapter, I will make some general observations about possible relationships between crime, learning and personality.

4 Crime: Learning and Personality

There is a vague impression that criminals — particularly those whose crimes arouse repugnance — are somehow sick, perverted, or in an indefinable way unbalanced, and that some positive disturbing factor is therefore to be sought which has affected a potentially healthy individual. This is to confuse sickness with abnormality, and partly with moral transgression as well. Except in a tiny, well-defined minority, most anti-social behaviour, however shocking, is 'abnormal' only in the literal sense that a viable society will generally have restrained it by training, disapproval and enforcible laws.* Moral and legal codes of course undergo change. But in those socially abnormal situations where little or no training in any values has been given, and legal controls fail to operate, acts which we class as grossly anti-social will be committed by the most psychologically ordinary individuals.

This draws attention to a second misconception, which is that crudely expressed in the endless and sterile argument about whether man is 'naturally' good or 'naturally' evil. Outside a genuinely theological context, such as the doctrine of original sin, it is meaningless to ascribe moral categories to the motivations of pre-social man, even supposing we can make any clear sense of the latter concept. But if we must picture the individual prior to social learning, then it must be conceded that this being behaves neither lovingly nor hatefully but simply in a manner most advantageous to his own survival, and the gratification of his desires, whatever

---

*We are all surely familiar with the reassuring myth — repeated even by the educated — that Hitler was 'insane'. In the complete absence of anything resembling medical insanity in his biography, this usually amounts to the tautology that he must have been insane simply because 'sane' people could not commit such atrocities or cause such destruction. Simple faith of this kind is scarcely a good guide to understanding history or modern society.

this happens to involve: only obstacles, painful repercussions, easier alternatives — in short, an environment — prevent him doing literally anything. And with humans, the most instructive and influential environment is other humans. If the dispute about man's 'natural' tendencies illustrates anything, it is that in the case of human beings we cannot talk of highly specific, goal-directed instinctual instructions in each individual, comparable to the hunting behaviour of cats or the homing behaviour of pigeons. Unfortunately or otherwise, there is no such fixed pre-social human nature.

Since violence is a potent instrument for attaining our ends and since its consequences are obviously drastic, all human groups have had the elementary tasks, among others, of controlling violent conflict and distributing scarce resources. It is important to stress here that 'scarcity' denotes not just distinct economic shortage, but the fact that in any social situation — including those considered prosperous — the available quantities of whatever people happen to want are finite, and therefore impose limits on the satisfaction possible to each individual. The recognition of this must lead to the creation of some regulative rules. Again, the notion that there are always fairly fixed, normal things which people want and fairly stable quantities of these which will broadly satisfy them, seems very questionable. Apart from undeniable minimal biological requirements, the reformer's concept of a sufficiency — whether three acres and a cow, the Beveridge minimum decent living standard, or the two-car family — has unfortunately proved singularly useless, in economic theory at least, where it is recognised that wants are largely a function of availability and opportunity, and must therefore be considered theoretically as infinitely expansible. Goods are not all desired for the obvious purposes of useful consumption such as security, comfort and pleasure, but will often be sought for ostentatious, prestigious, wasteful or even destructive purposes quite beyond what may be considered a person's rational and proper 'needs'. Scarcity then, in the sense defined here, is to be seen as a permanent feature with which social rules must cope. In saying that human groups have to develop social and moral rules for these purposes, we are not of course saying that the content of any particular rule is good or just; only that social human existence would be impossible without such rules in one form or another.

Areas of social control vary with the type of group or society. At one extreme is the group that cooperates briefly for mutual advantage (which may be the efficient plundering of less united people), to whom the rules of conduct apply only as long as this adantage is served. At the other, perhaps, is the stable and fairly permanent nation embracing all who live in a certain area, speak a common language and share a common culture, containing enduring instructions for the division of labour and function and the impersonal cooperation of large numbers of people over wide territories. In both cases there will be people outside the group who are not covered by its rules — and towards whom almost any behaviour is permitted. This is illustrated by the fact that murder has never been synonymous simply with deliberate killing, but only with deliberate killing of those deemed to be within some social, legal or moral category. The killing of outsiders is often seen as morally neutral (for example, the treatment of Negroes by seventeenth and eighteenth century Europeans), and sometimes even as positively good (the attempted exterminations of heretics, infidels, Red Indians, Tasmanians or Jews, not to mention wars of every kind).

The nature and extent of social controls vary enormously, even over short periods of time. The collapse or corrosion of social institutions, for reasons external or internal, can render life unpredictable or hazardous. On a less grandiose level, the addition of a new sphere of activity to the lives of individuals, such as motoring or the — to some societies — novel habit of consuming alcohol, demands the evolution of a quite new set of rules to coordinate the activities of those participating. Very generally, the greater the diversity of situations an individual occupies and the greater the anonymity between the persons in that situation, the more he must depend on socially rule-governed behaviour to ensure absence of clashes and compliance with expectations.

In other species, the problems of allocating limited resources and avoiding violent conflict such as would undermine the viability of the species, are solved (as are most other basic problems of survival) by elaborate, rigid, instinctual patterns of behaviour: in this case, behaviour patterns that can perhaps be denoted by the blanket term 'territoriality'. If intra-species conflict occurs at all, it is usually as an automatically stylised part of the over-all territorial behaviour, and seldom reaches the uncontrolled, destructive proportions it can attain in humans (though there are some exceptions). Humans, not having highly specific instinctual instructions of any kind, have no such built-in checks on these either: social controls have to be substituted, which naturally are acquired after birth and may therefore be transmitted inefficiently.

It is precisely the absence in man of such instinctual behavioural patterns as territoriality, that renders the individual so malleable by social learning, as the great diversity of human culture illustrates. There have been claims recently by ethologists such as Ardrey, to the effect that man's propensity for excessive violence and warfare is a result of his supposed instinct for territoriality. Not only is there no evidence for the existence in man of the territorial behaviour frequently observed in birds and other mammals: on the contrary, it seems that it is the very absence of any natural mechanism for allocating resources and controlling breeding (for example, non-fatal, ritualised conflict as the instrument to these ends), which has allowed man's history to be so bloody.

This discussion reinforces the point made previously about the importance of recognising that delinquents, though deviant, are not *sick* in the same sense in which psychotics are sick. The psychotic and neurotic are still socially orientated; they try desperately — and fail — to adjust to others, and suffer for their efforts. But the typical delinquent quite conspicuously makes no such attempt, and suffers, if at all, only as a result of the retribution of others. His delinquency is only a defect from the viewpoint of the surrounding society, not from that of the individual himself.

Thus the training and education of a young person to eliminate anti-social behaviour is done in the first instance because his society demands it, and not because he himself wishes it or needs it for his personal stability. Delinquent children are often referred to as children with problems or difficulties. The blunt truth is that delinquent children *are* problems and difficulties — for others.

Any review of criminological studies suggests that, on the whole, there are differences between delinquents and non-delinquents in environmental circumstances. I suggest that the wide range of environmental conditions (some of them apparent opposites) frequently found associated with delinquency, all share in common the fact that they constitute poor learning environments. A rejecting, broken home may not provide the correct behaviour models and necessary controls and reinforcements for good conduct; but, on the other hand, merely a loving and secure atmosphere in the home may, by omitting socialisation, produce as great a problem of delinquency in children. But I also suggest that personality differences between individuals make the control of impulsive behaviour and compliance with norms more difficult for some people than others — even given an initially promising environment.

It is necessary now to look a little more formally at psychological concepts of learning and their relation to personality patterns.

A large part of experimental psychology is governed by Learning Theory, derived from the original discoveries of Watson, Pavlov and others. The theory is based on the paradigm models of how connections are created and extinguished between stimuli and responses, mediated by the organism.

There are two basic models. In *classical* conditioning, the subject, who naturally responds in a certain way to some stimulus, comes to respond in the same way to another, previously neutral, feature of the environment, by a process of association with the first stimulus. The best-known examples are, of course, Pavlov's dogs who came to respond by salivating at the sound of a bell which had been systematically associated with food. The reverse process — dissociation of the two events — gradually extinguishes the conditioned response in the same straightforward way. A very great deal of human and animal behaviour is known to be acquired in this manner. A good example is the cause and cure of neurotic disorders: by maladaptive conditioning, some quite harmless or ordinary situation (and the thought of it) has come to arouse incapacitating levels of anxiety in a person. This is gradually lowered, by a step-by-step therapy of dissociation, or reassociating the feared situation with pleasant and relaxing experiences.

The second model is *operant* conditioning, whereby some otherwise neutral behaviour by the subject is followed a number of times by a rewarding event, and thus becomes systematically repeated by the subject. The occurrence of the 'reward' and its effect in strengthening the particular behaviour that brings it about, is termed reinforcement. There can be punishment as well as reward, negative as well as positive reinforcement. The best example of operant conditioning is probably the way animals come to learn discriminatory actions such as pressing sequences of levers or running through mazes when the 'correct' action is regularly followed by food. The two forms of conditioning have a number of sub-categories, and in fact are distinguished primarily by the structure of the experimental set-up in which they occur. For simplicity I will refer to both as behavioural learning in future.

The doctrines of the early workers, and of some contemporary ones, are widely known as Behaviourism — an approach which confused a view of scientific method with a theory of mind. The extreme, metaphysical doctrines of Behaviourism (for example, that the introspectible events of consciousness are fictions, or that all mental operations are combinations of S—R connections) are mainly of historical interest, but in any case are not entailed in learning theory. They are rare among experimental psychologists, at least in Britain.

Although the two models are extremely simple, the actual learning processes which have been explored with their help are very diverse and elaborate. A recent researcher distinguishes for convenience four types of classical conditioning and eight types of operant conditioning.[1] These include patterns of anticipatory conditioning in which a 'cue' stimulus comes to be associated with the expected reward and elicits the behaviour previously elicited by the reward, thus coming to serve as a signal for it; discriminated conditioning in which the circumstances attending the anticipated reward are slowly made more complex so that the subject learns to discriminate very elaborate combinations of features; and so on. Even without such deliberate controls, specific behavioural learning generalises very easily to similar situations, and generalised reinforcers, capable of guiding a whole range of behaviour, come to operate very early in the human child's life. Again, imitation often acts as the initiator of the behaviour to be reinforced, thus shortening the time needed to establish the 'correct' sequence of behaviour.

The processes described by learning theory are not just a more scientifically documented version of the commonsense 'stick and carrot', or 'sparing the rod'. Many features which have been discovered in the learning process are far from obvious, and contradict what conventional wisdom would expect. For example, it is definitely established that the time interval between the behaviour and its reinforcer is far more important in establishing the connection than the strength of the reinforcer. It has also been found that behaviour is more tenaciously established (more difficult to extinguish) by partial reinforcement (less than a hundred per cent of occasions) than by total reinforcement (one hundred per cent).

The basic conditions which determine what kind of reinforcers are relevant to learning are (1) the discriminative capacities of the child, which depend obviously on its degree of maturation; (2) the intensity and frequency of the reinforcers, the patterns they form (that is, their connection with other conditioned reinforcers, their over-all consistency, etc.), and the time-lag between the relevant behaviour and the reinforcing event, and (3) the accumulated experience of past learnt behaviour in the child, to which new learning must be related; (4) in addition, it is known that children vary in their degree and type of amenability to behavioural learning – their teachability. And this constitutes a basis of differences in abilities and in personality-type. This last point is of considerable importance, and one to which I shall return.

Just as it is not to be identified with mere stick and carrot or trial and error, behavioural learning is likewise not to be identified with the rational, prudential calculation used in pursuing whatever our goals are. It is certainly true that there are strong parallels: many of our motives and strategies can be seen as seeking reinforcers such as worldly wealth, esteem, etc. But the intervening processes – in particular language, higher concept formation and rational thought – are increasingly unlikely to be explainable solely in behavioural learning terms. This is not to say that the processes of behavioural learning do not operate among adult, thinking, interacting members of society, for we know that they do, most pervasively: only that they are probably not the complete story. A full scientific explanation of how higher conceptual, cognitive operations work – a science of the mental – just does not exist. And until a very great deal more progress has been made, it is at best metaphorical and at worst misleading, to classify just any kinds of motivated human action in behavioural learning terms, as if they exhibited the same lawlike features that have been so convincingly demonstrated for elementary types of learning.

What can be said is that the processes described by learning theory are a necessary, though probably not a sufficient, basis for all acquisition of skills, of whatever sort. Learning theory itself is gradually being modified in some aspects and is by no means free of problems. But it is probably the only psychological approach to these questions so far which has generated clear and fruitful research: the only one which by and large has been proved to work, to have produced repeatable experimental results which have unambiguously settled certain questions among empirical psychologists. Its discoveries have been piecemeal and perhaps mundane, but they have been cumulative. They have not yet answered some of the really interesting questions of psychology,[2] nor produced any grand theory of mind. But as far as they go, they are undoubtedly the most secure psychological explanations which we have.

I have already discussed the fact that enduring personality characteristics in the general population should be regarded as bi-polar and normally distributed. Sufficiently high correlation between otherwise independent kinds of behaviour leads to the postulation of an underlying 'trait' (about whose actual nature researchers need not at that stage commit themselves). Two prominent workers in the field of psychometrics are R.B. Cattell[3] and H.J. Eysenck.[4]

Cattell has isolated fifteen basic 'dimensions' of human personality, which have been derived from correlations between detailed traits, derived in turn from correlations between behavioural items. These dimensions overlap considerably, and it is possible to factorise their inter-correlations further to yield six second-order factors, or large 'surface traits'. The two most important of Cattell's surface traits resemble closely the two axes of personality Eysenck uses, that is, introversion—extraversion, and stability—instability (to which he applies the general term 'type' to distinguish these major dimensions from the traits composing them). It is of some interest that traditional historical descriptions of the main personality types approximate quite closely to the two dimensions isolated by modern statistical methods, for example, the Hippocratic system of personality, elaborated by Galen in the second century. One modern psychometrist, Vernon, whose standards are very exact and who is critical of much of trait analysis, none the less has no doubt that a simplified method of personality allocation which he has proposed (which would eliminate some of the anomalies and duplications of previous research), will reveal as major dimensions of personality the two axes of introversion—extraversion and of stability—instability (which he calls ego-strength).[5]

Most people will, of course, lie near the centre of any dimension, with different clusters of attributes. In the case of the two major dimensions with which I have been dealing, it is postulated that the extravert whose personality falls at the unstable end of the other dimension is likely to be excitable and restless, being touchy and aggressive rather than cheerful and lively. The introvert at the unstable end is moody as opposed to being calm and even-tempered, inflexible in attitudes and unsociable. In general, introverts are more or less anxious people, while extraverts show distinct amounts of impulsive behaviour and have difficulty in sustaining attention for any length of time. (I am greatly oversimplifying here because of lack of space: I am also for convenience giving the traditional psychometrist account of the relationship between the two axes. Recent work suggests that the postulated relation between these axes may need revising.)

The point of central importance to criminology is the recognition that introverts condition far more easily than do extraverts, given an equal amount and intensity of training. As children, they will be easier to train in hygienic personal habits, polite manners and law-abiding behaviour (whatever specific form these may take), will gain control more quickly over impulsive and aggressive behaviour, learn more easily to postpone immediate gratification for long-term benefits, and be taught more readily to recognise rights and feelings in others. But, precisely because he conditions far more easily, the introvert has a tendency towards those personality problems loosely termed neuroses — namely, anxiety states, depressions, phobic fears and compulsive habits. For example, in a highly introverted personality, the parental training which in others would produce altruism, sympathetic response to others and an ability to handle situations without undue antagonism, instead may produce a person so lacking in self-assertion that the very thought of crossing the wishes of others generates intense anxiety. (Roughly the same result could be produced in a mildly introverted personality by an excessively strict upbringing, continually emphasising the individual's duties to others at the expense of himself.) In keeping with this easy conditionability, very introverted children tend to be nervous, shy, easily frightened, withdrawn, and to indulge in introspective day-dreaming. Very extraverted children tend to take longer in toilet training and commonly show enuresis, and to act in violent, destructive and rude ways. Such problems of conduct can be seen as the opposite of the types of disabilities suffered by introverts.

Extraverts appear to combine relative imperviousness to stimuli with a need to seek it out. They are poor at tasks involving concentration for prolonged periods, or low levels of stimulation, and are consequently classed as having 'low arousal' in comparison with introverts. Arousal is not to be confused with activity, but is defined as ability to give sustained attention without being distracted. In his state of 'stimulus hunger', together with the greater likelihood of social mixing, drinking, enjoying loud music, etc., the extreme extravert will be prone to involve himself in rash, thoughtless and perhaps socially reprehensible behaviour such as reckless driving, fights, and — particularly as an agile juvenile — various criminal escapades. It has often been

suggested that the activities of juvenile delinquents spring
from boredom — that is, from a desire for stimulation which
cannot in their case be satisfied by such things as study,
hobbies, conversation and the kind of amusements normally
provided by youth clubs. To this must be added the greater
difficulty in applying social training and in setting up
internalised norms of conduct in the young extravert.

Now, personality shows intimate connections with bodily
build and this connection has received much attention from
criminologists. The study of types of bodily build in the
human population has been conducted very extensively in
this century by the American anthropologist and
psychologist W.H. Sheldon. From his research Sheldon
postulated the existence of three main bodily types (which
can be seen as refinements of the types suggested by earlier
workers such as Kretschmer). These are (1) The
Mesomorph — thick-set, heavily boned and muscled, strong
and stocky; (2) the Endomorph — more lightly boned and
muscled but well-endowed with fatty tissue, a round, soft,
bodily build; and (3) the Ectomorph, often called the linear
type, with a long and rather delicate bone structure, lack of
fatty covering and large surface area relative to mass. People
are rated in these three dimensions on three seven-point
scales, and given a three-digit number as score. There are thus
three hundred and forty-three possible ratings in all, but
Sheldon reports only seventy-six encountered by him in
practice. As might be expected, environment plays only a
subordinate part in determining a subject's somatype: a
mesomorph, for example, will not become an ectomorph by
losing weight — his heavy frame will be even more in
evidence. Sheldon claims he has not encountered a change in
somatype due to any metabolic or nutritional changes.[6]

These types correlate with personality traits sufficiently
highly for the two to be considered constitutionally
associated. The mesomorph generally has poor intellectual
attainment, is assertive and aggressive and inclined towards
impulsive and rash behaviour. The endomorph is associated
with a strong liking for social life, friendliness and a need for
approval and companionship, a tolerant and easy-going
nature; he is a sociable extravert in contrast with the
mesomorph, who is more aggressive, interfering and bullying

in his socialising. Ectomorphy has been repeatedly associated with scholastic leanings, preference for intellectual activity, anxiety, avoidance of social life, self-consciousness and restrained behaviour — traits which combine to produce what psychometrists would call a typical introvert.

5 Criminological Research

The most famous modern criminologists are probably Sheldon and Eleanor Glueck. Their enormous surveys of delinquents and recidivists cover follow-up spans of fifteen years. Because of the size of the samples, extensive follow-ups and the multitude of variables covered by the Gluecks in their work (as well as the highly important fact that they are often referred to by other researchers, including Maternal Deprivation theorists) they deserve (despite some methodological faults) priority of space in this brief survey of the prominent factors that have commonly emerged in research of criminality.

The Gluecks' work began in the 1920s with a careful study of one thousand delinquents[1] who had appeared before the Boston Juvenile Courts during the years 1917–22, when the average age had been thirteen and a half years. In later years the individuals were carefully followed up as adults in their twenties and thirties and their histories compared.[2] From 1942 onwards another very intensive study of five hundred delinquents and five hundred controls was undertaken.[3] The material in this study was used later for a highly detailed three-way statistical analysis for interrelations between family environment, psychological traits and physical characteristics.[4] The follow-up study of this set of delinquents appeared recently and is closely concerned with the outcome of penal and rehabilitative methods.[5] The salient factors which have emerged from these studies have led the Gluecks to devise a series of predictive tests, both for the future delinquent in the general population, and for the recidivist in the delinquent population.[6] The results of experiments with these tests have been very impressive: even when they are used in widely differing cultures they give a consistently high predictive accuracy for future criminality.

The five hundred delinquents and five hundred controls in the 1942–50 sample were boys aged eleven to eighteen; they were matched for intelligence, racial origins and residence in underprivileged districts. The Gluecks' decision to match their subjects in this way resulted from dissatisfaction with the inconclusive character of previous work, which they surmised was partly the result of its theoretical assumptions.

On the one hand, the influence of the French sociologist Durkheim led workers to view the comparative rates of crime of different areas (cities, regions or countries) as social manifestations, irreducible to individual events. On the other hand, a Marxist conception of society composed of classes with opposed value-systems, saw 'crime' as the label attached to working-class values by the dominant bourgeoisie. There was also the Fabian alternative of regarding the phenomenon as the result of poverty or other socio-economic grievances. Many today still assume that crime will go away when we reach a certain (unspecified) level of economic growth and prosperity.

The consensus produced by these two main orientations is that crime is caused by a mass social stimulus to behaviour, as reflected in the particular culture of the region or class under study. At a certain level of social analysis the 'mass stimulus' approach is valid, but the nature of the stimulus is likely to be different from that proposed by sociologists – mainly Marxist ones. The traditionally higher rates of crime in the working class are more likely to be related to concepts of masculinity than any revolt against capitalism. At present we have a 'mass stimulus' away from socialisation, emphasising the freedom of the child, which affects all classes. But as the Gluecks maintain, individuals are affected *differentially* by such culture pressures. We see this in our own society where the breakdown of normative standards is faster and more widespread among people having certain characteristics rather than others. To the Gluecks the mass stimulus outlook shuns discussion of three points, which they felt would have to be tackled if a researcher was really going to get anywhere near the heart of the problem of criminality. These points could only be properly examined if a more individual approach was instituted. They were that: (1) even in the most adverse circumstances or 'subcultural' group, many individuals do not

commit legally prohibited acts; (2) in any given culture there
are always individuals who do not conform to many of its
standards, whatever these are taken to be; and (3) in any
given culture, individuals respond differentially to many
elements in that cultural complex; indeed, culture itself is an
on-going interaction between individual personalities and the
social milieu. As most popular schools of criminology have
avoided discussion of the individual, it was no wonder that
they could offer nothing in the way of predictive devices to
isolate the future delinquent. The Gluecks thus began by
insisting on the simple fact that in every social class, ethnic
group and income bracket, many people do not commit
delinquent acts; their task was to discover the features within
these groups which distinguished the criminal individuals
from the others.[7]

In the 1942—50 study which is under consideration, the
Gluecks compared the delinquents and controls on a total of
four hundred and two measurable factors, classed as
biological, psychological, psychiatric and socio-cultural.
Examples of these features were the qualities and conditions
of family life, degree of affection shown by either parent,
type of discipline, quality of school life, quality of
community life, type of intellectual ability, character and
personality structure (unfortunately relying too heavily on
the Rorshach test, even though it is backed by other data),
bodily type, medical condition, general health record of
subject and family and so on. Rather than being designed to
test any given hypothesis, the study was simply looking for
whatever significant correlations might emerge among all
these factors and sets of factors when the two groups were
compared statistically. A number of important correlations
did emerge.

First, as far as the individual himself is concerned,
anthropometric analysis gave a very high incidence of
mesomorphic dominance in the delinquents' body structure
compared with the non-delinquents, who showed
considerable incidence of ectomorphic dominance. On top of
this possession of a dominantly mesomorphic body build, the
delinquents also showed a general retardation of the early
adolescent growth spurt, yielding a picture of over-all
physical immaturity.

The Gluecks also found that a higher proportion of the delinquents was reported as being very restless as young children and a considerably higher proportion of them had been persistent enuretics. As delinquent adolescents they were out-going and assertive: 'The delinquents have been found to be considerably more extraversive in their trends of action, more vivacious, more emotionally labile or impulsive (as opposed to stability of emotional expression), more destructive and sadistic, more aggressive and adventurous.'[8] These characteristics involved them in friction with others, but had little inward counterpart in the sense of leading to obsessional phobias or any heart-searching concerning personal relationships: their rate of neuroticism was far lower than for the non-delinquents. The latter not only easily learnt to control anti-social impulses, but equally easily learnt pieces of behaviour useless to society and uncomfortable for themselves. The delinquents' life style was described by the Gluecks as one of action, not of the mind

> ... with tendencies to restless and uninhibited expression of instinctual affective energy and to direct and concrete rather than symbolic and abstract intellectual expression. It is evidently difficult for them to develop the high degree of flexibility of adaptation, self-management, self-control and sublimation of primitive tendencies and self-centred desires demanded by the complex and confused culture of the times.[9]

From such indices a pattern of pronounced extraversion appears, but although strongly extraverted people are difficult to train, the fact remains that most will learn eventually, and also that not all delinquents, by any means, are *high* on extraversion. This alone cannot account for delinquency. However, the Gluecks found that the correlation of delinquency with extraversion was supplemented by the striking correlation with poor home discipline. By 'discipline' the Gluecks meant the training in social behaviour which is administered by a parent or parent-substitute who has looked after the child continuously since about the age of three. They divided the patterns of discipline into four over-all types, which might be provided by the mother or father or both. These were (1) Lax: negligent and indifferent to what the child did; (2) Over-strict: harsh, unreasoning, compelling obedience through fear; (3) Erratic: inconsistent response to the child's behaviour which vacillated between (1) and (2); and (4) Firm but kindly: consistent discipline, supported by reasons rather than merely by threat of punishment. Each of these types was further defined where necessary.

It was also noted that the parents of the delinquents were lax in many other ways besides the discipline they provided. Although their economic position was much the same as for the parents of the non-delinquents, their management of money and household resources was feckless and haphazard, their hygiene was poorer, and there was generally an absence of any planning for the future and any conscious aims in their lives. This clearly overlapped with another main correlation found by the Gluecks, namely, poor general medical condition. Not only did the health circumstances tend to be worse (for example, poor hygiene and diet), but the biological legacy of the delinquent parents and children was poorer than that of the non-delinquents, showing substantially more serious physical ailments, emotional disturbance, mental retardation and alcoholism. To this should be added the over-all physical immaturity of the delinquents, compared to the controls, which has already been mentioned.

The last main cluster of differences between the delinquent and non-delinquent groups concerns the high levels of intra-family hostility found in the former. This factor was obviously operational in leading to the large number of broken families in the delinquent group. The hostility operated in all ways, that is, parent—child, child—sib and parent—parent.

It was observed that as many as 60.4 per cent of the delinquent homes had been 'broken' (normal family life permanently disrupted) by separation of parents, divorce, desertion, prolonged absence or death. This compared with only 32.2 per cent of the controls. All types of breach, including death of a parent, were more common among the delinquents. Now this finding of the Gluecks has been used by adherents of the Maternal Deprivation and similar theories to demonstrate the validity of ideas which relate crime to early trauma in personal relationships.

There is indeed a strong correlation between broken homes and delinquency: but all the additional evidence suggests that the causal link is very different from that which is usually suggested today. It is not that loss of love (or suspected loss of love) due to parental separation causes delinquent development: rather, the indications are that barely socialised parents, often strongly extravert, and not infrequently of poor mental and/or physical endowment, produce similar children by simple heredity and then are quite unable to provide the persistent, painstaking guidance and training which those children will require. The same impulsive and relatively inconsequential patterns of life which fail to socialise the children, result in the parents' absence of stable goals, incapacity to cope with many domestic problems, unmanageable clashes, choice of immediate change and excitement rather than constructive solutions, which lead in turn to more frequent home desertion, separation or just irresponsible abandonment of the home when the mood takes them. Naturally, once separation has occurred a delinquent development in the child is even more likely, simply because it is more difficult for one parent to provide training and supervision than it is for two.

Very recently research findings from the Institute of Criminology, Cambridge, showed high rates of broken homes amongst delinquents. But as Farrington points out, this is because both the delinquent and the marriage breakdown are related in general familial inadequacy.[10] The self-reinforcing circle of poor conditionability and/or erratic parental supervision and training can account for the strong association between broken homes and delinquency. The 'broken home' *per se* cannot produce a delinquent outcome.

The foregoing discussion has been intended partly to suggest that heredity plays some role in the distribution of personality patterns in human populations. Some of the most direct evidence for this (as in most heredity—environment arguments), is provided by studies of twins, a couple of which can be briefly summarised here. Shields[11] in 1962 made comparisons of the following samples: (1) forty-four pairs of monozygotic twins (genetically identical twins originating in a single fertilised egg) who had been brought up apart;

(2) forty-four pairs of monozygotic twins brought up together; and (3) twenty-eight pairs of dizygotic twins (genetically no more alike than any two siblings, having originated in two separate fertilised eggs) who had been brought up together. The samples were matched for age and sex.

If environmental influences are dominant in shaping personality, one would expect the dizygotic (fraternal) twins to be more alike than the monozygotics reared apart, since they shared the same home environment. The results of two self-rating tests and a structural interview scale for personality showed significant resemblances between the identicals reared apart as regards extraversion, neuroticism and a variety of quite detailed personal items such as mannerisms and smoking habits. The identical twins brought up together also showed significant resemblances, though these were actually less than for those brought up apart. The fraternal twins were far less alike than either set of identicals. Intelligence tests were also applied, and the identicals in both groups showed very high resemblance, while the fraternals showed substantially less — although in this case the degree of resemblance among the two groups of identicals was virtually the same. Neuroticism and extraversion appeared to have a smaller environmental component than intelligence, although in all three dimensions heredity appeared dominant.

Eysenck[12] conducted a similar study in 1956, comparing thirteen pairs of male identicals and thirteen pairs of female identicals with an equal number of fraternals, the mean age of all subjects being a hundred and sixteen months. Again, significant differences appeared between the identicals and fraternals in the degree of resemblance for intelligence and extraversion. This followed earlier work of Eysenck and Prell in 1951, which showed that identical twins resembled each other more than did fraternals on the scale of neuroticism.[13]

Virtually all the main findings of the Gluecks have been repeated by other researchers. Gibbens's study of the somatypes of fifty-eight Borstal boys showed bodily measurements placing nearly all of them as predominantly mesomorphic, or endomorphic mesomorphs.[14] And Sheldon and his colleagues, in a study comparing the somatypes of two hundred delinquent youths with those of four thousand college students found the former massing in the mesomorphic-endomorphic sector, while the latter appeared mainly in the ectomorphic sector.[15]

There are many other studies which show the predominantly extravert characteristics of delinquents compared with non-delinquent controls; in particular the difficulty of habit-training and general restlessness are noted again and again. In 1939 Healy and Bronner[16] compared one hundred and five delinquents with the same number of controls. The striking difficulty experienced by parents of the delinquent group over toilet-training proved a tell-tale sign of the subject's general difficulty in forming conditioned responses. Even after eight years of age, enuresis was found in twenty-two delinquents as opposed to only four controls. The researchers considered this most significant and probably not due to lack of training. Extreme physical aggressiveness, impulsiveness, hyper-activity and restlessness were recorded for forty-six delinquents but for none at all of the controls, who tended on the contrary to be subdued, retiring, quiet inactive and non-aggressive, caring little for excitement. The delinquents' great urge towards crowd companionship also contrasted with the controls' tendency to seek solitude. In 1950–51 Roper's comparative study of 1,428 prisoners and 828 controls noted a high incidence of neurosis in the control group, while the prisoners often appeared unable to acquire the most basic social habits.[17] Warburton's study of recidivists in the Joliot Penitentiary in Chicago also showed his subjects to have high extraversion and instability scores on Cattell's personality scales.[18] R.G. Andry's[19] study of personality correlates for recidivism among offenders serving less than three months, and Gibbens's study of two hundred Borstal boys (part of which was mentioned above), both demonstrated high levels of extraversion among offenders.

Poor health and physique were reported by Sir Cyril Burt as slightly higher among the delinquents, but the difference was not highly significant.[20] Healy and Bronner's study[21] showed the delinquents as having worse developmental health histories than the controls: in general there was between twice and three times the incidence of marked underweight in early childhood, frequent or severe illness, and sickness of the mother during pregnancy, and similar observations have been made by other researchers over the years.

Turning now to more environmental factors, defective discipline has been noted by many criminologists in the backgrounds of their delinquents, together with unstable and hostile family relationships. In his classic study of two hundred young offenders and four hundred controls in 1925 (a study whose high reputation has weathered well over the years), Burt summarised his findings thus:

> These, then so far as they can be classified at all, are the chief conditions met with in the young delinquent's home . . . Altogether, vice in the home [direct training by criminal parents] was noted in twenty-six per cent of the cases; poverty with its concomitants in fifty-three per cent; defective family relationships in fifty-eight per cent and defective discipline in sixty-one per cent. Poverty, however, as we have seen, together with defective family relationships, was noted with much frequency among the non-delinquent; hence they have less significance than might be thought. On the other hand, among the non-delinquent, vicious and ill-disciplined homes were comparatively rare, the proportions being only six and twelve per cent respectively. As before, we can take the two sides into account by contrasting, not the raw percentages, but the calculated coefficients of association. The order of importance is then somewhat changed. The coefficients are: for poverty, 0.15; for defective family relationships, 0.33; for vicious homes, 0.39; and for defective discipline, 0.55. The figures speak for themselves.[22]

The types of defective discipline listed by Burt in ascending order of delinquent productive effect, are (1) Overstrict; (2) Weak and easy-going; (3) Capricious (the most frequent in the sample); and (4) Lack of any discipline whatever (the most harmful). In view of later work in behavioural learning theory it is perhaps less surprising now than in 1925 that capricious discipline should be worse than lax discipline. Capricious discipline, according to Burt, is where 'The child is petted and then smacked, one minute coaxed and cajoled into good behaviour, and the next minute abusively scolded or incontinently whipped; where the mother worries, weeps, loses her temper and hysterically tries every emotion in turn, but never thinks of calm, consistent, rational restraint.[23]

As far as defective and divisive family relationships go, the Maternal Deprivation theorist, Mary D. Salter-Ainsworth, has maintained that the Gluecks' 1942—50 study (see above) gives a strong support to Bowlby's hypothesis. She claims the 'Studies by Glueck & Glueck and Wardle tend to support Bowlby's hypothesis.'[24]

First, the Gluecks give no figures for the kind of maternal separation that is effective, Bowlby claims, in producing the affectionless thief (i.e. separation of three months duration or more). There is just no information about the comparative distribution of this antecedent factor in the delinquent and control groups. Ainsworth therefore looks to the material on serious and permanent breaches of family life due to death, desertion and so on. The percentage of broken homes among the delinquents was almost twice that of the non-delinquents, affecting 60.4 per cent of the delinquent sample compared with 34.2 per cent of the non-delinquent.

These, she suggests — when rejecting the work of Naess and Andry,[25] both of whom found that maternal separation *per se* was unrelated to delinquency — are the kinds of separation experience that Bowlby *really* regarded as the harmful ones. Her enlisting of the Gluecks as allies in this context suggests that the Gluecks' research satisfies the criteria for '. . . the very sort of deprivation experiences that had led to Bowlby's original findings and to his hypothesis that prolonged mother—child separation in the first five years of life "stands foremost among the causes of delinquent character development".'[26] And it is presumably because the Gluecks look at the *right sort* of deprivation experiences that their research supposedly confirms Bowlby's hypothesis. But even if we concede that he meant these drastic and permanent separations, the Gluecks still scarcely serve Ainsworth's purpose. This 'very sort of deprivation experience' which they examine includes separation from the father as well as from the mother; and while the Gluecks do not distinguish the two, it is more reasonable to suppose that most would be father—child separations, since in Western countries with nuclear families men are in a far better economic position to desert, and mothers are usually given custody of young children in divorces or legal separations. Indeed, this very failure to distinguish loss of mother from loss of father is pointed out by Ainsworth in criticism of the Gluecks' study itself. Also, in considering another study by Rowntree[27] which compared young children in broken families with those in intact ones and found but one temporary difference (more enuresis in young middle-class children), Ainsworth defends the Maternal Deprivation Theory by objecting that in Rowntree's broken families, the mothers were still in sole charge of eighty per cent of the children, so that nothing is demonstrated. She thereby draws the proper distinction between the specific situation of maternal deprivation, and the very general one of a broken home. It is, then, inconsistent to appeal to the Gluecks' findings as supporting the Maternal Deprivation Theory.

Next, it must surely be insisted upon that the Maternal Deprivation Theory maintains that the critical period in which separation is damaging is before five years of age. Ainsworth says of the Gluecks' study:

> Glueck and Glueck found that loss, before a child's fifth birthday, of either parent through death, divorce, separation or prolonged absence was an antecedent condition twice as frequent in a delinquent group as in a matched group of non-delinquents ($P<0.001$). Similar loss occurring between five and ten years of age also had a significantly higher incidence among the delinquents ($P<0.01$), but loss occurring after ten years did not. (The Gluecks' report unfortunately does not distinguish loss of mother from loss of father.)[28]

Now, the statistical significance distinguishing the delinquents and controls is entirely between the sum totals of broken homes and intact homes at different ages and not at all between breaks occurring under and over five, which should show a marked difference if Bowlby's hypothesis is true; if we compare the percentages of homes broken before and after five for both delinquents and controls, the case does not look so good.[29]

	Broken under five	Broken under nine	Others
Delinquent broken home (= 60.4% of all delinquents)	56.3	28.1	15.6
Non-delinquent broken home (= 34.2% of all non-delinquents)	46.7	31.0	22.3

Separation under five was generally higher for both groups. The Gluecks observed these differences as showing: 'a considerable likeness between the delinquents and non-delinquents in respect to the time at which the physical cohesion of the families first suffered a blow'. [30] Again, while broken homes from all causes were significantly higher for the delinquents, and while all types of breach were numerically higher, there were important differences in the distribution of types of breach.

The *percentages* of first breaks due to death, illness, legal separation and divorce (though not, of course, the absolute numbers) were higher for the non-delinquent broken homes than for the delinquent. This pattern fits the Gluecks' explanation of the correlation between broken homes and delinquency, but cannot be accounted for on a maternal deprivation hypothesis. It appears from the figures that the parents of delinquents resort to the more unofficial and less respectable ways of breaking up the home, such as desertion by one spouse or desertion of the offspring by both parents. Recently the Institute of Criminology, Cambridge[31] found that although there was a high incidence of broken homes in the backgrounds of delinquents, loss of parents through death did not produce a significantly high number of delinquent children.

If we are prepared to include in the class of the maternally deprived, children whose home life has been permanently disrupted in any way, at any age under nine and with the loss of either parent, and entirely ignore all other correlations with delinquency found in the study as well as the explanation offered for broken homes, then the Gluecks can be beaten into a just passable grist for the maternal deprivation mill. So could very nearly any other criminological study. (Perhaps it should be mentioned too that the predictive tests which the Gluecks evolved out of this and other studies, do not include anywhere in their critical indices for future delinquents or for recidivists the absence of a mother or permanent mother-substitute for a period during the first five years of life.)

Ainsworth refers to the Gluecks' study as 'Evidence derived from retrospective case studies of persistent delinquents'.[32] This it certainly was not. It seems likely that she has in mind the other main Glueck study published in 1940, which followed up one thousand boy delinquents who had first been convicted nearly twenty years earlier.[33]

The total follow-up study spanned a period of fifteen years. The main emphasis was examination for the amount of recidivism during a five-year period following completion of penal treatment. There followed a second investigation of the same subjects ten years later. First, there were many aspects in which the reformed delinquents and the recidivists did not differ. The Gluecks found that

> The same proportion of those delinquents who ultimately reformed as those who continued to recidivate had in childhood enjoyed the affectionate regard of their mothers. In both groups, also, the proportion of mothers who had to work to supplement the family income was the same. The two groups further resemble each other in being the product of homes which had been broken by the desertion, separation, divorce or death of their parents before the appearance of the boys in the Boston Juvenile Court. The two groups were to a uniform extent reared in homes and neighbourhoods in which the conditions of life were poor and difficult. The families from which the reformed and unreformed sprang were of equal size, and the same percentage of each were compelled to seek the aid of social welfare agencies during the childhood of the boys.'[34]

The very significant differences which did emerge were as follows: (1) the reformed group were more favourably endowed biologically, possessing higher intelligence, less mental disease and less measurable personality liabilities; their families also demonstrated more mental disease and defects; (2) the reformed group were less likely to have had parents who had applied consistent and reasoned discipline or consistent and strict discipline (the parents of recidivists in serious crimes proved to have been the most negligent of all in applying discipline); (3) an excessive proportion of the recidivists were the sons of Irish-born fathers and to a lesser extent Irish-born mothers, compared with boys whose parents belonged to other immigrant national groups of America; (4) the religion of the parents of the unreformed was more likely to be Roman Catholic than Protestant or Jewish; (5) the unreformed were also more likely to have caused trouble at school; and (6) they were more likely to have got into trouble with the law at an earlier age than did the delinquents who were later to reform. Whether affection or hostility existed between the delinquent and his family, whether he had the support and interest of his parents, and whether they were concerned or not to preserve an intact home, appear to exert no influence when he is grown up and no longer living with them. They may have been important factors when he was a child because they constituted his immediate environment, but they no longer do when he moves away from home and another set of relationships becomes his present, and therefore most important, concern.

From this work, and from additional data (reported in their work *Five Hundred Criminal Careers* and *Later Criminal Careers*)[35],[36] the Gluecks concluded that the physical and mental changes that comprise the natural process of màturation provide the chief explanation of the improvement in conduct with passing years. This theory is partially supported by the finding that, regardless of the age at which delinquency begins, delinquent careers run a fairly steady and predictable course. We know already that extraverts take longer to reach the state where conditioning in acceptable social behaviour can be said to have 'taken' — that is, where, given the level of reinforcement provided by the surrounding society, they can be depended on to behave normally without supervision. Those delinquents whose parents had applied discipline for part of the adolescent's life — though often in vain — have a more advantageous learning situation than those whose parents abandoned the whole socialisation process to state agencies, or just to *ad hoc* social situations that might have a crude conditioning effect on behaviour as personality gradually becomes more mature and amenable. Those delinquents with an environment conducive to the acquisition and reinforcement of non-criminal habits will, naturally enough, acquire them quicker than others of the same level of maturation. But, nonetheless, the Gluecks report that: '. . . with the passage of years, a differentiation seems to occur between the offenders whose delinquency and criminality is due more to adverse environmental and educational influence than to any deep-seated organismal weakness'.[37] That is, the individual who offends simply because his environment has not provided the necessary training or because he is late in maturing sufficiently for the training to be effective, is obviously capable of altering his conduct if the appropriate influences are exerted later. Reformatory treatment, army service, the pressure of acquaintances, employers or workmates can be effective in establishing in him certain standards of conduct later in life.

However, as the Gluecks observed, there will always be those who are 'inclined never to reach a stage of maturity sufficient to enable them to abandon criminalism, and who will either die as criminals or end their days in almshouses or on the street'. [38] This sombre group, who are virtually unaffected by educative procedures, are scarcely identifiable with Bowlby's hypothetical unreformable thieves.

From the evidence there seems little to conclude about the connection between delinquency and maternal deprivation except that it may, in some circumstances, form an index of parental inability or abdication from responsibility for adequate socialisation.

Naess (1962)[39] came to much the same conclusion in the later extension to the study already discussed. It will be remembered that here the factor of maternal deprivation was the only variable one, the homes of delinquents and controls being otherwise identical. Maternal separation was actually less in the delinquent group than in the controls.

What happens to the amount of maternal deprivation among delinquents when other factors are allowed to vary, that is, when delinquents and controls are not brothers sharing the same parents and home? She selected another group of delinquent boys from the files of Oslo Barnevernsnemnd (Child Protection Council) with initials from P to S, using the same criteria with which she had selected the first delinquent group, except that they were not required to have non-delinquent brothers. As would be expected, the boys who did not have non-delinquent brothers (because, among other reasons, if they possessed brothers near in age these were likely to be delinquent also), were more delinquent than the group selected for the 1958 study, having more police referrals. The amount of maternal separation among these delinquents was higher than for the original delinquent sample of 1958, being far nearer to that of the non-delinquent controls; it stood at 27 per cent for six months or more separation during the first five years of life, and 31 per cent for at least three months during the first five years of life. (The original figures for the 1958 study were as follows: 10 per cent and 15 per cent for the delinquents and 20 per cent and 24 per cent for their non-delinquent brothers.) The slightly higher figure for the second delinquent sample is, however, not significant. Similar figures for separation are also found for a group of children attending a clinic for psychiatric treatment and a group under observation in a psychiatric hospital. (Naess only included clinic or hospital patients who had stealing noted in their records.) These lie between the figures for the control and the second delinquent group, being 24 and 25 per cent respectively for the clinic group and 25 and 30 per cent respectively for the hospital sample. It appears that maternal separation rises in delinquent samples only if other environmental factors are allowed to vary, such that it can be seen as an incidental function of these. The important family factor that rises (according to Naess, from her analysis of Norwegian delinquent samples) with the seriousness of delinquency, is that of the broken home, with mother—child separation being one form of such disturbance, causally related to other forms, such as father's imprisonment or desertion.

Naess's conclusion that mother—child separation is not a

cause of crime in itself, but is part of the picture of an
unstable family life, is similar to that of Barbara Wootton,
who suggests that the only diagnostic value of maternal
deprivation lies in the fact that it can be one way of spotting
a rejecting mother.[40]

The findings of Naess are repeated in the 1971 study of
Rutter.[41] He investigated two groups of children for any
after-effects of separation experiences. One group was
composed of nine- to twelve-year-olds in families from a
community of small towns in the Isle of Wight, and the other
was a representative group of children from London families
in which one or both parents had been under psychiatric
care. The first group had been selected originally for a
large-scale investigation of the educational, physical and
psychiatric handicaps of school-age children. The second
group had initially been selected for an investigation of the
difficulties experienced by families when one member
becomes sick. Rutter found that separation from one parent
was unconnected with the rate of anti-social conduct. Indeed,
although it was a difference short of statistical significance,
he found (like Naess in her original study) that, if anything,
fewer of the separated children showed anti-social conduct.
(This may be due to children gaining from socialising
experiences outside the family.) There was no difference
between maternal or paternal separation, and no difference
was made by the age of the children at separation. The
comparisons were repeated for neurotic disorders and, again,
no association was found between separation from one
parent and any type of psychotic or behaviour disorder.

There was, however, an association between separation
from both parents and anti-social conduct. To isolate other
possible variables operating here, Rutter took ratings for the
quality of the parental marriage. He found that it was only in
those homes where there was marked discord and disturbance
that separation correlated with anti-social tendencies.
Children from such homes were likely to be separated from
both parents and put into care, or they might be abandoned.
Children who were separated from both parents because of
holidays or illness showed no more anti-social tendencies
than those unseparated. Age was irrelevant. The pathogenic
factor is thus not separation but lies in the events preceding

some instances of it, such as hostility, quarrels, parental psychosis. The separation and the anti-social conduct were attributable to parental irresponsibility and inadequacies.

6 Criminal Character

The theory we are looking at in detail is one in a tradition that makes much of the idea that crime is a symptom of a sick personality, produced by bad environmental influences. If the latter are absent is it assumed that humans naturally grow up obedient to the *mores* expressed in the laws of twentieth-century Britain? True, the theory does not maintain that all crime is committed by those of the affectionless personality type, only one third of it. What of the other two-thirds? One explanation often given for them is that they are due to other parental failures of a less serious variety: generally that the mother does not consciously love the child enough. Alternatively, if she does appear to love it, her shortcoming is said to be 'unconscious'.

The notion that crime is a result, an expression, of a deformed personality, has led some supporters of the Maternal Deprivation Theory to suggest that the studies of criminal behaviour we have already quoted are of only limited value, and do not disprove their contentions. We must not, they tell us, start with criminal behaviour and then see if the criminals have been separated from their mothers to a significantly greater degree than the control group. We must, instead, start by investigating the personality, and see whether the persons diagnosed as affectionless were separated from their mothers, after which we see if they also show a significant degree of delinquency. But if the hypothesis is that one-third of delinquents are of the affectionless personality type, and that this is caused by maternal deprivation, then, whether we look separately at the thieves for the incidence of affectionlessness and/or maternal deprivation, or whether we take the maternally deprived and/or affectionless and examine their lawbreaking activities, we should expect to find this proportion of one-third maternally-deprived criminals — which is significantly higher than the proportion of criminals in the general population and also, presumably, significantly higher than the proportion of the maternally deprived in the general population. This applies particularly to the researchers we have looked at, who have frequently used far more serious offences than Bowlby did to separate delinquents from controls. It is not denied by Ainsworth[1] that some maternally deprived, affectionless people do not become criminal (although Bowlby explicity states at one point[2] that stealing is a necessary condition of affectionlessness), but her claim still entails that the proportion who do not become criminal will be significantly smaller in the deprived than in the non-deprived.

(It would be made a lot easier if some public criteria were provided for the identification of affectionless characters. We are told of a mysterious clinical knowledge which we must possess: personality questionnaires, behavioural observations, are held to be of little value compared with 'reliable clinical history-taking methods').[3]

Still, if we must not start from the delinquent link in the causal chain, let us please the supporters of the theory and start by looking at the affectionless personality first. We are going to see if any non-clinical researchers have come across any affectionless subjects in their work and whether these appear to be of the same personality type as Bowlby's affectionless thieves.

Hilda Lewis (1954)[4] undertook a complex study of five hundred children admitted to the Mershal Reception Centre. Children were admitted to this centre because of parental neglect, cruelty, loss of parental care due to chronic physical or mental illness, or because the child was uncontrolled or delinquent. The ages of the children went up to twelve in the case of boys, and fifteen in the case of girls. This sample was obviously composed of children with great environmental handicaps. Ninety-nine fathers of children in the sample, and one hundred and eighty mothers, suffered some form of mental disability; twenty-three per cent of the children were illegitimate, four times the rate for the general population. Lewis used Hewitt and Jenkins's tests for deviant childhood behaviour.[5] This early test for maladjustment in children, similar to the Stott[6] guides, was derived from statistical analysis (by means of multiple correlations) of children at the Michigan Guidance Institute. Three main sorts of behaviour emerged, in each of which certain activities or traits occurred so frequently together that it could reasonably be assumed that they formed a consistent pattern. Hilda Lewis distinguished children who have high ratings for a complex of behaviour from those who rate lower for the individual items that compose it.

Lewis defined temporary separation as separation of a child from the mother for a period of not less than three months and not more than two years. Cases where children had been in the care of adoptive or foster mothers since early life were excluded. There is also lasting separation, which was defined as continuous physical separation of the child from the mother for more than two years immediately before admission to the reception centre. Most children in this group turned out to have been separated from their mothers all of their lives.

Testing of the children in the Centre produced the following results:[7]

Behaviour	Number	Percentage
Normal	119	24
Mixed	37	8
Unsocialised aggressive	52	10
Socialised delinquent	57	11
Over-inhibited, neurotic	80	16
Slightly 'unsocialised aggressive'	25	5
Slightly 'socialised delinquent'	19	4
Slightly 'over-inhibited, neurotic'	111	22
	500	100

The number of children with only mild departures from the normal (155) is high. According to the theory, the worst damage should be done to children who have been separated from their mothers for long periods in the first couple of years. A total of 174 children had undergone temporary separation. There was found to be no statistical difference between the behaviour of children separated from their mothers for periods up to two years and those having undergone no separation up to the allocation to the reception centre. Now 142 children among the 500 had suffered lasting separation, 54 before 2 years, 54 between 2 and 5 years and 34 after 5 years. Lasting separation before the age of two showed a statistical significance between the behaviour of those separated and those unseparated. The behavioural differences between those lastingly separated and those who were not consisted mainly of mildly disturbed behaviour.

Now from this study we find no damage at all accruing to children as a result of separation from the mother of up to two years duration. Why mild disturbance after this period? If separation is harmless up to two years, extra time should hardly make a difference. Lewis points out that the difference between children who have never had a home and probably never will, and those with temporary arrangements, are considerable. In the backgrounds of the former are to be found the chronically mentally ill or defective parents, the child itself often having suffered complete rejection and abandonment: some children had been exposed to six or eight moves. Maladjustment in such cases could hardly be laid solely at the door of separation from the mother. There is the additional fact that these children did not even constitute a representative sample from such appalling backgrounds, for many were at the Mershal Centre because they had actively caused considerable trouble to the institutions or foster parents with whom they had been placed, and had therefore been referred to the centre for diagnostic advice. Children 'doing well either in foster homes or institutions were only infrequently referred to the centre'.[8] Not all the children in the permanently separated category even showed mild disturbances: although they had suffered repeated separations and rejections, many were quite normal. Very poor heredity and alternative environmental considerations offer a far simpler explanation for mild disturbances.

Of what nature were these mild disturbances? Affectionlessness, perhaps? Actually there was

...no clear connection between separation from the mother in early childhood and any particular variety of disturbed behaviour ... [so that] In the scarcely significant association...the trend is for the children separated from their mothers to fall into the aggressive group rather than the group of socialised delinquents among whom most of the juvenile thieves were to be found: as far as definite neurotic disturbances are concerned, the children separated from their mothers tend to behave like the other children.[9]

All observations failed 'to confirm the belief that a characteristic form of delinquent personality, recognisable on psychiatric examination, commonly ensues upon a child's separation from his mother in his early years'.[10]

Were there no affectionless subjects at all among the five hundred children? Hilda Lewis found that 'Nineteen of the five hundred children were judged to show morbid lack of affective responsiveness, the judgement is, however, inevitably subjective, as can readily be discerned in the last sentence of the quotation from Bowlby.'[11]

However, even with these nineteen it would be 'misleading'

. . . to imply that all nineteen children showed a universal lack of affective response to adults and children: this was most exceptional. In the majority their detachment and devices for avoiding emotional involvement were selective, being displayed more towards some individuals or classes of people than others, and their mostly unemotional behaviour was punctuated by lively expressions of feeling, such as an out-burst of temper.[12]

Ten of these children came from the 184 subjects who had never been separated for more than a few weeks before the committal to the Reception Centre, 4 came from among the 174 who had undergone temporary separation and 5 from the group of 142 that had suffered prolonged separation. Only one had suffered separation before two years.

Stott's findings[13] are similar to those of Hilda Lewis. In 1956 Stott studied 141 backward children, 25 of whom had been separated from their mothers for at least ten weeks during their first four years of life. Teachers used the Stott Bristol Social Adjustment Guides (an objective test for maladjustment in children) and interviews were carried out with mothers and the relevant institutions. The illness rate was high with these backward children, as one would expect;

some were born weakly or ill, others needed special medical attention because of their failure to thrive and gain weight in infancy; others suffered from gross physical neglect, serious convulsions and proneness to accidents of a fairly serious nature. As many separated children would have been separated because they were ill, a comparison was made between the 25 separated children and 28 others from the 141 who had had serious illnesses without being separated from their mothers, in order to gauge the role of illness in personality deviations. The group who had been ill but stayed at home showed about the same amount of maladjustment as the separated children and were somewhat more 'unforthcoming' than the separated group. Stott does not regard the differences as significant because of the small sample. In the entire sample of 141, 51 children were assessed as socially unforthcoming (corresponding to the over-inhibited category of Hilda Lewis). Among these only 2 were separated without being ill, while 15 were ill without being separated. As Stott remarks, people 'are normally lacking in "go" after being ill'.

In the case of sixteen other unforthcoming children there was neither separation nor serious illness under the age of two years; these may have occurred later, as did anxiety-producing family relationships observed in many cases. From Stott's work we get little indication that separation is a pathological factor without the accompaniment of severe illness or bad parental treatment. When separation occurred in the context of parental attempts to get rid of the child, of which it was aware, then it was a predisposing factor to maladjustment, of course. Stott gives an interesting account of separation of twins: one is diagnosed as well-adjusted, the other as demonstrating unsettled behaviour. The latter had experienced what the former had been lucky to avoid — namely, having been scalded badly as an infant, then being treated in hospital for ringworm, which involved as part of the treatment having the head shaved, with no familiar person present.

Stott finds it difficult, if not impossible, to call any of these children affectionless. Exceptionally bad experiences with people had made some wary, but 'Even then they were not affectionless: they had a burning need for affection, alongside the rejectional hostility which they always kept ready to hand in case their need for love was not met.'[14]

And affection Stott characterises as not '. . . fondling or treats or indulgences . . . but affection in the sense of loyalty which induces a parent or other adult to stick to the child through thick and thin and neither relinquish the child to other care or appear likely to do so.[15]

Cruel rebuffs can obviously lead to a withdrawal from inter-personal contacts; but the fact cannot entirely be ignored   that individuals may vary considerably in their desire   for   social   intercourse,   due   to   innate,   not environmental, factors. It may simply be asking too much of some people that they generally behave in a positive manner towards others. Sociability is certainly one of the most stable of measured personality traits. Clare Hyman[16] found that personality tests on parents who battered their children and on those who did not, revealed (among other things) less willingness in the former to participate in social situations. Supportive evidence suggests that genetic origins cannot be entirely ruled out. There are, of course, some very important environmental circumstances also associated with child abuse (which I shall deal with later); but the fact still remains that it may not be a very good idea for those who have little need for, and tolerance of, the company of others, to have a job involving people (in this case parenthood) and certainly not an unsupervised, unshared one. It is a cliché that bad, violent parents produce in turn bad, violent children, so that a cycle of deprivation rolls on down the generations. This recurrence of the same problems in one family could be as attributable, at least partly, to genetic as to environmental factors, although this explanation is unfashionable and, on the surface, pessimistic.

I now want to take up the theme of the interaction of genetic and environmental variables in the following discussion of the origins of a personality type almost as common in the Maternal Deprivation and other popular child-care literature as he is on the police files — the psychopath. Said to markedly lack affection and concern for others, he fails to learn from experience and is a violent, irresponsible parent almost as much as he is a violent irresponsible citizen.

7 Affectionlessness and Psychopathology

In the work of the Maternal Deprivation theorists the term
psychopath is often used in place of affectionless, as well as
the term 'delinquent character structure', which also appears
as a synonym. Thus Bowlby: 'These responses, which are
probably the result of frequent separation or of prolonged
separation occurring before about two and a half years of age
and without a substitute mother—person being available, are
the forerunners of the grave personality disturbances (known
technically as psychopathic) which are described fully in the
next chapter'.[1] The use of the term psychopath to describe
the after-effects of maternal deprivation has probably been
more efficacious in causing alarm among sensitive parents
than the less well known term affectionless. It has a
ready-made structure of cultural associations to call upon. It
is a term intrinsically bound up in the public mind with
violence. It may be felt that absence of maternal presence or
failure to give the right quantity of love, will produce an
outcome far more sinister than that conveyed by such terms
as 'neuroticism' or 'insecurity'.

The only way of dealing with such fears is to examine
rationally what is meant by the term psychopath and to
investigate, as far as possible with our present knowledge,
what its causation is likely to be. As we do this, it will
become apparent whether the psychopath is identical with
Bowlby's affectionless thief and whether the condition is
caused by maternal deprivation.

Maternal deprivation researchers have made use of
this word as an alternative to affectionless, because it has
long been noted by writers on psychopathology that the
psychopath usually forms only the most fleeting relationships
with people and often appears to lack affective or altruistic
feelings towards them. More old-fashioned terms which the
reader may have come across, are 'moral imbecile' and

'sociopath'. After a review of the literature on psychopathy McCord and McCord[2] in 1964 concluded that the two central features of this personality are lovelessness and guiltlessness. At much the same time (1965) Craft[3] named the essential features as lack of feelings or affection for others, combined with a tendency to act on impulse without forethought.

There are many more inclusive, lengthy descriptions of the characteristics of psychopathology, for example, that of the American psychologist Gough[4] (1948). In his view psychopaths are characterised by a failure to postpone immediate goals for long-term objectives: impulsive behaviour involving an apparent incongruity between the strength of the stimulus and the magnitude of the behavioural response: poor judgement and planning in attaining defined goals: lack of anxiety, embarrassment or distress over social non-conformity and disruption: a tendency to blame others and take no responsibility for failures: meaningless lying, even though the person is quite aware that he will be found out: lack of dependability or willingness to assume any responsibility: inability to form any persistent attachment to others, and unconcern over the rights and privileges of others where they might interfere with personal gratifications. A simplified definition was provided by a 1962 conference of prison medical officers and practising psychiatrists, who were asked which important clinical features they would consider diagnostic of psychopathy in order of importance. These were to be considered independent of convictions. They listed: (1) aggressiveness, (2) liability to act on impulse, (3) a defect in feeling or affection for other humans, with, perhaps (4) a failure to learn from experience or profit from punishment.[5]

The impulsiveness, desire for change in personal relationships, the aggressiveness of many, the search for powerful stimulation and the dislike for any introspective mental activity leads one to class the psychopath as an extreme (unstable) extravert. His behaviour, as Michael Craft[6] is at pains to point out, after a review of writers on the subject, consists of extremes in behaviour variables from a normal of which there are infinite gradations. But to say simply that he is an extreme (unstable) extravert is probably a gross over-simplification, since the trait term introvert—extravert covers a number of component traits which vary in strength from one individual to another. Thus, on blanket tests for extraversion, psychopathic samples have given conflicting results.[7] What the experimental material tends to point to is that so-called psychopaths are high on some indices of extraversion, particularly impulsiveness and aggressiveness and are nearer to the mean for normal population samples for factors such as sociability. The axis of introversion—extraversion is probably too wide to be an adequate descriptive tool in some cases and could be broken down into at least two component personality traits without necessarily becoming cumbersome.[8]

Experimental evidence shows that psychopaths do not develop conditioned responses readily. Their behaviour seems to be immune to the possibility of unpleasant consequences; they are neither motivated nor guided by them and past events have little or no effect on present behaviour. Their lack of concern for others, egocentricity, the self-indulgence in things immediately gratifying, the lack of moral standards, the fleeting nature of their interests and their distractibility has often led others to compare them with young children. Unfortunately an adult with little or no control over his impulses is more of a menace than a young child, and psychopaths occur frequently in criminal samples. As Roper[9] remarks, it is useless to think of them as adults, except in so far as they have the adult's strength and cunning. Indeed, EEG (electroencephalogram) studies of psychopaths show that many have the slow brainwave activity associated with children.[10] This has led many to postulate that the psychopath suffers from a cortical immaturity, which prevents him learning from his experiences in the manner of the normal adolescent or adult. People certainly do become less extravert as they get older, and as we saw with the Gluecks' investigation of recidivism, many people do grow out of their delinquency, acquiring controls as they become neurologically mature enough to accept them.

But the fact that many psychopaths have immature EEG patterns does not allow us to dismiss psychopathology as a disease or organic defect like epilepsy. That some people have a make-up that prefers many but transitory contacts to a few long-lasting and complex relationships is not in itself pathological, for it would be theoretically possible to regard the latter as equally so. That we prefer people to make few but stable contacts is to be recognised as a cultural value-judgement and not a criterion of human mental health, no matter how justified this judgement may be. In some societies, the personality attributes held to be desirable closely approximate to those which we term psychopathic; and where the person is not endowed by nature with these attributes it is requisite for his status and possibly survival that he learn to imitate them. Take for example, the cannibal Mundugumor of the Yuat River in New Guinea:

> These robust, restive people live on the banks of a swiftly flowing river, but with no river lore. They trade with and prey upon the miserable, underfed bush-peoples who live on poorer land, devote their time to quarrelling and head-hunting, and have developed a form of social organisation in which every man's hand is against every other man. The women are as assertive and vigorous as the men; they detest bearing and rearing children, and provide most of the food, leaving the men free to plot and fight.[11]

Military regimes throughout history have attempted to foster such traits, and the behaviour that is admired and encouraged in boys as masculine often verges dangerously on the psychopathic. Contempt for any life of the mind, aggressiveness, callousness, insensitivity to the feelings of others, rashness and impulsiveness are all desirable signs of crude virility.

Society is also prone to admire enormously the psychopathic character, who, having been born in a favourable station, has escaped the broad and easy road to prison that is travelled by similarly endowed individuals of a less favoured class. Ruthlessness in business and politics are seen as signs of courage and skill; aggressive military policies which disregard gentlemanly rules and employ terror in all its forms are widely admired as tough and realistic and countless films and books identify courage with mere brutality.

Psychopaths do not appear to differ in intelligence from normal samples; in fact, as R.D. Hare[12] remarks in his excellent review of all the research into psychopathology, as a group it is possible that they may score higher, since IQ tests on psychopaths have usually only been given to detainees (that is, the ones who get caught). There is a certain amount of evidence that this may be so. Psychopaths appear to perform tasks under stress better than normals; they seem to be physiologically immune to much pain and stress and recover very rapidly from any adverse stimulation which they do feel. This under-reactivity of the psychopath is the polar opposite of the responses of the very introverted (who can easily suffer from neurosis), where all the neurophysiological correlates of fear or stress subside very slowly. The latter may be crucial to the formation of conditioned responses, which, of course, the very introverted acquires easily. The under-reactivity of the psychopath also leads him to seek exciting, highly stimulating situations (often dangerous or violent ones) and to be oblivious to many of the subtle cues and considerations that guide others in their interpersonal relationships. The fact that he seems to suffer from under-arousal rather than over-arousal perhaps makes the description 'unstable extravert' a misnomer. This term would seem more descriptive of the behavioural consequences of his low arousal which seem to us to be reckless. As Hare argues, it is probably preferable to call him a stable extravert.[13]

That the psychopath is shallow in his relationships with others, is often brutal towards them and frequently sacrifices them to his impulsive gratifications, might justify tentative use of the term affectionless to describe this personality type. Michael Rutter[14] in his critical review of the Maternal Deprivation Theory equates Bowlby's affectionless thief with the psychopath; this appears to be largely on Bowlby's word, since little in the way of genuinely independent correlations are brought forward. Even here it is difficult to see how the studies he considers (of the behaviour of institutionalised children and Harlow's socially isolated monkeys — see chapters 9 and 16) can give any independent support for the existence of an affectionless personality unless the interpreter is uncritical of the popular use that is made of the studies. This is the weak part of an otherwise very thorough book. Rutter finds that such a personality as the affectionless (that is, psychopathic) one is not a consequence of maternal separation as such, for it has failed to show up in studies of children having undergone this experience; and he then tries to ascertain what other origins it might have. This avoids two important questions: whether Bowlby's affectionless character can be seriously equated with the psychopath (which seems unlikely, as we shall see) and whether such a character exists at all.

It is highly doubtful whether Bowlby's affectionless thief can be equated with the psychopath because other traits possessed by the typical psychopath do not fit the descriptions of affectionless children which Bowlby gives. For example, in his *Forty-Four Juvenile Thieves* there is little indication that it is only those with pronounced extravert traits that are being described, since some of his affectionless children are, as far as one can gather, frightened, withdrawn and quiet. His hyperthymic group of children appear to come closest to the extreme extravert. Other authors who have tried to clarify what Bowlby means by affectionless take it to mean, partly at least, a pronounced form of apathy and unresponsiveness to contact — which contrasts sharply with the psychopath's continual active search for stimulation. Hilda Lewis[15] interprets it in this way, as does Stott.[16] Lewis tested for psychopathic personality separately, and found only fifteen of her children with this type of personality, three per cent of the sample. This figure is not exceptionally low considering the number of extreme aggressive, impulsive extraverts in the general population, despite its disproportional cultural influence via the cult of masculinity. The percentage is, of course, higher in prison populations, but even here hardly reaches the thirty to fifty per cent given by Bowlby as his estimation of the number of affectionless individuals among recidivists.[17]

The second natural question arises: is extreme extraversion, even if it could ever be equated with affectionlessness, a product of maternal deprivation?

An experiment to ascertain the role of adverse factors in the early lives of psychopathic criminals (who do not, of course, include the whole population of criminals or of psychopaths) was undertaken by Michael Craft (1966).[18] The early adverse factors used were three which could be checked for from case notes: illegitimacy, absence from parents for over one year prior to the age of ten (from the mother if illegitimate, from either parent for the others) and brain damage (defined as prolonged unconsciousness, properly documented head injury, or present neurological signs). The three groups of psychopaths were studied alongside four other groups of non-psychopathic individuals.

A significant association was found between predicted rank order of psychopathy and the three factors of illegitimacy, separation and brain damage in combination. The factor of parental separation itself was not found significant, nor was age at separation, the separation experiences being fairly equally divided between 0–5 and 5–10 years. Craft postulated that parental attitudes might be a better measure than the number of years of separation. So here he used a five-point scale to rate each parent's relationship to each of the one hundred and one admissions to the Balderton Psychopathic Unit (in Nottinghamshire), and then graded the patients in four grades of psychopathic severity. The result was significant; absent, lax or hostile parents were very high in the extreme psychopathic groups. There was a significant relationship between degree of poor parental relationship and severity of personality disorder.

A study by Oltman and Friedman in 1967 showed high levels of parental loss amongst psychopaths compared with normals and groups of other subjects in various psychiatric classifications (alcoholics, neurotics, psychotics, etc.).[19] Yet if one looks closer at the type of loss, death of the parent does not differentiate the psychopaths from the other groups (indeed, normals suffered parental loss through death in 26·9 per cent of cases, alcoholics 29·3 per cent psychopaths in only 20·6 per cent). Loss through death is usually postulated as the most traumatic form of separation by those in the psychoanalytic tradition. The high levels of parental loss among psychopaths in this study were related to other forms of separation and moreover (compared with the other groups), to separation from the father. (Actually, if one is determined to see separation *per se* as a crucial variable in the causation of anti-social behaviour, the evidence from so many studies suggests that *paternal* not maternal separation is the vital factor.) The Oltman and Friedman study parallels Rutter's and Farrington's in finding death irrelevant, but other forms of separation linked to later difficult behaviour. And like Rutter and Farrington, these authors postulate that the disturbances in the family prior to separation are more important than the separation itself:

> The parent (usually the father) who deserts his family is presumptively unstable, irresponsible, and heedless of the children. He may be alcoholic, physically abusive, promiscuous, shiftless. Is it not credible that the impact of these factors upon the child exerts an adverse influence equal to, or greater than, the physical absence of the parent?[20]

A study by Robins[21] (1966) described the adult social and psychiatric states of 524 persons who had been referred to a psychiatric clinic thirty years earlier — 406 of them for anti-social behaviour. Twenty-two per cent received an adult diagnosis of psychopathic personality compared with two per cent in a normal control group of 100 subjects. Broken homes were common in the backgrounds of the psychopaths. This seemed to be strongly related to the fact that most of the psychopaths also had fathers who were either themselves psychopathic or alcoholic. Robins notes that the consequences of having such a father are lack of adequate discipline and family discord — again the circumstances surrounding separation are more important than the breach itself. Many might say that it is the child's sense of rejection, of being unloved, that is the variable involved in the broken home—separation complex, which leads to later anti-social behaviour. But Robins found that cold, unaffectionate fathers tended to have fewer psychopathic children than others — such fathers were usually strict disciplinarians and it appeared to be the factor of strict or adequate discipline, above all, that considerably lessened the chances of adult psychopathy. From the studies, the chief predictor of psychopathy would seem to be having an anti-social or psychopathic father.

Nonetheless, as Hare[22] points out, such grossly inadequate parental behaviour is neither a necessary nor a sufficient condition for the development of psychopathy. It must be remembered that most people who come from very discordant homes do not become psychopaths. And even where we find such background, we are unwarranted in seeing the causal connection entirely in environmentalist terms, that is, simply inadequate socialisation. There is now a considerable amount of evidence available for important neurophysiological differences between normals and psychopaths. I have already mentioned the immature EEG patterns possessed by many psychopaths, and one investigation of these also tested the parents and foster parents of psychopaths. There was a significant tendency for psychopaths with slow waves to have parents (but not foster parents) with slow waves.[23]

It could, of course, be postulated that brain-wave patterns have an environmental origin in parental behaviour towards the young infant. If maternal deprivation leads to psychopathy, could separation from the mother in early life produce low cortical arousal status (slow, high-voltage activity)? It is difficult to conceive what the causal mechanism might be if such a connection were ever found. Slow wave patterns could theoretically be produced by the parent rewarding behaviour associated with low-arousal states and thus encouraging slow waves, but learning is not a mechanism in favour in the psychoanalytical tradition.

Shield's study[24] of identical twins shows no relationship between later ratings for extraversion and early separation. He studied twenty-six pairs of twins, where one of each pair had remained with the natural mother while the other had left in infancy or early childhood to go elsewhere. It was postulated that those who left the mother might have been affected in some way, possibly adversely. The findings [25] can be tabulated in the following way:

	Higher	Equal	Lower	Not tested
Intelligence	13	—	11	2
Extraversion	14	4	8	—
Neuroticism	17	2	7	—
	Poor	Equal	Better	Not rated
Mental health rating	13	1	10	2

These findings mirror the negative picture that emerges when we look at the case histories of notorious criminal psychopaths. In some there is early maternal separation, in others there is not: no meaningful pattern is discernible. Straffen,[26] born in 1933, spent his early years in India, where he was separated from his father fairly often but, as far as we can tell, never from his mother. In England he was first placed on a probation order at eight for stealing, it being then remarked on that he had no idea of right and wrong. At eighteen he killed two girls in one evening, attending a film show in between. In escaping from Broadmoor, he killed again. Neville Heath, born of middle-class parents, also appears not to have undergone any separation from his mother. His career involved various offences, including theft, house-breaking and forgery. In 1946 at twenty-nine he began sadistic attacks on women, ending by killing and mutilating two. At the trial he showed no remorse, being quite without feeling for his victims and equally unconcerned at the prospect of execution.

What the work of Shields and others demonstrates, is the strong role played by heredity in personality differences. The British expert on the subject of psychopathy, Michael Craft[27] agrees that genetic endowment is probably the most crucial factor in its origins. There are also subsidiary factors involved, both organic and environmental. The main organic factor is brain damage, usually occurring before and during birth. This, as we have already seen, handicaps learning ability and emotional control. Many researchers have noticed the occurrence of sickly pregnancy and difficult birth in children who later present behavioural problems as well as health ones; the literature is quite extensive.[28] For example, Drillien[29] (1959) investigated 92 children whose birth-weight was under 3lbs; 22 per cent were found to have a major physical handicap at follow-up, and only 13 per cent had average or above average IQ ratings. It appeared that, below a birth weight of 4½ lbs, the lower the weight, the higher the incidence of physical, intellectual or behavioural handicap. The work of Stott,[30] [31] [32] on samples of difficult children clearly shows a connection between maladjustment and other constitutional defects. Indeed, if a child suffers from one or more defects or weaknesses it is increasingly more likely to suffer from others. These impairments may include damage to the nervous system which affects general behavioural stability.

With considerable advances in medicine in this century, that have reduced the infant mortality rate to a level where usually only the most grotesquely deformed now succumb at birth, the numbers of damaged infants that survive is obviously large. Prechtl (1963)[33] gives figures of twenty per cent for boys and nine per cent for girls in a population survey of elementary school children for minimal brain damage, and this is only for limited symptoms. The figure for signs of minimal brain damage rose to two-thirds for children who had birth complications. Brain damage not severe enough to make the child incapable of joining in everyday life, or to require it to have close medical attention or institutionalisation, nonetheless presents problems in child-care. Such children are often aggressive, accident-prone, inattentive and unsettled, their neural impairment preventing them from learning efficiently from past experience or envisaging the consequences of their actions. Application of the Bristol Adjustment Guides for maladjustment to samples of British children[34] in different regions reveals that between 11 and 15 per cent of boys (depending on region) and about 8 per cent of girls score highly. There are a further 20 per cent of children who, although not severely maladjusted are certainly not stable on any criteria, and show the symptoms mentioned above which are known to correlate with medical signs for minimal brain damage.

Although we have dealt with these organic factors separately from inherited personality traits, it is still relevant to ask whether and to what extent such organic defects also have genetic origins. We have seen the connection between brain damage and birth complications: mothers who have difficult births may be poorly endowed genetically themselves, so that both the birth complications and the defective baby are products of this. Thus the under-weight baby who later shows behavioural and intellectual handicaps, may owe these not to his unfortunate birth, but to a mother who is herself of low IQ and poor physique. In opposition to this view, circumstantial evidence can be quoted that the serious complications of birth and pregnancy, such as toxaemia, haemorrhage, prematurity and stillbirth, are more common in very young mothers, and the reason suggests itself that these mothers are too immature physically[35] to bear healthy children. But, here again, those females who become mothers when very young are on the whole likely to be the more poorly endowed. They mature later, and at any age would be likely to produce less healthy children. Good physique and high intelligence are known to correlate with early physical maturity,[36] but girls so endowed are likely to undergo a longer education and to postpone childbearing, often for ten or more years beyond menarche. It is for this reason that comparisons between females, in order to sort out the role that early childbearing (apart from poor genetic endowment) by an immature mother exerts, is made so difficult.

Environmental factors in psychopathy again are such as to suggest that some may initially have genetic origins. Craft[37] found hostile and rejecting familial situations in the backgrounds of extreme psychopaths, and this adds to the findings of criminological research that difficult family relationships are more frequent in the families of delinquents. But it is too easy to conclude that the difficult personality that emerges from such families owes its origin always to parental mismanagement and rejection. While the Gluecks[38] found that certain psychological traits appeared to correlate well with given factors in the family environment throughout the range of somatypes, they are nonetheless wary about attributing these to environmental causation. It could equally be held that a trait in the child produces fairly characteristic parental behaviour towards it. It has been observed how common it is for mothers of infants to take their cues from the baby for the manner in which they will respond to it and the regimen that they will adopt. For example, Prechtl[39] makes the observation that a baby with minimal brain damage can be more irritating and disturbing for the mother to care for than a more obviously damaged child, over whom she would consult a physician. The mother of the former type of baby may have to cope in lonely bewilderment, feeling she has nothing definite enough to report to a physician, or that she may be blamed for mishandling the infant. Such a child would put particular strain on very young and less intelligent mothers, to whom many such infants would probably be born.

The backgrounds of psychopathic individuals are full of

conflict that often appears to be initiated by the child rather than the parent. This is an unpopular conclusion to draw from the evidence, as the tendency today is always to blame the parent unthinkingly when things go wrong. The expectation is that the parent should show indefinite patience and capacity for self-sacrifice, and that any expression of actual dislike for a child whose behaviour may be intolerable is inherently wicked. If such dislike ever is expressed it is automatically taken as evidence that the child's impossible conduct must originate in parental rejection, conscious or 'unconscious'. (Even 'inconsistent discipline' may mean simply that some desperate parents have tried everything in turn.) In a study of maladjustment by Stott children

> ... had been disturbed or otherwise abnormal in their behaviour from their earliest infancy. Their tiresomeness or failure to respond to affection was in some cases too much for their parents: they became rejected children or the black sheep of their families. Their insecure family situation had been created by their initial emotional handicap. It was not so much the cause as the result of their maladjustment. Naturally the position would get worse in a vicious circle, until the maladjusted child had created a bad situation against himself. All that could be said against the parents was that they lacked the nervous resources, or had too many other burdens, to be able to cope with an emotionally disturbed child. We cannot in consequence assume, even when we find parents who actively reject a child, that their rejection is the sole or even the primary cause of the maladjustment: more likely it has served to aggravate a predisposition present in the child from birth.[40]

Edelston,[41] whose background is psychoanalytical, equates psychopathology with Bowlby's affectionless delinquent, but finds that although in clinical practice he has dealt with twenty to twenty-six children who could be thus diagnosed, only one has 'a history of any prolonged separation in early life'. These children, who were 'to a greater or lesser extent immature, in that their behaviour, grossly abnormal at their present age, would be accepted more tolerantly in much younger children',[42] have characteristic background histories. Dennis, aged 11½, is described by his mother as a 'right rough lad since he was tiny'.[43] Emphasising the difference between him and her other children, the mother claimed that 'you can do nothing with him. . . I don't think that he has any love in him'.[44] Maurice, aged 12½, 'was the eldest of four children in a respectable, good working-class family. According to his mother he was difficult right from the beginning, always crying and discontented.'[45]

The child's difficult and unrewarding behaviour can so tax parental patience that the child is emotionally rejected and may provoke parental violence. As Edelston remarks, the fact that separation from the parents or frequent changes of foster homes may be observed in the backgrounds of some children could be a result of the child's difficult personality rather than a cause of it (as could harsh punishment).

If such a child can be a strain on fairly conscientious parents, how much more tumultuous will be his history when his family background comprises parents whose personalities are like his own, or who are incapable of coping because they are ill, mentally dull or too weak. The very consistent and strict training, the controlled supportive environment that he may require over long years to establish some self-control and socially acceptable behaviour, will be absent. But there will, unfortunately, be children who are so difficult to handle that to expect any parent to cope is simply asking too much of parental labour and affection:

> In their preoccupation with the child (or the child in the adult, in cases of later neurosis) psychoanalytic, i.e. Freudian writers, have unwittingly postulated the existence of the perfect parent as a solution. . . The best parental love is not indefinitely extensible, and that in the problem parents usually (but not inevitably) associated with the worst problem children it may not allow itself to be extended very far. Taking even the average parent, by and large I suspect there will always be a fair number of difficult children who are too much for their natural parents and who will need special homes or institutions to deal with them.[46]

While repudiating the theory that the affectionless personality (which he equates with psychopathy) is caused by separation from the mother, Rutter[47] nonetheless concludes that it is due to never having formed a 'bond' with anybody in early life, attributable usually to institutional rearing or frequent changes of homes. Leaving aside the consideration as to whether Dr Barnardo's has been unwittingly turning out cohorts of psychopaths over the years, what is significant is Rutter's neglect of the evidence on the role of genetic and organic factors in the genesis of psychopathy. He may be putting the cart before the horse in claiming that failure to make a 'bond' gives rise to a psychopathic personality, rather than that the child's possession of a psychopathic personality makes it impossible for anyone to establish a 'bond' with him. The existence in ordinary, affectionate homes of children who exhaust their parents' patience and love ought to be enough to throw serious doubt upon this hypothesis.[48]

In an excellent biographical study of a psychopath's life and death, Lloyd and Williamson[49] illustrate the complex and interrelated genetic, organic and environmental strands that made Harry the man he was. Harry had been born by a forceps delivery that damaged his head, to a small, thin, sixteen-year-old mother, who had been overworked, underfed and viciously assaulted by the sadistic bully with whom she lived; this father had recently escaped a manslaughter charge when a man whom he had beaten up died. Harry grew up — if one can really talk of Harry growing up at all — impulsive and violent. The exceptions to this description were when he was in the controlled, protective environment of the Approved School, and a galley boy on a ship, where he was both happy and an asset to the community. He looked after the younger approved school boys and claimed that he felt for them. Otherwise his life was one of violence to himself and others. An accident aboard ship may have caused further brain damage which spoilt the progress he was making, and Harry died from a ridiculous and infantile self-inflicted injury (swallowing open pins) some years later. Before his death he heard about the progress of a son whom he had never seen, but who is growing up just like his father and grandfather before him.

Histories such as that of Harry must not be allowed to detract from the fact that many people with personalities like his do alter considerably and even spontaneously with advancing years.[50] The full maturation of the organism that occurs in the twenties and thirties causes personality changes away from extreme extraversion, and environmental influences have a greater chance to affect conduct[51] [52] The prognosis is better with those psychopaths who have immature EEGs than those without.

It might strike many as quite impossible that a person who for many years has shown no concern or affection for others and no guilt over his wrong-doing, should ever change such traits. Bowlby's statement that he can diagnose an affectionless character at three[53], a diagnosis that could be permanent, strikes deep chords in our culture's attitudes to personality. Educated according to articles of Freudian faith about the crucial first five years of life, where personality traits result from the mother's suckling, bowel training, fondling, etc., it is difficult for us to accept that considerable changes are possible, and indeed common at later ages. If a person has not 'learnt' affection by early childhood, our attitude is that the receptive and sensitive period is past, never to be repeated again. This revealed religion is reiterated everywhere: 'There can no longer be much doubt that, broadly speaking, healthy human development is founded on an infancy spent in a complete, stable, loving family.'[54]

And

> Normal behaviour presupposes that the child in the home should have met first with stable and secure affection. This is a biological need without which he cannot develop normally... For his social development the most important of these is that, lacking affection in his early years, his capacity to return affection is atrophied, stunted or distorted.[55]

Yet, powerful as such statements might appear, in some the capacity does not become inexorably atrophied, stunted or distorted. As they grow older they acquire capacities and talents that are the fruits of maturity, not infancy. Craft, for example, is confident that more people than we give credit for have considerable room for growth and change beyond infancy:

David: Born illegitimately to a prostitute, he was an unwanted marasmic child, removed from his mother at six months when she was jailed for child neglect. Adopted at two, by his true but guilty father and newly-married wife, there was a stormy infancy with violence and hostility on both sides and many screaming temper tantrums. On starting school at five, he clung to his school-mistress's skirt and clamoured for the love and attention that he had always wanted. He clawed any child who came within range to dispute his need at school, just as he did at home with the siblings who came later than him. School continued for a month, and then he was forwarded to the first of many psychiatrists and admissions to child and psychiatric units, of which the next seven years were full. He entered the ESN schools and those for the maladjusted, and was as often expelled. The final expulsion was at twelve when camping in North Wales he was refused the attention he wanted from the master and found a couple making love in the heather. Unknown to the others, he loosened a larger boulder above them and levered it off so that it started down upon them. Fortunately, the boulder was large and made much noise, so that the couple were able to extricate themselves. David was so furious at their escape that he attempted to knife the master who remonstrated with him.

He returned home, drank his father's whisky, exposed himself to neighbours and varied traffic lights on a foggy night so that a Liverpool bus fell into a ditch. The country was scoured for special units without success and at thirteen he was admitted to the adult ward of the local mental hospital where he learnt much from the men and where he was diagnosed shortly after as an aggressive psychopath. Certified as morally defective, he was admitted to Balderton, where he was noted to be illiterate, to have an IQ of 87 (Wechsler), to be rational but extremely impulsive, to be without feeling for others and extremely aggressive. It was noted that although he had repeatedly stolen he had never been convicted, and showed neither remorse nor shame for his actions. At Balderton, David was a principal leader in the formation of the new self-governing group psychotherapy ward for psychopaths, and became very upset at the admission of a brain-damaged lad similarly unable to see others' point of view, had an excited furore and became violent.

He was so excited that he had no clear recollection of what had happened, and was so confused that he had first to be treated in the ward for the mentally ill. Some time later he was tried in lodgings and work, but reverted to his enuresis, work shyness and aggression, and this last secured a Borstal sentence at seventeen. The care was excellent, his reading age soon advanced to twelve, staff allowed for his instability and his personality improved markedly. At nineteen he was replaced in employment, but a hostile landlady resulted in further unnecessary larceny (earning £16 a week this was an expression of resentment) and his admission into a rigid Borstal resulted in such a furore that he had to be contained within the hospital wing in a maximum-security Borstal. Following discharge here, he committed another ostentatious larceny, and rejected by two hospitals, entered a third.

By twenty-two his IQ had risen to 113, he had held the same job for two years, was married to a sensible and stable girl and accepted by the new family. On a follow-up visit to North Wales his play and care with a baby called Timothy Craft made it clear that he enjoyed the company of children. He has developed a feeling for other humans, the Liverpool workers report his impulsiveness to be minimal, and his developing shame and guilt over the past are such that he no longer wishes to discuss it. By 1966, he had children, job, house and was accepted as a normal citizen by the community.[56]

8 The Spitzian Scare

'Children are either brought up in a home, or in an institution.'[1] This is a familiar and decisive dictum. The exclusive alternatives exhaust all the possibilities. The institution — cold, impersonal, inhumane, with heavy overtones of the Poor Law: a semi-penal place like the workhouse, to which those who fail to conform to the conventions of respectable society are 'sent away'. Another, more modern spectre of the institution is unfailingly raised when there is any talk of creches, kindergartens or nurseries — the spectre of Brave New World: rows of hygienic cots, hungry mouths fed by mechanical arms, flashing lights, robot voices, all producing robot people faithfully parroting the slogans of the totalitarian state. The result is the end of love and personal relationships and the throttling of all that is vital and beautiful.

From the lair of the institution emerges that dangerous character of the last chapter, the psychopath, and his brother, the pathetically inadequate individual. There is much agreement today that a background of institutionalisation inevitably ruins a person. If the criminal, the baby batterer, the addict is found to have had such a background, no other explanation is needed: 'He was brought up in an institution' — and we nod knowingly and sadly.

Do people even come out alive from institutions? It is frequently claimed that babies actually die in them, not from starvation, disease or cruelty, but because they have no mother. This is represented as a pining away from lack of 'love' or 'mothering', which a real mother diffuses simply by her mere presence. Babies need love just as they need food, and many child-care books advise the mother that virtually continual physical interaction with her infant is essential for its survival.[2] It is in studies of institutionalised children, that the greatest confusion occurs between the need for a single mother and the need for 'mothering' and all it implies.

Even if the institutionalised infant is not in danger of death (a point over which there appears to be some disagreement), the necessity for a devoted mother figure in the early years is held to be demonstrated by the large amount of mental (and physical) retardation, as well as the emotional damage, to be found among ex-inmates of institutions. This contrast between the institutionalised and the family baby is commonly cited as striking evidence of the vital importance of intensive care in the early years; and supposedly vindicates the environmentalist against those who would give greater weight to organic and genetic endowment in human development and adequacy.

There are several considerations to be mentioned before we examine the evidence from institution studies. To begin with, I want to re-emphasise the necessity of using criteria of personal adequacy based on population norms, not ideals. All too frequently (and particularly now in relation to arguments about environmental retardation of IQ) a very high standard is set for 'normality'. It appears to be assumed that the 'natural' level of IQ is somewhere over the 120 points level, and that children with IQs around or below 100 must have been retarded by their environment, and somehow failed to achieve their potential. To show that institutionalised children are not retarded, we would have to demonstrate that they are no better or worse than a comparable, controlled sample from the general population.

Secondly, if institutionalised people are inadequate compared with family-reared population samples, this by itself does not of course prove that the fault lies in lack of a permanent indivisible 'mother figure' or lack of her 'mothering' (whatever this may mean). There are institutions and institutions, and the regime of one may be radically different from another. One could well be lacking in some necessary developmental factor which has nothing to do with mothers or mothering, such as a proper diet, or language teaching. It is equally possible that this factor could be lacking in a home where the child is exposed to a continued maternal presence.

Thirdly, and very important, if an institution sample is compared with a family-reared sample, some of the differences which emerge may be due to constitutional differences present in the children since birth. If other evidence strongly suggests that mental retardation or psychosis are related to genetic and organic factors, then a preponderance of children with these defects in an institution does not demonstrate that they are caused by that institution's regime. Children abandoned to institutions may have been abandoned because their mothers were too mentally backward or psychotic or handicapped to look after them.[3] Children who succeed in being adopted (and are thus removed from the institutional population into families) are likely to be healthier, more intelligent, and better endowed genetically than those left behind. Attractive, alert infants without physical handicaps are far more easily placed with adoptive parents.

These, then, are factors which must be controlled in comparing the institutionalised with the family-reared. But even apart from statistical observations it is important to bear in mind that an institutional upbringing is not regarded socially as an acceptable manner to rear normally 'wanted' children, but is notoriously a fate for the unwanted. For this reason it differs radically from say, the Israeli kibbutz or the communal child-care arrangements of religious groups such as the Hutterites, which are the normal forms of upbringing for ordinarily wanted children. This means, as suggested above, that institutions will tend to be a dumping ground for the physically and mentally handicapped, the poorly endowed, the problem children, who are often unwanted precisely for these reasons. It also means that anyone known to have an institutional background will have their adequacy called into question far more, which will impose greater demands on them in ordinary social life. Institutional upbringing, lack of a normal home and family, carries an undeniable stigma today, corresponding almost exactly with the older stigma of illegitimacy. No blame attaches — perish the thought — but rather the same pitying air of sanctimonious, manufactured 'tragedy'. This is a point to which I shall return.

The claims, still widely broadcast, that institutional evidence demonstrates the vital necessity for one unbroken relationship with a mother figure, without which infants die or only survive as grossly retarded and inadequate, appear to be based almost entirely on the work of the psychoanalyst, René Spitz, in the 1940s. On the evidence put forward by Spitz there has been a loss of confidence in the institution and day-nursery in western Europe.

The Spitz research I shall consider is the famous series of papers published in The *Psychoanalytic Study of The Child.* The first of these was 'Hospitalism: An Inquiry Into the Genesis of Psychiatric Conditions in Early Childhood' (1945).[4] Here Spitz contrasts the development of two sets of infants in contrasting institutions which he names Nursery and Foundling Home.[5] He compares them in development (measured by the Hetzer-Wolf tests), in background, in physical development, in the care they received in the institutions, and the amount of contact they had with their mothers. Spitz's second article, published one year later,[6] describes the development of the Foundling Home Infants in the two years following the original study. These descriptions were compiled by an investigator who visited Foundling Home at four monthly intervals. Only 21 out of the 91 original infants were still available for the study at the end of the two years. Spitz contrasts the development of these with that of 122 infants from the other institution, Nursery. Only 69 infants were present in Nursery in the original study, so that 53 new cases had subsequently been added.

His third article is entitled 'Anaclitic Depression: An Inquiry into the Genesis of Psychiatric Conditions in Early Childhood, II' (1946).[7] (His term 'anaclitic depression' denotes a psychiatric syndrome of depression which he observed in some of the infants in Nursery, in severe form in nineteen of the infants and a milder form in twenty-six.) Later articles elaborate on the theme and findings of these earlier three.[8]

In comparing the two groups, Spitz concludes that children develop various physical and mental disorders from being separated from their mothers after six months. Many die from the same root cause. The infants in Foundling Home developed a syndrome he terms 'hospitalism', because their mothers left them at about six months of age, when they were weaned. The infants in Nursery, on the other hand, developed normally. Their mothers continued to bring them up after they were weaned. This mother and infant bond was broken temporarily for 95 infants in Nursery, 45 of whom developed anaclitic depression, which we are told in a later paper (1951)[9] is a milder version of hospitalism, although Spitz apparently did not realise this at the time.

The hospitalism syndrome is constituted by a drop in the development quotient (DQ) as measured by the Hetzer-Wolf baby tests (a sort of infant IQ). The children are also held to have emitted blood-curdling screams or to have been frozen and immobile when confronted with a stranger. In later writings Spitz claims that they hit their heads and tore their hair out 'by the fistful', that they could not assimilate food and became insomniac.[10] Pinneau, who undertook an extensive, critical examination of Spitz's research techniques and data[11] draws attention to descriptions that give infant behavioural states ranging from stuporous deteriorated catatonia to agitated idiocy.[12]

Other symptoms of hospitalism included retardation of skeletal development, of sitting and walking, of development of social skills and of language. At the follow-up Spitz claims that 5 could not walk at all, 16 walked by holding onto the furniture, 12 could not eat alone with a spoon, 20 could not dress alone and only 6 were toilet trained. Six could not talk at all, five had a vocabulary of two words, one a dozen words, and only one actually spoke in sentences.[13]

Thirty-four of the children in Foundling Home died. In his first two reports from Foundling Home, Spitz mentions that the main cause of death was a measles outbreak. But in his later writings this reference to measles gives place to the explanation that 'The progressive deterioration and the increased infection-liability lead in a distressingly high percentage of these children to marasmus and death.'[14]

'Progressive deterioration' is attributed to maternal separation and nothing else. The children pined and wasted away because they had lost their 'object', that is, their mother. This made them incapable of assimilating food properly, and in a perverse manner (although an infant cannot directly commit suicide), they directed aggression against themselves, thereby bringing about their own destruction.[15] Apparently no infant died in Nursery.

Some of the children in Nursery[16] who were separated from their mothers also suffered a drop in their DQ. Those who were separated, but who showed no apparent signs of deterioration, were not tested. When the deteriorated group were reunited, they reversed their decline, although Spitz also states that some later started to decline again (but not to such a low level).[17] The affected children became weepy and apprehensive, with immobile, frozen faces. They appeared immune to their environment. This was accompanied by 'oral', 'anal' and 'genital' 'auto-erotic' behaviour. (I assume this means thumbsucking and masturbation.) Not every symptom was present in each case or at the same time in any one child; first one and then another might dominate.

Let us now look at Spitz's methods and material. (Some of the points which I shall make are in agreement with those already put forward by Pinneau[18] in his excellent and thorough article on Spitz's work. I am particularly indebted to his statistical analysis and background to Spitz's use of the Hetzer-Wolf baby test – the DQ scores.) Spitz has claimed that the drop in DQ he recorded for Foundling Home babies coincides with the final departure of the mothers, who were leaving their babies predominantly in the sixth month when they were weaned. The mothers in Foundling Home are generally shadowy figures, and even prior to weaning they do not appear to have much to do with their babies – except that they instead of the nurses fed them. But Spitz has claimed that this does not matter much, since a mother who is present simply to breast-feed gives the infant immeasurably more than one not there at all: 'As soon as the babies in Foundling Home are weaned, the modest human contacts which they have had during nursing at the breast stop, and their development falls below normal' and this weaning begins to occur at 'the beginning of the fourth month',[19] and 'the separation from the mother took place beginning after the third month, but *prevalently in the sixth month*'. [20] (Italics mine.)

However, an examination of the DQ scores for these infants shows them falling from the second month of life. Indeed, the graph falls from an average of 131 in the second month to 72, with 43 points of this drop occurring by the time the children were in their fifth month with a majority of the mothers still present! The retardation was obviously well under way by the time the mothers left.

Similarly, little conclusive evidence can be found to support Spitz's argument that the Nursery group of children also suffered when their mothers departed for three months when they were seven months old. Of the 95 who were separated, 45 showed (in addition to anaclitic depression) a decline in DQ which was later reversed when the mothers rejoined them. The separated children not showing depression were not tested for DQ. But in an earlier work Spitz gave DQ figures for most of the infants in Nursery, separated and unseparated: and from the two sets of figures Pinneau[21] deduced statistically what must have been the DQs over several months of all the children who did now show depression. These, he claims, show even more marked fluctuation than those of the anaclitically depressed, maternally separated group.

Reading Spitz's articles gives one the impression that the findings are based on longitudinal data (that is, a single identical sample being re-examined at intervals over a fairly long period). He talks of the Foundling Home sample deteriorating .over two years, and of the Nursery sample remaining healthy and developing well, except when some were separated, who recovered on reunion. The picture of change and development suggests that the same children are being studied over the two-year time span. However, closer examination shows that this is not so, and that Spitz's conclusions are probably based on a cross-section of children at different ages, studied for a short period of time. These criticisms were developed in some detail by Pinneau.

At the beginning of the study of hospitalism the number of children below 2½ years is 88, with only 45 of these under 1½ years, that is, there would be on average only 2.5 children at each month of age from birth to 18 months and less than 4 at each month from 12 to 24 months. If each was followed longitudinally, the development graph for the first year could not have been based on more than a fifth of the infants. Pinneau holds it to be impossible that the DQ graph recorded the performance of a constant sample of 88 children, but that it rather represented the average DQs of different children chosen at different ages. Spitz mentions that he first visited the institution two years prior to the follow-up report — yet the follow-up period is this two years. The original study must have taken very little time. No tests were applied during the follow-up period, so that conclusions based upon the DQ graph apply to observations of children at different ages, made possibly during only a few weeks or less of observation and recording.

In his reply to Pinneau's criticisms Spitz[22] says that the time period spent on the initial study of Foundling Home was over three months.

To come now to the follow-up: Spitz speaks of 91 Foundling Home children being followed-up for two years. Yet it appears that only 21 were actually followed-up, because 34 died and 36 could not be studied as they had been taken back by their families or adopted. This leaves a far less informative sample for follow-up, less than a quarter of the original, and its representative character is strongly open to question.

Similar considerations apply to the Nursery sample. In his 'Anaclitic Depression' article Spitz says 'In the course of a long-term study of infant behaviour in a nursery we observed one hundred and twenty-three unselected infants, each for a period of twelve to eighteen months.'[23] Yet in his first article we have 69 in the Nursery group,[24] in the second article 122,[25] in the third 123[26] and a further article speaks of 196.[27] There is little indication of the ages at which new cases were admitted. As Nursery had apparently been in operation for ten years the children could not have all been admitted at the same time. The 69 in the first study who were compared with Foundling Home children must have been of different ages. There is thus no longitudinal study of infants from one age to the next, as Spitz would seem to suggest. In the 'Anaclitic Depression' study (123 children), 50 infants have been added, so it would have been impossible to have studied them for very long. Add to this the fact that many of the original group were also not studied during much of their first year, so that the total number of children followed during this first year of life is probably less than half the sample.

Where is Nursery? Spitz has refused to reveal the location of both this and Foundling Home except to say that they are in two different countries in the Western hemisphere.[28] Later, when exposed to criticism, Spitz restricted the geographical range to the 'western world, including Europe'[29] explaining his refusal even to locate the institutions in a specific country as a doctor's duty to respect the confidences of his patients. But clearly, the location of such institutions is of vital importance since conditions in a poor or backward country are likely to be radically different from those in modern Britain, and conclusions drawn from them may not be applicable to our case.

In connection with Foundling Home, Spitz talks of a 'Latin background'.[30] Now if we were to locate this, for example, in Italy, then we know that general Italian orphanage conditions are far removed from British. Considerable information from Italian courts in the last few years suggests that orphanages run privately by religious orders are not infrequently places of the most horrifying cruelty, filth, starvation and neglect. Children are seen as sources of profit, to be rented out as beggars: they are locked in among vermin and refuse and scavenge there for food: they are tied and chained, flogged and tortured.[31] Italian institutions have indeed produced their crop of injuries and deaths, which appear far more obviously related to starvation, infection and punishments that would do pornography proud, than to any 'separation trauma'.

From clues given in articles later than Spitz's main three, it would appear that Nursery is somewhere in New York State. The more elusive Foundling Home[32] is possibly in Latin America, although it cannot completely be ruled out that it is in Italy, Spain or Portugal.

The children were placed in Foundling Home because their mothers were unable to provide for them financially. The mothers were present in this institution for several months, but appeared to have little to do with their babies — the reason is not given. Spitz maintains that the genetic endowment of these infants is better than that of the Nursery sample. That the mothers could not support themselves and their children is held as 'no sign of maladjustment in women of Latin background'.[33] A somewhat arbitrary statement. If these women were married, why were the fathers not supporting them? If they were widowed, why were their kin not giving them support? If they were unmarried, is not loss of virginity and getting pregnant rather aberrant conduct in women of 'Latin background'? How were they so careless — or unchaperoned? Were they women of the lowest economic—social class? Were they prostitutes? Had they been assaulted, or were they simple-minded girls who had been seduced? All these questions — which could have a bearing on the genetic endowment of the children — are left unanswered.

Nursery, on the other hand, is given as an institution for delinquent girls. We are told that all Nursery infants were cared for by their mothers for the first year of life: yet in a later report it appears that a considerable number were separated from their mothers for a period of three months, for reasons not given.[34] When this happened, another mother or pregnant girl looked after the infant. Spitz describes the mothers as socially maladjusted, feeble-minded, psychically defective, psychopathic or criminal, although at the same time they gave the child 'everything a good mother does and beyond that, everything else she has.'[35] This is in contrast with Foundling Home, where a case is argued that the infants had better genetic endowment, but that an absence of mothering nonetheless led to disaster: illustrating the child's need for the mother (even a defective one), over and above all other factors. But in a later paper Spitz gives the conflicting account that the mothers in Nursery 'came there because of a failure in social adaptation. In a large percentage of these cases this maladaptation is not severe, consisting mainly in sexual indescretion at the wrong age'[36] — and he goes on to say that they would differ little from any urban population sample. The children's poor endowment is now questionable. On the whole, I am inclined to agree with Pinneau[37] that if there is anything to choose between the genetic and organic endowment of the samples, that of Nursery is probably superior. However, we have no real evidence. This omission weakens the value of the survey, but it is by no means the greatest defect. That we shall turn to now.

Spitz not only argues that the sample of children in Foundling Home are of superior genetic endowment, but also that the care in Foundling Home was of an excellent standard. Food, hygiene and facilities, he says, were good, the medical care 'impeccable'[38] the nurses who looked after the children are described as 'unusually motherly, baby-loving women'. Yet, despite the excellent care, the children failed to thrive and somehow thirty-four died.

But more detailed descriptions of both institutions do not square with these claims. In Nursery the babies were transferred from cubicles at six months to rooms for older babies containing four to five cots, where they could play together. The cubicles were well lit and the whole place far better furnished than Foundling Home. It was exceptional for a child ever to be without one or two toys. Over-all the place 'gives a friendly impression of warmth. This is probably because trees, landscape and sky are visible from both sides and because a bustling activity of mothers carrying their children, tending them, feeding them, playing with them, chatting with each other with babies in their arms, is usually present'.[39] Even when in cubicles, as well as being cared for by the mothers, the babies could see each other simply by turning the head.

In Foundling Home, by contrast, the babies were kept in cubicles for fifteen to eighteen months. After they were weaned there was no human contact except when they were fed. Sheets were hung round the cots so that all they could see was a white ceiling (when they could see at all, for some of the cubicles were badly lit). They had no toys and played only with their hands and feet. They saw no other baby. They were kept entirely on their backs so that a hollow was worn in the mattresses by the second part of the first year of life, which stopped them turning in any direction. Even after eighteen months these infants appeared to be left either lying in bed or stumbling around, ignored by the nurses. And this was where the nurses were described as 'unusually motherly, baby-loving women'![40]

Some years later Spitz completely contradicted the strange claims about the conditions in Foundling Home by saying that he had to study an institution in this particular (unspecified) country because conditions so bad are no longer found in the United States.[41]

Considering that the only thing the Foundling Home nurses did for the children was to feed them, that they lived out their infancies in hollows they had made in the mattresses, looking only at a white ceiling, if they looked at anything at all; that they had little to play with and, until they were eighteen months or so, saw no other infant, heard little or nothing in the way of human voices, it seems scarcely surprising that these children were not toilet trained, could not speak, could not walk, etc. Is it really supposed that these things come completely without any learning or practice? Children reared in such isolation from their own kind, suffering acute sensory deprivation hardly provide evidence for Spitz's astonishing conclusions that their incapacities were due to maternal deprivation. There is very much more missing in these children's environments than an unbroken maternal presence.

The most obvious fault of the study, then, is Spitz's complete failure to isolate maternal separation from other far more likely causes of retardation. When confronted with the very obvious suggestion that this backwardness was due to lack of stimulation, Spitz replies that 'We do not think that it is the lack of perceptual stimulation *in general* that counts in their deprivation.' The reason given for this view is that 'The presence of a mother or her substitute is sufficient to compensate for all the other deprivations'.[42]

A mother, Spitz tells us, exerts an almost magical influence without any direct learning and no more stimulation than her mere presence. It is thus that the child becomes endowed with the skills to deal with his environment.

I suggest the far simpler explanation that these children's deficiencies came about because of a total absence of opportunity to practice basic motor and manipulative skills such as walking, and a total absence of learning in the case of language and social skills. The capacity to initiate and sustain social relationships with others is largely part of this dependence on taught skills. If this is not the case, if maternal presence is sufficient in itself, one would like to know how Spitz and his followers explain the presence in so-called 'problem families' of children similar to the ones he described in Foundling Home.

Any individual will appear backward if his environment does not provide features which allow his behaviour to be reinforced, shaped and modified in more complex flexible patterns. It is these which enable him to cope with and utilise his surroundings — animate and inanimate. Where no one is willing to encourage (and in some directions limit) and stabilise certain behaviour in a child, that child will acquire little or nothing in the nature of useful skills, social or otherwise. Someone, or some people, must start by taking an interest in the child and reciprocate his attentions (if this willingness to take interest is to be identified with affection or 'love' for a child, well and good). It should be clear that the biological mother (or her substitute), may or may not be one of the people undertaking this task. If she is the only person a child is exposed to and she does not attempt this process of 'socialisation', either because she is uninterested or antagonistic, or because the nature of her attentions do not build up sequences of generalisable social behaviour, then that child will be incompetent and inadequate. Precisely the same result will be achieved in an institution where duty towards the charges ends with sustaining physical life, and nobody involves themselves with the children to develop and reinforce social and other skills. Spitz inadvertently gives support to this contention when he mentions in a later article the existence of a child he omitted to mention in his early accounts of Foundling Home:

> The one who could speak, walk, dress itself, and eat alone, and who was toilet trained, was of an angelic beauty — just like an angel by Raphael — and no person who came into that nursery failed to stop at the child's bed and talk and play with it. Every nurse stooped down to tickle its chin, every doctor stopped and spoke to it, and so this was the one child among these Foundling Home children who really did get something in the nature of emotional interchange with another human being.[43]

If the other separated children's difficulties are not due to lack of stimulation and learning, then why was not this separated child also in a state of Hospitalism? Spitz does not ask what was the difference in circumstances between this child and the others, since all were without a mother.

In the light of what we have seen in connection with Foundling Home, it is an open question whether an institution where children were trapped in hollows in the mattresses had 'impeccable' medical provision. By comparison, there was not a single death in Nursery, which was 'visited by no epidemic'.[44] Measles was a great killer of children in and out of institutions in the developed West well into this century.

It must be remembered that, historically, institutions have been not merely places of social death but physical death as well. The death rates for institutionalised infants in eighteenth- and nineteenth-century institutions in Britain and abroad (principally France) were enormous — actually, in some cases, reaching one hundred per cent. Demographically, as Malthus himself pointed out[45] they acted as a damper to the sharp population rise of that time. Infants abandoned to these institutions rapidly succumbed to exposure, infection and starvation. It is well to keep this in mind when dealing with institutions for foundlings in the poorer half of the world today.

Now, if the suspicion is correct that Foundling Home was visited only for a short time when Spitz's first report was drawn up, another potential source of error appears. For this, on Spitz's admission, was the time when measles was rampant. If, as seems reasonable, a significant number of the children tested were suffering from measles, this condition would obviously depress the DQ scores.

At all events, however the low DQ scores for the Foundling Home group were caused, it must be emphasised that this by itself has no bearing on the possible future development of these children, and certainly cannot be taken as evidence that any irreparable damage is being done. It is generally known now that DQ scores are not (as was once mistakenly believed) very good predictions of later development. They are unrelated to performance at school age, and certainly cannot be taken in any sense as predictions of later IQ. The DQ scores essentially measure motor control in infants, which is the result of autonomous physical maturation plus opportunity for practice.

As to the poor skeletal development, we have already seen that the genetic and organic endowment of these remaining twenty-one children was unknown; that they had little motor practice and that there is reason to question the elementary medical and dietary standards of Foundling Home. In view of these the unusual claim that maternal separation affects

skeletal growth can hardly be regarded as established. There
are plenty of cases of children from neglectful homes, who
have never been taken away from their mothers and who
suffer from malnutrition and the growth retardation this
involves. Experimentally, no growth retardation has been
found in human infants who are maternally deprived yet
adequately fed. Whitten *et al.* (1969)[46] undertook an
investigation of the role of diet and 'mothering' on the
physical growth and well-being of thirteen infants who came
from neglectful homes and were markedly underweight for
their age. The absence of 'mothering' was simulated for two
weeks in the hospital by solitary confinement in a
windowless room (in fact social and sensory deprivation), but
the children were offered a good diet. Eleven of them showed
an accelerated weight gain, and two failed to eat. Following
this period of sensory and social deprivation, the infants were
given a high level of stimulation and personal attention, with
the diet remaining the same as before. There was no change
in the rate and pattern of weight gain: the two who did not
gain during the period of deprivation still did not gain.

If it is objected that Spitz claimed that the diet was good
in Foundling Home, we will consider another study by the
same researchers. Here three underweight infants of mothers
who maintained that they fed them an adequate diet were
fed at intervals in the presence of an observer. No move was
made to alter maternal handling of the infant and the
experiment was disguised as an investigation of calorie intake.
All the infants rapidly gained weight, although the food
handed to the mothers by the experimenters to feed their
babies was a duplicate of the diet which the mothers claimed
they fed their infants! If mothers are often so mistaken about
the amount of food they feed to their children, how much
food reached the infants in Spitz's notorious Latin
orphanage?

Spitz has claimed that the theoretical background to his
Hospitalism studies was laid in 1936.[47] From his enthusiastic
references, one can reasonably surmise that this background
was strongly influenced by the writings of Margaret Ribble,[48]
who could be claimed as the originator of the concept of
'mothering'. She claimed that a mother's suckling, cuddling,
fondling, kissing and gentle lullaby singing, are necessary for

the new-born infant to breathe properly, to enable its
digestive and other systems to operate, its brain to grow, etc.
– so that lack of mothering could have dire consequences.[49]
She presented no studies of much worth to demonstrate her
remarkable claims. Spitz's studies appear to be an attempt to
provide Ribble's sentimental prose with a more substantial
backing. What is certain is that he considers the truth of his
theory to be established prior to, and independently of, his
empirical studies. He says of Pinneau's criticisms of his
institutional study

> . . . the experimental psychological and statistical material
> in the five articles discussed by Pinneau was not
> introduced by me to *prove* my point, as the articles are
> addressed to medical readers. They were used as supportive
> evidence, subordinated to the clinical data – an
> illustration, as it were, of the description presented.
> Dismissing the statistics as inadequate would not therefore
> invalidate my clinical findings.[50]

The nature of this all-important 'clinical' (that is,
psychoanalytical) approach to the subject of study, on which
Bowlby also relies heavily, is dealt with later in this book (see
Chapter 13).

Leaving aside the credence that can be given to the claims
of Spitz and Ribble, we must ask if backwardness in DQ
caused by early lack of practice and stimulation (deprivation)
can be later compensated for. This is necessary because the
notion of the irreversibility of all forms of early retardation
has now become so popularly entrenched as to be regarded as
contemporary common sense.

At about the same time as Spitz's work a series of papers
by Dennis also appeared on infants reared without
'mothering', or much stimulation or chance to practice motor
skills. For example, a study of Hopi Indian children[51] who
spend most of their first year on a cradle-board and thus have
little practice in standing, creeping or crawling, showed that
they develop quite rapidly when allowed to practice. It must
be remembered that customs such as swaddling or strapping
infants to cradle-boards, which severely limit opportunities
for movement, manipulation, and exploration, have been

extremely widespread historically and geographically — among Greeks, Romans, Jews, Arabs, in north-western Europe until the nineteenth century and Eastern Europe until the twentieth, and universally among Indians of both Americas. No evidence has come to light that these practices had any detrimental effect whatsoever (on personality, intelligence, etc.) on the individuals treated in these ways as infants. From his observations Dennis postulates an opposing hypothesis to that of Spitz — that DQ measures relatively superficial factors governed by opportunity to practice: as long as the organism is not neurologically damaged these can be made good later.

More recent observation in Guatemala has led the eminent American child psychologist Jerome Kagan to doubt radically the truth of the current doctrines on early experience and (especially), later intellectual performance.[52] The children of San Marcos in Guatemala spend their infancies in the tiny dark interiors of their parents' huts, neither spoken to nor played with, with no toys and mothers who do not find it necessary to engage in any reciprocal behaviour. In a perhaps Spitzian manner, the infant of San Marcos, in contrast with his American or European counterpart, appears passive, fearful, extraordinarily quiet and he seldom smiles. He is well behind his foreign peers on formal behavioural tests. Yet, surprisingly, at ten years of age, performance on tests involving perceptual analysis, perceptual inference, object recall and recognition memory was comparable to American middle-class norms. Children of this age in San Marcos are also apparently quite happy and playful.

In contrast to this rather dramatic evidence against the theory of the vital importance of infant experience for later development, the evidence brought forward by its proponents of late seems increasingly meagre and tenuous. For example, it is fashionable now to make absurd analogies between 'deprived' infants and kittens whose eyes are sewn up to prevent them opening at the biologically programmed time[53] — an operation which has permanently bad effects on feline eyesight when the stitches are later withdrawn.[54] Obviously if you destroy the physiological basis or so grossly interfere in order to thwart its development, you can for ever destroy or maim the capacity involved. The correct human analogy is with practices like Chinese foot binding or castration. Even in San Marcos a comparable deliberate, multilating interference with sensory development is hardly undertaken. Unfortunately it is all too common for people who compare such experimental interference in animal development with human deprivation to employ this concept of what it means to be 'deprived' in a very loose, slippery way. From experimental kittens we not only go to babes in Dickensian isolation and neglect but, also typically, to those in virtually every well-provided-for, well-cared-for, small, Western working-class family.

At present the evidence points increasingly in favour of a picture of the human brain as astonishingly sturdy in early life, with intellectual development very plastic well beyond infancy. The critical importance of early experience for intelligence and many other capacities is very far from being the unassailable and substantiated thesis that so many dogmatic and often-repeated pronouncements would have us believe.

9 Extra-familial Upbringing

Absence of learning and stimulation is not necessarily part of an extra-familial upbringing, but has only been associated with it because of the ideological environment in which institutionalisation operates. There is no reason at all why an upbringing outside the nuclear family need involve a bar on human intercourse and relationships, and on all teaching, even of language. But such, unhappily, has been the common condition in our institutions until very recently.

The explicit code of the British 1834 Poor Law (which still covered institutions for children up to the welfare state legislation in the 1940s), was that the condition of an institution's inmates was to be, and to be seen to be, worse than that of outsiders in order to discourage applicants. The status of the institutional child was impressed upon him and others by distinguishing clothing (as with Jews and other pariahs in certain times) and he was educated at separate schools, if he was educated at all. In 1861 Frances Power Cobb[1] wrote of a children's institution run by two ancient women (one paralytic), whose 'first object [was] to hush their charges into the state of stupid, joyless inactivity which gives them the least fatigue and trouble' — the children spent their days sitting or lying still. On leaving this institution in adolescence they could not hold a plate, use a knife and fork or carry a glass of water, never having manipulated or balanced objects: they tripped over mats and fell on staircases, never having walked on either; objects like trains and activities like travel terrified them. One girl, having seen snow on roofs through the institution's window but never having touched it, enquired 'How will the dust be got off the trees?'

The Curtis Report of 1946[2] revealed conditions in children's institutions that had scarcely changed over the century, with defectives, seniles, homeless adults and children sharing the same drab wards. The attitude dies hard that kindness, concern and interest in other human beings is somehow the proper reward of decent family life and should be reserved for those in that situation. The British Poor Law and similar principles governing institutions abroad (particularly in Catholic societies) had and have a policy that those without a respectable family should be subjected to a semi-penal treatment for this failing. And well after the decline of this deliberate principle in Britain, the studied cultivation of an impersonal atmosphere in institutions, where the personal and social lives of the inmates are in permanent suspension, continued in very many cases. It is not entirely extinct today: institutions for the aged still exist in this country where married couples are separated.

A children's institution is still viewed as providing a kind of waiting-room until parents can take a child back or it can be placed in a foster or adoptive home. The eagerness to do either, with little regard for the family's ability to care for a child properly for any length of time, frequently means that the child is passing backwards and forwards between institution, home and foster home, a process yielding little but miserable confusion. The powerful moral conviction that human relationships and basic social skills should only be provided in 'a family', does far more to explain any observed backwardness of institutionalised children than any inherent inability of institutions as such.

The Poor Law orphanages, such as that described by Frances Power Cobb, and Spitz's Latin Foundling Home, represent an extreme of detachment and suspension of the inmates' existence, demonstrating nothing about maternal deprivation but illustrating a very wicked way to treat human beings. Other institutions described in the literature may not have such appalling regimes, but there is still frequently a pronounced and deliberate lack of interest in the children beyond their basic physical requirements. Even today there is a dire shortage of institutionalisation for neglected, delinquent and abandoned children which attempts to provide a stable learning environment, with interested staff willing to enter into social relationships. Instead, prompted by anti-institution studies such as those of Spitz, children tend to be either left in bad homes or in a series of foster homes. One suspects that our failure to develop an adequate number of such institutions stems not just from a sincere, if misguided, view of child welfare, but also from a reluctance to raise up possible competitors to the family.

Another influential worker in the anti-institution movement has been Goldfarb. In nine studies of institutionalised children (five of which involved the same group of fifteen children and fifteen controls) Goldfarb[3] compares children who spent their early years in institutions and were then placed in foster homes, with children who went straight from their mothers to foster homes.[4] Here again, conditions in the institution were very bad from the point of view of learning and social interaction.

During their first year of life the infants lived in almost total social isolation, enjoying human contact only when being fed and cleaned. For the next two years or more, before they went to the foster homes, conditions were little better. Before they took the children, the foster parents were informed about the 'meagreness' of the institution and warned that a child coming from it would have poor verbal ability, would find its new surroundings strange, and that it had had no opportunity of forming social relationships. It is therefore not surprising that these children were backward in speech compared with the uninstitutionalised controls. Nor is it any evidence that their backwardness resulted from maternal, as opposed to simple social, deprivation and absence of teaching necessary to acquire skills such as language. A later study to investigate why all institutional children were not still poorly adjusted after a while in foster homes (some adjusted well, which has to be explained if maternal deprivation or institutionalisation are to be posited as automatically harmful), found, not surprisingly, that adjustment was connected with the length of time spent in this depriving institution — the longer the stay, the poorer the adjustment.[5]

Like Spitz, Goldfarb did not identify the institution that his children came from, and the criteria for selecting both the institutional group and the foster-home group are not properly specified. According to another worker, Bender,[6] both Goldfarb and Lowrey — a researcher who also gave poor reports on the development of institutionalised children[7] —

did their work in the same institution. If this is so, Lowrey's accounts suggest that many of the children in the institution in question suffered from adverse heredity (having psychotic or defective parents, for example). This is a very important consideration since Golfarb[8] claims that maternal deprivation depressed the IQ of his institutional sample. Goldfarb gives the IQ of the institutional sample as 68 at 34 months, and that of the foster home group, 96. When retested at 43 months, after the institution group had been in foster homes for a period, the respective scores were 75 for the institution group and 101 for the controls. The relative positions are virtually unchanged. As one critic, O'Connor,[9] points out, who is to say that this difference was not also present at 4 months (or at birth), before the children went their different ways?

The personality differences Goldfarb claimed for his institutional sample of children compared with the foster-home controls are supported mainly by the Rorshach test (administered and interpreted by himself). The response of a subject to certain shapes supposedly gives an insight into internal personality structure, but in the absence of backing by other evidence, this yields little in the way of predictions about behaviour which could be tested, so that it is impossible to tell conclusively whether an interpretation is correct or not.[10] Goldfarb's statements that the institutionalised children 'craved affection' and that they easily complained, are, as O'Connor argues, very subjective and unreliable unless rigorously checked and counterchecked by others who do not know of the hypothesis.[11-12] Craving for affection and attention-seeking are held to be symptoms of personality damage. Bowlby equates them with his Affectionless Thief syndrome. But only one of Goldfarb's institutionalised children stole. One might also think that a child who can crave affection and attention is decidely not affectionless. But Bowlby maintains that: 'This contrast is probably more apparent than real. Many "affectionless" characters crave affection, but nonetheless have an almost complete inability either to accept or reciprocate it.' [13]

The handling of affectionate interchange, reciprocity and the formation of relationships is itself a process of lengthy learning and experience, for which there was little opportunity in this case for a considerable time. The children's ineptness in personal relationships is no evidence for Golfarb or Bowlby that the capacity for them was not there. It is surely demonstrated by the fact that they craved attention and affection. If, on the other hand, these institutional children had been quite cold and emotionless, can we be sure that Bowlby would not have take it as evidence that they were affectionless? Instead they try desperately (and clumsily) to make contact with an adult, and Bowlby still classes them as affectionless.

Children in large families will often be attention seekers, frequently trying extreme and bizarre manoeuvres to get the ear and eye of an adult faced with a chaos of clamouring children. These attempts will frequently be reinforced, because they do attract attention in circumstances where there is stiff competition, and only appear peculiar where there is not. It has been noticed that institutionalised adults, too, will try desperately to make contact with other humans in an impersonal setting. William Sargent[14] describes the reactions of long-term mental patients, abandoned and largely ignored in a pre-war mental hospital, where a doctor touring the wards might be 'surrounded by a crowd of patients, dragging at my clothes and jealously hitting out at each other':

> In the wards reserved for the worst cases, a visiting doctor would as a rule be greeted with tremendous hubbub; but although patients might come up to challenge or threaten him, or appeal tearfully for help, they seldom used violence. Most of them were merely trying to remind him of their existence, but the nurses would always find some trick or other to free the doctor of his more persistent or aggressive charges.[15]

Recently Rutter[16] has accepted that the affectionless character exists, and that affectionlessness can be equated with 'affection craving' (also with psychopathy, as discussed in chapter 7). He holds that it is not produced by separation *per se,* but probably by absence of any opportunity to form a 'bond' in early life through being, for example, in an institution. Thus, according to Rutter, the first two or three

years or so are crucial to the capacity to form later
relationships; if a person does not have a relationship then to
act as a template for others, he cannot build any later — the
critical period is past. One telling sign that a child is probably
going to be incapable of relationships is, Rutter says, the
indiscriminate friendliness shown by institutionalised
children. But he produces no studies of such children in
institutions who have been given objective tests for
psychopathy and ignores the more solid evidence for an
organic or genetic basis to this personality type. He presents
no studies of adults institutionalised as children and tested
for psychopathy. The latter is critically necessary to back up
this claim, which otherwise rests on rather arbitrary surmises
about the meaning of certain child behaviour patterns and
predictions (so far untested) about their relation to adult
conduct. Nor has Rutter attempted to give an explanation of
the nature of this mysterious 'bond' which must form in
early life: how it forms and why it influences all future
affective capacity.

   Let us look a little closer at one interesting case which
Rutter notes. This concerns the child of a deaf-mute, reared
in a dark attic until the age of six and a half. Upon discovery
the child was devoid of speech, rachitic, her behaviour
towards strangers that of a wild animal. She was 'apparently
utterly unaware of relationships of any kind. When presented
with a ball for the first time, she held it in the palm of her
hand, then reached out and stroked my face with it. Such
behaviour is comparable to that of a child of six months',[17]
By the time she was eight and a half she had caught up
educationally with other children of her age. Her social
adjustment was good, even a year and a half after her
discovery giving the impression of a very bright, cheerful,
energetic little girl. At fourteen she was as normal as her
classmates in all respects. Yet despite evidence such as this,
Rutter argues for the dubious contrary thesis that there are
critical periods in early life.[18]

   (As I will argue in greater detail later, relationships are not
duplicates of some mysterious 'bond' of early life. They arise
essentially from the stimulus-seeking of the human organism.
Other humans provide us with lots of desirable stimulation
and satisfactions, and we thus seek their presence and

attentions over and above inanimate objects. In interaction with them we build up sequences of learnt behaviour which are useful in creating and sustaining other relationships. As well as being the only known process to have a long-term effect on human behaviour, learning is not limited to critical periods. The capacity to form the initial relationships in which we build up the sequences of behaviour which generalise successfully to others, need not, therefore, be confined to the first few years of life, although in normal circumstances that is when these initial kinds of learning will occur. The behaviour learnt is partly determined by the person's culture, which is often precisely why it is generalisable. A relationship in itself, no matter how intense, will confer little ability to form further ones if the relevant learning does not take place within it.)

As a child gets older inexperience in handling relationships is likely to be cumulative because, for example, people expect quite sophisticated skills from a ten-year-old as compared with a ten-month-old, and will accordingly have little patience or understanding with a child who is, after all, only trying to communicate on an elementary, untutored level. If the relationship breaks down it is an unwarranted assumption to blame it upon a permanent defect in the child. If the child is fortunate enough to spend a lengthy period with amenable adults, there is no reason why the necessary social skills for building and maintaining relationships should not develop.

After consideration of the evidence, Rutter quite rightly comes to the conclusion that the linguistic and intellectual retardation of children in poor institutions is likely to be due to an absence of stimulation and learning unrelated to separation from 'the mother', or absence of 'a mother'. One wonders, then why he singles out social skills as a special independent case, not governed by learning but by an obscure 'bonding' process.

When all the evidence which we now have that the backwardness of institutionalised children is due to lack of stimulation and teaching is considered, it is impermissible to go on regarding it as due to the absence of a 'mother' and curable, as Ainsworth holds in true Spitzian manner, not by 'environmental stimulation' and teaching, but 'mothering by one mother-figure'.[19]

Many years ago the Iowa studies (unmentioned by Bowlby in his monograph) demonstrated that children in a very poor orphanage improved markedly and often surpassed their peers from the same social class, living in the parental home, when they were given extra attention and academic training.[20] Many later studies also demonstrate that providing a more stimulating environment and educational facilities (nursery school, personal attention, encouraging verbal expression, etc.)[21] raises the IQs of children in bare, overcrowded institutions in which there was little or no personal attention. Ainsworth appears to assume, as many others do, that children become capable human beings through some process of spontaneous growth. That children who are taught nothing learn nothing seems to provide many people with an endless source of puzzlement and gives rise to the most ingenious explanations to account for this peculiar condition. Berger aptly sums up the situation: 'The presence of disabilities may, however, suggest little else than the possibility that "the environments which these individuals have experienced" have been rather inefficient in capitalising on what the research evidence demonstrates, namely, that children brought up in institutions are educable!' [22]

Although I have concentrated on the bleaker type of institution, or rather those researchers who found institutionalisation harmful (because these have been so influential), it should not be overlooked that others have reported no adverse findings for children reared in institutions, or have found adverse findings for some capacities but not others. Garvin and Sacks (1963)[23] actually found an average gain of nearly nine points IQ in children admitted to an institution for short-term care. Rheingold and Bayley (1959)[24] claimed to have found no cognitive or emotional defects in children following institutional care. Institutionalised children need to be compared with groups of children reared in a variety of different homes, for example, big families, not just favourable or even average ones.

Hilda Lewis[25] asserted in the light of the evidence from her Mershal sample that although striking adverse reports on institutionalised children might have the power to arouse interest, they also mislead. Children in the Mershal sample had come from exceptionally bad early circumstances often to spend the rest of their childhood in institutions, yet as adolescents many were as normal and happy as those reared in the average, intact home. Years before, one psychoanalytically inclined researcher, who might not be disposed to such conclusions, found that children brought up in a wartime camp were neither deficient, delinquent, nor psychotic.[26] Six children whom Anna Freud studied

> ... had come to form a more compact group than the usual homogeneous age group. These six children had all their security in the group and they had no interest in anything in the world outside. They neither had nor wanted to have parents: for quite some time they were not interested in the adults who looked after them, but they were enormously interested in each other. They were so interested in each other's characteristics that they fulfilled each other's wishes and needs just as a mother fulfils the needs of her child ... What impressed me most, however, was that when the children went for walks they carried each other's coats, and bent the branches back in the wood so that the other children could walk through, which I have never seen done among mothered children.[27]

Evidence is accumulating that institutions as a whole are not as bad as they have been painted and that some of the worst conditions are (certainly now) likely to be found among families. For example, the case of Keith[28], a boy who emerged from the maternal presence at five behaving like a wild animal, incontinent and without speech (his family conversed in grunts). After four years at school he learnt to speak fairly well, had a higher IQ (87), and his personality had considerably improved. Removing boys like Keith to an institution at an early age would produce a beneficial rather than a detrimental effect.

The studies of the Clarkes[29] on certified feeble-minded cases coming from very poor homes (where the circumstances usually involved cruelty and advanced states of neglect) have accumulated impressive evidence that relief of these living conditions brings about marked and apparently permanent improvement in IQ and personality, giving better social behaviour. Their early work showed that over a two-year period since removal from very bad environmental circumstances, adolescent and young adult feeble-minded cases admitted to an institution showed an average IQ increase of 10 points (with a range extending up to 25 points) in contrast with a control group of patients and a group of feeble-minded patients from poor but less adverse circumstances, who both made an average IQ gain of 4 points. The picture suggested is that IQ increments were common, and that many adolescent and young adult patients coming from very bad circumstances went towards and sometimes achieved an IQ well within the normal range.

Further studies undertaken by the Clarkes confirmed the findings and the long-term nature of the improvement. In all, longitudinal data on about two hundred feeble-minded adolescents and young adults has been collected over the last eight years. It is significant that those patients who had been nurtured in the worst conditions had a far better prognosis both intellectually and socially than those drawn from less adverse or normal circumstances. It would appear that very bad environmental conditions suspend the normal growth processes, whereas people reared in the range of environments provided by satisfactory family homes have matured more or less to the limit of their genetic endowment.

The research suggests that the gain in IQ and personal adjustment comes about because adverse conditions that act as a break on maturation are withdrawn, rather than because the new environment is a positively rich one. Deliberately providing a more stimulating environment than the day-to-day reality which constitutes normal surroundings for the bulk of individuals does not itself accelerate or enhance the growth of IQ. The Clarkes gave some feeble-minded cases a special, very stimulating environment, but found little difference in the IQ and personality gain compared with those who had simply been removed from very depriving and stressful conditions. These findings corroborate those of other researchers on motor skills in young children reared without opportunity to practice them: once restrictions are lifted development proceeds normally. Recovery from early deprivation appears to go on until about the age of thirty.

The certified feeble-minded are a definable group whose members frequently have histories of gross neglect and ill-treatment because of defective parents. However, the findings on the reversibility of intellectual retardation from adverse circumstances suggests that it can happen throughout the IQ range.

Over-all, the Clarkes estimate that the most adverse social conditions, characterised by cruelty and neglect, retard intellectual development by at least 16 points. A bare institutional regime without either the continual stresses of neglect or the stimulations of everyday life would retard development by at least 10 points.

The specific stresses imposed by neglect, cruelty, sensory deprivation, restrictions on movement and malnutrition seem to be the ones responsible for retarded development. From the literature on both bad family homes and institutions it seems also that frequent and confusing changes of environment, such as are involved in continually shuttling a child back and forth between natural parents, foster parents and institutions, are additional sources of stress and apparent retardation. Patterns of behaviour and preferences built up in one environment may be inapplicable in another, so that learning starts virtually from scratch again. But before it can do so there is the chaotic and confused period where old learning is being broken down through lack of reinforcement (extinction), and a child may never remain long enough in one place for any adequate pattern of behaviour to become established. To this is added his lack of control over the environment in which he is placed, which represents a failure of the organism to 'cope' successfully and is known as a potent source of stress in both humans and animals.[30] If sustained, this confusing state of affairs in turn engenders nothing but fearful expectations, which further heighten the now almost constant state of stress and tension. Often nothing is left to the individual but primitive attempts to manage, namely aggression or withdrawal (fight or flight).

This primitive behaviour is widely recorded (although frequently in anecdotal form) for children who have undergone a series of disrupting changes. The adverse factor of continual transfer between home, foster home and institution, as well as poor genes, organic damage and domestic cruelty and neglect, have all biased samples against institutional upbringing, since in their different ways all these deficiences are attributable to its failure. But nothing we know of the learning process indicates that the stage of confused fight or flight is permanent, or indeed that it has residual damaging effects in later life. Extension of the 'extinction' phase of learning, which this state of confusion represents, is indeed stressful and thoroughly upsetting to the individual; but its very confusion, the very inability for settled patterns to form, demonstrates that learning capacity is intact. It is biologically essential for us to be able to break down old learning and acquire new. Placed again in a hospitable and stable learning environment, the stress-ridden, fearful individual can in time make good his retardation by acquiring new and fruitful behaviour patterns. We have no evidence that going through such a period, painful though it is, leaves any long-term psychological scars; nor, more generally, that there is any particular period in the individual's life which is crucial for acquisition of basic learning.

Probably the only study that we have on a sample of adults institutionalised as children which is controlled for genetic factors is that of Heston, Denney and Pauly.[31] Here a family control group was used, together with objective tests for personality and IQ. The study again demonstrates the unfortunate backgrounds of those committed to institutions and undergoing frequent changes of home afterwards. It also shows that, whether caused by the environment of the institution or other adverse environmental factors such as we have listed, retardation of maturation due to deprivation was made good by the time the individuals reached their twenties.

The study was of 47 adults who had been in foundling homes from their birth for a mean period of 24·7 months, and 50 adults who were either never in child-care institutions or who had spent less than three months in such care. The subjects were born between 1915 and 1945, and were selected from records for a different study, designed to test the genetic contribution to schizophrenia by comparing groups where children had been reared apart from their biological mothers. Of the subjects reared apart, many (about half) were cared for in foundling homes, while the balance were reared in families. This provided an opportunity to test also for any long-term effects of institutional care. The subjects were divided into four groups:

Group A had been born to schizophrenic mothers in Oregon State psychiatric hospitals, and cared for in foundling homes pending adoption or other disposal — total 25.

Group B had also been cared for in foundling homes but born to parents who had no known history of psychotic disorder. These were located from records in the same foundling home which cared for subjects in group A, and were matched for sex and length of stay with subjects in group A to within ±10 per cent — total 22.

Group C had been born to schizophrenic mothers but did not go into foundling homes, mostly being reared instead in the homes of paternal relatives — total 22.

Group D had been born to parents with no known history of psychotic disorder and chosen to match subjects in group C. None had had more than three months in a foundling home and all had been reared with relatives — total 28.

Groups A and B form the Institutional group to be compared with Family groups C and D.

The times the former spent in institutions is as follows:[32]

Months	Number
0 – 6	4
6 – 12	10
12 – 18	8
18 – 24	5
24 – 36	8
36 – 48	4
48 – 60	1
Over 60	7

This is an underestimate of the total time spent in institutions, since many were known to have been admitted to other foundling homes or readmitted to the same one, and some changed several times from foster homes to institutions. Subjects in family groups changed homes infrequently.

The quality of care in the foundling home reflects the general pattern for large institutions in pre-war years — common eating, sleeping and play areas, each unit caring for

20—50 children from 0—5 years.

The tests administered to the adults were the MMPI (Minnesota Multiphasic Personality Inventory); the MHSRS (Menninger Mental Health and Sickness Rating Scale: here ratings on three diagnostic scales received special attention, those for schizophrenia, psychopathology and mental deficiency); an IQ test; any tests from records of police, armed forces, hospitals, etc., and a personal interview. The information was evaluated independently by the three authors, two of whom did not know the subjects' genetic or institutional background.

The results demonstrated no difference in adulthood on any criteria for those subjects reared in families and those who had spent periods of their early lives in institutions. The MHSRS scores for all the Family group was 72.7 (in this test 100 is taken as unusually good psycho-social functioning, with the score going down to 0; a normal population sample would be expected to fluctuate around 75).

The score for the Institution group was 73.0. The MMPI scores showed no significant differences or, indeed, any suggestion of differences in the two groups. The IQ averages were 99·3 for the Family group, and 98·4 for the Institution group. The prediction that, the longer the stay in an institution the lower the resulting intelligence of the subject, was not borne out. The pattern showed instead:[33]

Time of stay in months	Mean IQ
0 — 6	111
6 — 12	104
12 — 18	101
18 — 28	102
24 — 36	95
36 — 48	100
48 — 60	121
+ 60	102

Similarly the predicted adverse effect on mental health and psycho-social functioning of lengthy periods of institutionalisation was not borne out. Those institutionalised but adopted from groups A and B achieved a mean score of 75·2 on the MHSRS. Those later reared in foster families achieved a mean score of 72·2. Seven subjects reared in the institution for five years or longer achieved a mean score of 63·7 (this included two mental defectives who were there for that reason; if they are withdrawn, the score is 79·1, which is above the psycho-social adequacy rate for the Family groups as well as for those institutionalised for shorter periods).

The social class-ranking in adulthood was no different for Family and Institutionalised groups. The rate of social mobility of both was similar to that of the general population in the twentieth-century West (roughly one-third changing class each generation). The class-ranking of individuals was related to their psychiatric health in a way which suggested that low achieved social class was at least partly a function of disability, rather than that low social class produced the disability.

The Institution group's records of schools, nurseries and foster parents, as well as personal recollection of their childhoods, frequently mentioned unhappiness, upset or withdrawal. Yet the study was to come to the conclusion that 'The human organism has the happy capacity of reversing the effects of childhood emotional trauma of the type connoted by institutionalisation.'[34] The following case-history illustrates the process:

A man, now twenty-four years old, was placed in a foundling home three days after birth. His natural father was a semi-skilled lumber worker, his mother was a waitress. He had no post-partum contact with either. Physical examinations at six months and one year of age were normal. From age two to four years he was in four foster homes, never longer than three months in any one home and in a foundling home between placements. At age four he is described as a 'difficult child', biting other children then 'sullen, withdrawn', and so restless at night that he required sedative medication. At age four years ten months he was seen by a psychologist for a pre-adoptive evaluation. A Stanford-Binet test yielded an IQ of 75. At five years two months a psychiatrist described him as a 'small, physically and emotionally immature youngster who failed on tasks requiring abstract thinking and judgment' ... At age six he was placed in a fifth home, and 6 months later in a sixth. The latter placement with a childless couple in their late 40's proved permanent.

After initial difficulties and adverse reports from school and the foster mother, (who on one occasion asked to have him transferred to another home):

> At age fifteen his high school IQ was 95. The subject was a participant in athletics and other high school activities and is remembered as a popular, active boy. There is no record of disciplinary action or social maladjustment. After high school graduation, he worked steadily for three years, then was drafted into the US Army. He achieved the rank of corporal and was honourably discharged two years later. While in the Army, he married his high school girl-friend. He has worked since his discharge in a semi-skilled factory job; he has no police record and his credit rating [*sic*] is excellent.
>
> This man was interviewed in his home and was a willing participant. No evidence of psychopathology was elicited during the interview. He recalled little of his early years but did state that he was a 'mess' when he began school but that he 'grew out of it'. His MMPI profile was completely benign. He related warmly to the examiner and to his wife and infant daughter who were intermittently present. A MHSRS score of 94 was assigned. Because of the intellectual deficits predicted as a result of childhood deprivation, a full-scale WAIS [a test for different aspects of the IQ] was administered at a later date. The subject achieved a verbal IQ of 100. Performance 98. Full Scale 99, with no scatter of subscale scores.[35]

Given normal constitution and heredity, there appears nothing to prevent the person with a miserable, retarded institutional childhood from leaving this behind him and developing into a perfectly adequate, acceptable adult. So determined are we that an unhappy childhood shall leave recognisable scars, so prurient is our fascination with the tragedy of traumatisation and the inescapability of every infantile experience, that we are most reluctant to acknowledge just how resilient and adaptive most human beings are. And in this we do the institutionalised person insult as well as injury.[36] Having caused him unnecessary childhood unhappiness, we refuse to recognise his recovery from it. If we want to understand fully why present society has fallen so heavily for these kinds of myth, we must ask ourselves honestly whether we really want people reared in institutions to grow up just as adequately as those with good family homes, and to be indistinguishable from them. As we saw, a century or more ago respectable society held the attitude that children not coming from a family home should quite properly suffer for that fact and this viewpoint is not quite dead today. It used to be said that the prostitute is society's sacrifice on the altar of monogamy: it could equally be said that the institutionalised child is its sacrifice on the altar of the family.

Since Western institutions are not 'acceptable alternatives' to the home for bringing up wanted children, the only unweighted evaluation of the modern family as a form of upbringing would have to involve comparison with quite different rearing arrangements, which are normal to other societies. There is space here only for a brief mention of two such contemporary societies.

The Hutterites[37] are a traditional, conservative Protestant sect of long history, now existing as groups in North America. They practise common ownership and control of property, the community also assuming a great deal of responsibility for the welfare of each member. Infants are looked after by the mother until they are two months old, when she works part of the day in communal kitchens and gardens: an older girl is left in charge of the baby during her absence. At two and a half years of age the baby attends the communal kindergarten, and even on reaching school age spends most of his spare time as part of a group under the supervision of the Hutterite religious teacher. The teacher (male) is responsible for much of the child's socialisation. In Hutterite groups extensively studied by Eaton for psychiatric illness and crime, 131 youngsters who were medically screened by the field staff and for whom records were kept, showed no signs of severe habit disturbances or anti-social behaviour. The findings were equally negative for another 200 children, who were examined without records being kept. Physical aggressiveness of any sort is heavily frowned upon in Hutterite communities; children are taught from an early age not to fight, and any display of physical abuse in adults brings severe ostracism (the Hutterites are pacifists). The only time force is ever resorted to is in disciplining children. Eaton failed to find cases of murder, assault or rape involving Hutterite members in state crime records. Only petty legal offences were recorded, such as licence evasions. As far as he could tell only 12 had spent time in jail (and these were one-time offenders).

Hutterite experience indicates that neither extra-family upbringing nor early socialisation into a demanding and integrated social system (with all its restrictions and obligations) are, as is widely taught, measurably harmful to children. The wider American society, practising nuclear family upbringing with the minimum of restraint on children's behaviour, manages to produce an enormous rate of violence, behaviour problems and maladjustments compared with the Hutterite experience.

The Hutterites also compare favourably with the wider society in that child neglect is unknown because of their communal welfare arrangements; so also is neglect or lack of economic or medical care for the old, sick and infirm. No Hutterite becomes a public charge as long as he wishes to remain part of the group. Among adults the amount of psychosis is roughly the same as for the wider society (corroborating much other cross-society evidence which suggests genetic and organic origins). Where the Hutterites do differ, however, is in their treatment of mental illness, which carries no shame, disgrace or avoidance in their social groups. Symptoms of disorder are thus made more bearable for the patient, his kin and community, and the onset of disorder brings him and them immediate support and reassurance. Care for the mentally sick is shared by members of the group so that the family is not left to cope alone and as far as possible the patient is kept in work within his capacity. If recovery ensues, his past illness is no barrier to advancement to authority in the community or in his trade.

In contrast to the pious, conservative Hutterites, the kibbutzim[38] are products of modern egalitarian and socialist aspirations. Although kibbutzim differ, and many have altered over the years, the common pattern is for children to be reared in a separate children's house by a trained nurse, not in the parent's accommodation. Children can, nonetheless, go to their parents' quarters if they wish, and modern ideas have led the kibbutzim (compared with the Hutterites) to emphasise the necessity for children to receive a great deal of love and attention. Kibbutzim children also have wide access to interaction with adults apart from the nurse and parents, and if a child's personality clashes with his parents he does not have to visit them. As with the Hutterites, no child is neglected or ill-treated, since he does not have to stay with parents who might do these things — the community automatically providing care for all. The rates of crime and anti-social behaviour for those reared in kibbutzim are low. Personal relationships have often been singled out by commentators for their stability and degree of responsibility; openness, honesty and loyalty to the community and its principles are strong features of a kibbutz education. Contributions to public life in Israel by kibbutz-reared people are said to be more than proportional to their numbers. Bowlby maintains that, since in the kibbutz there is not a complete abandonment of parent—child relations (because the child visits his biological parents in the evening and on the sabbath and they enjoy one another's company), the lack of maladjustment or affectionlessness is no objection to his argument.[39] But if so, why does he oppose mothers working, or the provision of day nurseries, since here, too, the mother would see the child in the evening or weekend? Why do he and his supporters talk of a mother's task as full-time devotion to her child, since the kibbutz mother devotes her time to her own and the kibbutz's work? She is certainly not in her living quarters all day interacting with her infant: indeed, she can go away for months at a time on educational courses, leaving her child in community care.

Salter-Ainsworth says that there is always a 'mother-figure'[40] present for the kibbutz child, but she hhappens to be different people at differen times, such as real mother, teacher-nurse and age-peers. If this situation can be seriously taken as unbroken attachment to one mother, what imaginable situation could not? And what was the whole Maternal Deprivation Theory about, if communal or group child-rearing are allowed to be quite acceptable as long as we call the different persons separate components of a 'mother-figure'?

10 Bowlby's Sanatorium Study

The search for the Affectionless Thief has not so far proved fruitful; it is time we returned to the work of Bowlby in order to learn a little more about him and his origins.

In 1956 a study[1] was published in which Bowlby and colleagues attempted to substantiate the connection between maternal deprivation and affectionless delinquency. This research consisted of comparing sixty children who had entered a sanatorium for tuberculous patients before the age of four (the length of separation falling between six and twenty-four months), with a sample of class-mates matched for age and sex. The control group was three times the size of the research group (the sex distribution of the sample biases it towards discovering defects in the hospitalised group, as boys outnumber girls 41 to 19, and boys are known to react more adversely to stress of all kinds). The ages at follow-up ranged from six years ten months to thirteen years seven months. The data for comparison involved three items. There was an IQ test administered by a psychologist, who also gave a report on the child's behaviour in the test situation. Then there were the teachers' answers on a questionnaire concerning the child's school behaviour (the same teacher answered for a child and three controls of the same age). This questionnaire was in two parts: the first part comprised twenty-two items covering the child's relationships with the teacher, with other children, and his work and play activities. For each item there were two, three or four choices covering all likely manifestations of behaviour, only one or two of which could be regarded as indicating satisfactory adjustment, the others indicating deviations in different directions or degrees. The second part of the questionnaire form gave the teacher opportunity to note any symptoms which may have been observed, to comment on the child's attendances, health and school progress, on the child himself and his family. Each teacher completed this questionnaire for a sanatorium child and for three controls.

The teachers could not be kept ignorant of which child had been in a sanatorium and which had not. They were told that a follow-up was being conducted on sanatorium children to see how they were settling down on returning home. The psychological testers were also conversant with who had been in a sanatorium and who had not.

The selection of the controls was rather unsatisfactory. At first the teachers were left to choose the children, but the researchers found that they did not adhere to the age criteria, or only selected children who did well at school, etc. The selection was finally made by the researchers. In some cases (that is with some sets of four children), the researchers appear to have objected to the teachers' selection after the children were reported upon, so that a second set of reports had to be done, with different controls. Also in some cases, where two sets of reports were drawn up, both sets of controls were found to meet the criteria of selection (why in these cases there was objection to the teachers' initial choice, we do not know). Here the most 'reliable' set of reports was chosen.

Mention is made by Bowlby and his colleagues that the teachers and the psychological testers were very inadequately briefed. The teachers were not properly briefed about the use of the questionnaire, nor the psychological testers about the type of report that they were expected to make on a child, so that they proffered widely differing types. Conditions were bad for the IQ test, with inadequate accommodation and frequent interruptions. After outlining the inadequacies of the investigation, the researchers assert with confidence that such peripheral considerations would probably not affect the outcome, which they expected would be a strong confirmation of the Maternal Deprivation Theory: 'Nevertheless it was believed that the differences between the sanatorium and control children might be sufficient to be clearly manifest even with such a relatively crude instrument.'[2] Unfortunately, as Bowlby admits, this was 'a belief that was not confirmed', since none of the differences between the sanatorium children and the controls on the teachers' reports 'reached a level of statistical significance'.

Pleas for the publication of the actual figures have not, to my knowledge, been satisfied.[3]

The sanatorium children were found to be above average in IQ (with a mean of 107). The only statistical difference detrimental to the sanatorium group was found in the behaviour in the test situation. More children in the latter compared with the controls needed encouragement, or were completely put off when taking the test. Their nervousness is put down to their 'separation experience'. It is unfortunate that there is such an implicit assumption in this study that the Maternal Deprivation Theory is completely valid, so that any failings of the sanatorium group are attributed to maternal separation rather than to other adverse experiences.

There is also a rather strained attempt to square the findings with those of Goldfarb. Goldfarb found that his institutionalised children had a low mean IQ when compared with his foster home sample. Bowlby found that the sanatorium children had a mean IQ above average, but nonetheless, more sanatorium children than controls were in the lower ranges of the IQ spectrum (not statistically significant), so a case is rather tenuously made for similar damage (that is, mental retardation) in the two samples because of separation. Goldfarb found that his institutionalised children showed little capacity for sustained effort, faltering quickly under difficulties and inclining to be passive. The shyness and nervousness of the ex-tuberculosis patients are equated with Goldfarb's findings. The impression gained from Bowlby's discussion on how the damage seen in his sanatorium sample can be equated with the damage Goldfarb saw in his institutionalised group, is that with enough discursive interpretation this could be done with many observations, whether favourable or detrimental.

The study as a whole, then, hardly supports the claims of the Maternal Deprivation theorists for clearly discernible, permanent damage to personality and intelligence. The teachers' reports must have been particularly disappointing; high maladjustment rates show up neither in the objective test nor in their personal comments. Bowlby and colleagues suspected that 'in some cases, therefore, information felt by the teacher to be adverse to the child has certainly not been recorded',[4] although earlier the role of teacher bias had been discounted[5]. They had said (p. 216) that with 'the same teacher reporting on all four children . . . any unreliability or bias of the teachers would also be reflected in the control group'. And also, during discussion of how far the reports of the psychologists and the teachers might be affected by awareness of the hypothesis under investigation, it is stated (p. 219) that 'the consistency of the two independent sets of data in respect of certain deviations from the norm suggests that both sets are tolerably valid.'

This led to the teachers' reports being subsequently subjected to scrutiny and unreliable ones discarded. Five reasons were cited for rejecting a report: (1) Inconsistency in the teachers' checking of items on the questionnaire; (2) Inconsistency between the items checked on the questionnaire and the description given of the child by the teacher at the end of the report; (3) Inconsistency between the teacher's report as a whole and points later brought out in discussion with the research worker; (4) 'Strong suspicion' by the research worker that the teacher had 'mistrusted' the research and had 'covered up' difficulties in his report (this judgement again was made after discussion with the teacher concerned, and recorded in the report of the school visit); (5) Lack of discrimination in the reports of any set of four children rated by the same teacher — in particular, where all or nearly all items were checked identically for all four children, the items in question usually being those which indicated good adjustment. It is stated that two research psychologists studied the reports independently of each other before a decision was reached to reject a set. These 'research psychologists' appear to have been the workers carrying out the investigation.

Having discarded twenty-five sets of children because of the 'unreliability' of the teachers' reports, the psychological testers' reports on behaviour during the IQ test were also likewise restricted — to thirty-one sets, just over half the original sample. We are not told if these cover the same sets as the 'reliable' reports of the teachers.

Now these 'reliable' reports showed that on eleven items out of twenty-eight, a larger proportion of the sanatorium children than the controls were given marks for maladjustment. Out of these eleven measured differences, only five had any statistical significance, and two of these only when the behavioural manifestations appeared to have been thinned out: that is, a difference showed only on one or more of the component indices making up an item, but not on all. The items which showed statistically significant differences between the sanatorium and control group children were as follows:[6]

Item 27 'Day-dreaming'
Item 14 'He does not seem to know what to do
         unless told'
Item 11 'His attention wanders rather frequently'
Item 8 'He seems diffident about competing with
         other children' together with 'He does not
         seem to care how he compares with
         other children'
Item 9 'He is liable to get unduly rough during
         playtime'

Even if we do not agree with F. Kräupl Taylor (1958)[7] that the result 'is likely to indicate that bias did inadvertently — though perhaps inevitably — creep into this secondary selection of acceptable reports',[8] these differences are hardly evidence for great personality damage. Yet they are used to brand the children as virtually hopeless defectives: that they day-dream more than the controls and are not as good at competing leads Bowlby and colleagues to apply to them Goldfarb's damning description of his institutionalised children's whole personalities — that they are 'meagre and undifferentiated, passive and apathetic'.

Again, unless one has already made up one's mind which factor will be chosen to account for such minor faults, why arbitrarily assume that these children were affected by their separation experience? There is as much reason to put it down to hospital cooking or ugly nurses. Bowlby acknowledges that there were plenty of other disadvantageous factors in the backgrounds of these sanatorium children to account for the differences. But he seems strongly convinced that they are due to separation because they 'are similar in nature to those found by Goldfarb'.[9] If the work of Goldfarb or Bowlby is to have solid scientific validity, either of them should be able independently, with objective tools, to repeat the findings of the other — which has not been done here.

The investigators mentioned some rather disturbing facts about the backgrounds of the tuberculous patients compared with the controls: 'Very many young tuberculous children come from families where the members, especially parents, have tuberculosis (by whom they are affected) so that illness and death are common, with their attendant disturbed family relations and depressed economy.'[10] And while they were separated, 'the children were ill . . . and confined to their cots for rest during much of the time'.[11] Some children also underwent tonsillectomy, frequent taking of blood samples and gastric lavage (extraction of the contents of the stomach through the nose). Any reasonable and sensitive person should surely be aware that experiences such as these are unlikely to leave any child or adult completely unaffected — at least for a short time afterwards. To expect a child to emerge from tuberculosis bursting with vim and vigour is quite ludicrous. The remarkable fact to come out of this investigation is that it took so much sifting of the reports to produce these results. These children obviously have the most admirable capacities for endurance and recovery.

Not content with the findings, the researchers decided to take their own closer look at the children's personalities, using clinical (that is, pschoanalytical) methods. Visits were made to the home of each of the sanatorium children, to glean material about the child, his history and family, that would be useful to the researchers in ascertaining his degree of adjustment and his 'pattern of personality organisation'. More material was gathered by interviewing the teachers and making use of their original reports. No 'clinical' investigation was made of the control children to see how they compared. The material accumulated in this way was rated for maladjustment by 'three clinically orientated judges' — that is, the researchers carrying out the investigation, all believers in the theory concerned. They first assessed the information on each child independently, and then agreed ratings together. They had to rate the children generally as, 'clearly well adjusted'; 'child well adjusted on the whole'; child has 'some obvious problems present'; the child has 'problems present' which make 'treatment advisable'; or the child is 'severely maladjusted'.[12] Allocation to these categories does not appear to be based on any publicly standardised test for mental illness or maladjustment, so that it is impossible to repeat the researchers' procedures and thereby test their findings.

We are merely informed that these clinicians 'set a far more rigorous standard of adjustment than would the layman'.[13] Unfortunately we are not told what is meant by 'rigorous'. It is obvious that if one sets higher and higher standards for mental adjustment, one will eventually find oneself diagnosing one hundred per cent of the population as maladjusted. This would not only be pointless but contradictory, as abnormality would become the norm, and one would require new tests to differentiate those showing strong deviations from it.

There is similarly little logic in maintaining that: 'It is almost certain that, if deprivation causes psychological damage which is manifest in some cases, it will cause damage which is concealed in others,'[14] although it is claimed that more delicate techniques are needed to measure its extent.

The hints that we receive about the definition of maladjustment in the sanatorium study (and whether or not this is going to prove irreversible) are that this involves 'the quality of relationships made, particularly those with the mother, father and siblings' and 'anxieties, symptoms and personality difficulties'. All these are wide open to the most subjective evaluation. And even these elastic signs are merely symptoms, as it were, of hidden internal processes which may be going wrong and which will emerge later in life as character deformities.[15]

The clinicians, using their own methods, found sixty-three per cent of the sanatorium children maladjusted. They say that if they had been given even more refined techniques for measuring all the hidden disturbance, they would have found a higher rate still.[16]

From rates of maladjustment the clinicians turned to classifying the sanatorium children's 'personality patterns', according to the subject's 'object relationships', particularly with his mother. The more strained his relationship with her, the more estranged from her he is, the more aberrant his

personality. This does not appear to be because these subjects
necessarily have any other unusual traits, but because the fact
of not getting on with their mothers is in itself presumed to
be damaging.

The clinicians agreed on seven divisions to classify the
sanatorium children:

> Group A *Conforming:* children who, through good
> behaviour or achievement or both, are socially acceptable.
> Some but not all seem unduly concerned with winning the
> approval of adults by means of this behaviour.
>
> Group B *Over-dependent*: children who are more
> dependent on the mother than is normal for their age,
> showing it by clinging to her or demanding reassurance of
> her affection or approval. These are divided into two
> subgroups: (i) those who do not express hostility,
> (ii) those who express some measure of hostility to other
> people, including the mother.
>
> Group C *Withdrawn and over-dependent:* children who
> are not only extremely over-dependent in all their
> relationships but are also unable to mix satisfactorily with
> other children.
>
> Group D *Ambivalent*: children who show evidence of
> both affectionate and strongly hostile feelings towards
> their mothers and others, and who are not over-dependent.
>
> Group E *Mother-rejecting*: children who show both a
> pronounced lack of dependence on the mother and some
> hostility towards her, with preference for other members
> of the family.
>
> Group F *Affectionless*: children who show no apparent
> dependence on or affection for the mother and whose
> relations with other figures are also severely disturbed.
>
> Group G *Superficial*: children in whom there is little
> evidence of overt disturbance or difficulty, but whose
> relationships are suspected to be lacking in warmth and
> depth though at first glance they may appear
> satisfactory.[17]

The most striking point about this personality
classification system is that any category to which a child
could be consigned involves some defect or other in his

ability to make relationships. So, before we start allocating the children to the various groups, it is taken for granted that they are all going to be abnormal in some way or other. Even taking it from here, there appears, as with the procedures for assessing maladjustment, to be little in the way of firm criteria for judging whether or not, for example, a relationship is deep or superficial if

> . . . a basic and serious disability in making discriminating object relationships is masked by a superficial camaraderie; thus some good mixers are found in reality to make nothing but casual and undiscriminating relationships. It is at least possible that some of the sanatorium children reported as making friends readily fall into this category.[18]

This despite the fact that elsewhere this investigation showed, on the face of it '. . . no disability in this respect reported by teachers, but, more important because probably more reliable, at least half are reported by their parents to mix well and to make friends readily'.[19]

But in all this confusion one thing at least is a little clearer than it was in *Forty-Four Juvenile Thieves*, and that is how we might recognise a future Affectionless case. Affectionless children make up groups F, E and G, in that order of severity. In all of them

> . . . loving components in their relationships to their mothers are little if at all expressed, while hostile components or indifference are frequently prominent. Many are said to lack any feeling of attachment to their mothers and to get on well with strangers, known clinically as an ominous combination of features.[20]

The severest, Group F, have their 'feelings of affection' towards their mothers most 'deeply repressed', indeed they show 'no feeling' for her, although they get on well with strangers. Group E are not quite so bad:

> They are described as being 'independent' of mother, not at all affectionate towards her, and disobedient. Their relationships with father and siblings, however, are rather

better. Some flare into tempers when frustrated, others are defiant or obstinate . . . Their relationships with other children vary, some getting on quite well while others get on badly, but all seem unduly aggressive.[21]

Group G children are placed with Groups F and E because 'their relationships are suspected of being superficial, lacking in warmth and depth. At home they are described as being "independent of mother", and yet on good terms with her and the rest of the family.'[22] They are 'obedient and easy to manage, without any evidence of hostility'[23]. Nonetheless they still get on well with strangers.

The suspicions aroused in *Forty-Four Juvenile Thieves* are confirmed; we can also see why we cannot find Bowlby's Affectionless Thief in the work of other, non-psychoanalytic researchers. The meaning of affectionlessness is largely lack of love (or suspected lack of love) for one's mother. 'Other figures' have some subsidiary importance, but again, only if they are also immediate family members. Good relationships with friends or adults outside the family are discounted when they are not supplemented by good relationships within it — primarily with mother. It would appear that even if there is no mother to love, her absence — and hence the impossibility of the child having any relationship whatsoever with her — renders him *ipso facto* affectionless. This being so, it is at least clear that maternal deprivation could not cause an affectionless personality, for the simple logical reason that they are not genuinely independent concepts. 'Affectionlessness' is given no proper meaning except a good relationship with one's mother. But two things must be logically separate for it to be even discoverable that one causes the other.

A child may have been away from home for a long period in an institution or foster home so that he forms relationships with other people who are more real to him in the here and now than his parents. Common-sense views, uninfluenced by psychoanalysis, would see nothing extraordinary in this. However, Bowlby appears to be surprised by it. Of two of his thieves he said:

No. 27, Betty I. who was away in various homes from the age of nine months to that of nearly five years, was said nine months later to 'behave as though she had just come in to play and does not seem to belong'. No. 30, Norman K. whose mother had been in sanatoria for long periods was described as behaving as though he felt he did not belong to the family. [24]

Bowlby imposes precisely the same interpretation on the tubercular children who, after periods away from home, have to readjust to what are, to all intents and purposes, new relationships and ways of life. The family at home are in a similar position, and would usually have made alternative relationships (the parents may have had other children), so that difficult and sometimes unwelcome adjustments may have to be made on the return of the hospitalised person.

It also seems to be expected that a child's love should extend automatically to a hostile and even cruel mother. Now if an adult has no say in establishing a relationship, such as a forced marriage, and the person to whom they were tied is cruel and rejecting, we would normally be sympathetic should they wish to break free and make other personal relationships. Why should we not have the same reaction to a child in similar circumstances? One child, No. 34, Derrick O'C. in the *Forty-Four Juvenile Thieves* study, Bowlby noted as trying very hard to establish personal relationships outside his family, and as eager not to fail. He, however, was classed as affectionless:

> Over a long period of time he came regularly to see me once a week. He proved unexpectedly cooperative and did much to unearth the causes of his own stealing but was always pathetically anxious to please and was obviously worried when he was unable to answer some query I might make. (p.51)

Stott, in the investigation already quoted, speaks of a boy of thirteen who as a toddler had been some eighteen months in hospital and convalescent home and who (according to Bowlby) would probably be an affectionless character as he was not demonstrably affectionate to his mother who

> . . . had given birth to another child the very day he

returned from his long stay in hospital, so that the homecoming must have been inauspicious. Also she had the unfortunate habit of using threats to put him away when he was naughty; and for two years he had been waiting to go to a residential school.[25]

In another case the mother had said that she

> ... 'tried to get him away but we could not do anything about it. He was a drawback to me working in service.' All this was related in front of the child in a matter of fact way. It was evident that the child must have heard all the details of the steps she was taking to get rid of him.[26]

While these are not cases of physical cruelty, they are undoubtedly circumstances of clear hostility and rejection, in which it would be quite natural for any child to exhibit less than normal affection. To postulate a special defect of affectionlessness to explain such behaviour demonstrates a rather strange conception of ordinary human affection. If a victim continues to adore his tormentor we term it masochism, which denotes, not something normal and desirable, but something maladaptive and self-destructive.

Often when children (or anybody else for that matter) have no choice but to remain with those who show them callous disregard, they may pathetically attempt to solicit some favourable response, although the situation is hopeless.

> It was this unnatural situation during the years between six and nine rather than his early experiences, that was making him take refuge in affectionlessness. But he helped his mother with the washing up, swept for her, and 'starts to clear the table even before you have finished' — which shows that the term 'affectionless character' in this as probably in most cases is an oversimplification . . .[27]

Bowlby's original hypothesis, I scarcely need repeat, would predict a significantly higher incidence of stealing in the separated children than in the controls. In fact it transpired that only *one* of the sixty sanatorium children was reported as having stolen (by the teachers). However, Bowlby came to 'suspect' that the three severely affectionless cases may have pilfered. No suspicion fell on any of the control children, for the reason that similar interviews were not given to their families.

Yet in the sanatorium study only eight children could be placed in mother-rejecting categories E and F — three in the severe Group F (I am ignoring the five suspected mother haters in Group G as this seems a manifest absurdity). I can only conclude that this study reveals a remarkable degree of filial affection in children who have been separated from home for long periods. Taking this together with the negative result on stealing, we are surely entitled to say that this later study fails to support Bowlby's theory of maternal deprivation.

Although they were not included in one of the groups of affectionless children, the other sanatorium children apparently have inadequacies and deficiencies of some kind. Group A children (Conforming) may have 'a personality pattern [which] is often compatible with mental health', but it is 'sometimes the expression of an excessive need for gaining approval of other people and based on deep anxiety.'[28] Group B (the Over-dependent) have a 'marked need for reassurance of their mother's love, manifested chiefly by demands for affection, attention and approval from her and sometimes expressed by a tendency to cling to her.'[29] If detachment from the mother, or dependence on her and her love, are both deficiences, what to Bowlby and colleagues would constitute normal, healthy love for her? Group C clearly do not have it: 'There is a marked desire for physical contact, demonstrative affection and cuddling, which is extended in three cases to other members of the family and even to strangers.[30] Group D (Ambivalent) would seem to strike a healthy balance: 'in relation to mother, they are consistently neither over-dependent nor rejecting; instead, there is evidence of a positive affectionate relationship with her. . .'[31] But unfortunately this is 'accompanied by considerable hostility in the form of tempers or obstinacy'.

The whole research is summed up as follows:

Perhaps the principal value of this investigation has been to display the great heterogeneity of personality organisation which is consistent with having undergone prolonged separation experience starting before the fourth birthday. The patterns of personality found range from children who are noted for their good behaviour, to those who are near-delinquent.[32]

In other words, the whole range of faults and virtues, strengths and weaknesses found in the general population is also found in the maternally separated. In effect we are told that they do not differ from any cross-section of the population. 'Great heterogeneity of personality organisation' is doubtless equally found in those children who at one time go on school expeditions or believe in Santa Claus.

So can we at last breathe a sigh of relief? It was all a false alarm — maternal deprivation is not damaging to later personality after all? Alas, apparently we cannot. Because we have no evidence that a hypothetically postulated disease causes any damage, Bowlby claims this is all the more reason to guard against its consequences at all cost:

> There are also differences from the case of poliomyelitis, however. In that disease we not only have some idea of the incidence of residual disability but have ready and reliable methods of estimating its degree. In the case of personality disturbance following separation and similar experiences we have neither. Lacking a basis for calculation, therefore, we are in no position to take calculated risks.[33]

The most obvious reaction to this comparison is not: how much more insidious is Maternal Deprivation since we know so little about it — but, but do we even know that there is such a disease?

Furthermore, any experimental outcome can be made consistent with the predictions of a theory if a sufficiently high price is paid in its informative content. Thus, it can be claimed that many of the unfortunate aspects of human existence are really maternal deprivation. Bowlby (1967) in order to explain the presence of the psychopathic, the delinquent, the neurotic, the psychotic, and the mentally retarded among those who were not maternally separated, renders the term almost infinitely elastic: in the backgrounds of these subjects

> . . . there is often evidence that there has nonetheless been separation of another and more or less serious kind. Rejection, loss of love (perhaps on advent of a new baby or on account of mother's depression), alienation from one parent by the other and similar situations, all have as a common factor loss by the child of a parent to love and attach himself to. If the concept of loss of object is extended to cover loss of love these cases no longer constitute exceptions.[34]

Ainsworth, too, has taken the view that maternal deprivation is not just separation (and if we ever thought the Maternal Deprivation theorists said this, we are, she tells us, greatly mistaken.[35] [36]). It means virtually any adverse features of mother–child interaction. She divides adverse features into three broad types of deprivation: (1) discontinuity in relations brought about by separation; (2) insufficiency of interaction (how one interprets this would seem to depend on what one thinks is the ideal mother–baby relationship); (3) distorted interaction, or the wrong type of mother–baby interaction (except for obvious cruelty, conscious rejection and neglect, this too lends itself to all manner of interpretations). By these means, Ainsworth is able to deal with criticisms of the theory and accommodate the apparently refuting evidence of so many surveys. The evidence of other factors besides separation which might account for the observed phenomena can also be generously interpreted as evidence of maternal deprivation. And when no repercussions are observed at all, this can be put down to absence of one of the three conveniently vague factors during the separation experience. The variations are limitless. Such a volatile explanation of personal and social ills is as viable as that offered by Astrology which, given sufficient latitude of interpretation, will show any and every event in our lives to be the outcome of the ubiquitous machinations of the heavens.

The poor showing made by the 1956 study (see above) did appear to deflate slightly the assurance of its proponents. One has a right to expect some withdrawal after so much sound and fury:

> Meanwhile it is clear that some of the former group of
> workers, including the present senior author, in their desire
> to call attention to dangers which can often be avoided,
> have on occasion overstated their case. In particular,
> statements implying that children who are brought up in
> institutions or who suffer other forms of serious privation
> and deprivation in early life *commonly* develop
> psychopathic or affectionless characters (e.g. Bowlby,
> 1944) are seen to be mistaken.[37]

But the public did not notice. Two years later Bowlby says
that in 'including myself amongst those guilty of
overstatement, I may have been unduly self-critical . . .' and
that the 1956 study did not shake his faith in the theory: 'In
conclusion may I emphasise that the object of this letter is
not to persuade sceptics of the correctness of these views but
to discourage anyone from supposing that I have changed my
position in any material way. . .'[38] The theory had obviously
gained a popular momentum of its own by this time which
rendered such considerations as empirical verification
unimportant. *Without even having shown that lengthy
separation was harmful in itself, and certainly not that it
scars for life*, Bowlby in 1958 wrote a rather alarming
booklet to deter mothers from leaving healthy,
normally-loved babies for short periods.[39] Edelston is right to
remark that although we appear to have escaped the hazards
of maternal deprivation, 'One hazard which it seems we have
not escaped is the premature dissemination to the public at
large of opinions which as yet are not fully authenticated.'[40]
As the theory was repeated over and over again and became
eagerly incorporated into contemporary social mythology,
the necessity for proof receded before the acclaim. *Child
Care and the Growth of Love*, still selling, still influential, no
more contains any note in text or preface to counteract
unwarranted alarm than it did in 1951 in the form of the
original monograph.

In a social climate so conducive to this type of theory,
further work has proceeded on the assumption that the

Maternal Deprivation Theory has been established. Bowlby's *Attachment and Loss* (Volume 1 appeared in 1969) attempts a detailed explanation, utilising modern ethological knowledge, of the mechanisms of attachment operating between mother and child which render separation so harmful.

Bowlby is not attempting to test his hypothesis once and for all by undertaking a large-scale survey in search of a possible correlation between the extent of maternal separation and the extent of mental abnormalities in the population. He appears to assume that such a correlation is beyond dispute. Even in 1954, before the publication of the sanatorium study, he wrote that such a large-scale survey would allegedly be

> . . . an undertaking of such magnitude as to lie outside the limit of feasibility. Whether it would be worth undertaking on a more superficial basis is doubtful . . . On the other hand, starting with the assumption that separation has already been shown to be a pathogenic factor, it might fruitfully be used to answer certain sociological questions. Where in the population does separation occur most frequently and in connection with what problems?[41]

Instead he seems increasingly to incline towards the novel approach of working forwards from a 'pathogenic agent', instead of working backwards from the pathological condition to the agency or event in the past which caused it. He feels that this preferred method is vindicated by medicine:

> When a study of the pathology of chronic infection of the lungs is undertaken today, an investigator is no longer likely to start with a group of cases all showing chronic infection and attempt to discover the infective agent or agents that are at work. It is more likely that he will start with a specified agent, perhaps tubercle or actinomycosis or some newly identified virus, in order to study the physiological and physiopathological processes to which it gives rise.[42]

The reason why medicine may start with a specific agent is

that that agent, or ones closely related, have been known to be connected with later disease. It is preposterous to suppose that medical research would take any random bacterium about which no connection with later effects on the organism was known and start investigating it. Of course, in investigating millions of the myriad species of bacteria a pathogenic agent might be found, but then an ape, if it is given long enough to hit a typewriter will, it has been asserted, write the plays of Shakespeare. We can surely agree with Wootton[43] that this abandonment of any attempt to show that maternal deprivation has harmful effects, in exchange for the blind faith that it does, 'is certainly a council of despair as well as a grave breakdown in logic'. Instead we are informed by Bowlby 'that any new projects would be well advised to utilise the current study approach'. And so 'after spending several not very successful years following the first strategy' (follow-up method), he seeks the desired results by switching tactics 'to study the child's responses at the time of and in the period immediately subsequent to the [separation] experience'. This, he tells us, has shown itself to be 'much more rewarding'. These studies appear to take as their sole evidence for irreparable damage the emotively-charged details of young children crying for their mothers. This is apparently the pathogenic agent: this 'trauma' of separation.

11 The Emotional Sell

It has been frequently claimed that the behaviour of a child during a separation experience confirms the Maternal Deprivation hypothesis. A child in such a situation is supposed to go through a period of protest (when his mother first leaves him), despair (when she does not return), and then detachment. Leaving aside for the moment the consideration whether or not upset in infancy is connected with anything in later life, and concentrating upon what one might directly observe, unbiased by preconceived theory: what might the behaviour of a child left by his mother be like? It is possible that he would cry (depending on how used he was to being cared for by others): some children might then become withdrawn and weepy for a while (depending upon the availability of other adults to befriend them and, again, on the child's previous experience). What particular empirical observations reveal detachment? Here we part company with direct observation. Bowlby holds that during detachment the relationship with the mother is broken, not because the child has forgotten her, but because he has 'repressed' her image, sent it down into the dark basement of his unconscious, where from then onwards it will work mischief. This makes it impossible for the child to re-establish the previous relationship with the mother; and since this relationship is broken, he cannot, according to the theory, make any others, for the capacity to do so is destroyed: that is, the child becomes affectionless.

What is taken as evidence of this incapacity appears not merely to be the straightforward observation of a child standing aloof from social relationships,[1] but equally, contrary behaviour, where he begins to make new relationships. Bowlby tells us that the infant's speedy acceptance of other persons after his initial upset at separation is evidence of his intolerable grief:

He no longer rejects the nurses, accepts their care and the food and the toys they bring, and may even smile and be sociable. This seems satisfactory. When his mother visits, however, it can be seen that all is not well, for there is a striking absence of the behaviour characteristic of the strong attachment normal at this age. So far from greeting his mother he may hardly seem to know her; so far from clinging to her he may remain remote and apathetic; instead of tears there is a listless turning away. He seems to have lost all interest in her.[2]

To regard this behaviour as a 'defence mechanism', where the image of the mother is repressed out of anguish, is a rather extravagant explanation, involving a whole host of unverifiables. In the absence of other evidence for this process of repression, it would be far simpler to see the behaviour as evidence for the short memory of the young child and his uncomplicated, opportunist approach to relationships. That it may be distressing to the mother, who sees her relationship with the child in adult terms, is not denied.

This approach of heads I win, tails you lose, whereby one kind of observation is taken to confirm a theory, but equally, by suitable interpretations, the very opposite observation is also taken to confirm it, is sadly common among modern child-care experts. One important area for this acrobatic way of interpreting data is the general doctrine that events — even of a subtle kind — impinge upon and affect the child far more intensely and lastingly than they do the adult. If, in a situation where it would be normal for an adult to be distressed, a child is apparently unmoved, the conclusion is not drawn that the child may not possess the understanding and emotional capacity to be deeply affected, but that he is far more upset, so much so that none of it shows. We learn from some writers, for example, that a child can react to the loss of a sibling in very different ways, but all of them indicate profound grief. Thus 'The child may continue to play as before, read comic books and show no strong evidence of sadness. They may even ask whether the parents are going to get another child to take the dead sibling's place'. But contrary to the inferences of commonsense 'This behaviour represents the need of the child to deflect the impact of the death-loss in the various ways available to him, in order to avoid being emotionally overwhelmed by feelings of depression and sadness.'[3] However, had the child shown common signs of sadness, those would have been taken at face value as proving the point, without requiring special interpretation. It becomes very difficult to imagine what behaviour could ever count as absence of grief reactions in a child.

In a social atmosphere so influenced by psychoanalytic attitudes to child-care, many lay people, not surprisingly, have come to accept the implicit, almost unnoticed, argument that as long as any upset is seen in a child, this alone is sufficient evidence that 'damage' is being done. This has now come to seem so obvious that one need not appeal to the supposed operations of mother-image repression, or even be acquainted with them, in order to accept the following statements of Bowlby and Ainsworth:

> The balance of opinion, indeed is that considerable damage to mental health can be done by deprivation in these months [first half of the first year of life], a view which is unquestionably supported by the direct observations, already described, of the immediately harmful effects of deprivation on babies of this age.[4]

and

> Because of the distress they bring, discontinuities in attachment may have adverse effects on development.[5]

'Because of the distress they bring' . . . so that if a child is seen to be upset, is this sufficient proof that he will be inadequate in some unspecified way at a future unspecified date?

Public sensitivity to the vague dangers of childhood 'trauma', and in particular the readiness to identify present stress and upsets with lasting psychological damage, has opened the way for some interesting techniques of persuasion on behalf of the Maternal Deprivation Theory. It is most significant that, where the findings of investigations seemed unconvincing to many doctors and nurses, the pathetic child upsets of this 'direct study' material have become an effective means of persuading doubters of the indubitable truth of a theory which has the minor drawback of lacking any firm scientific basis:

> Three years of fruitless talk to doctors and nurses about the existence of acute and dangerous separation distress and how it could be avoided was, except in a few cases, of little use.
> This led him [James Robertson, psychoanalyst, Tavistock Clinic], despite his inexperience with a ciné-camera, to produce a short, understated documentary which shocked and angered many different people: it showed that a controlled, supposedly contented child was in fact in the depths of misery.[6]

The films of James Robertson, showing in detail the behaviour of a handful of separated children in hospital, nursery and foster homes, are widely shown to nurses, trainee teachers and social workers. As documentaries of the reactions of a very small number of children to various types of separation experience, they have undoubted value. But they tell us nothing about any future consequences. These questions can only be finally settled by comparisons of controlled studies of representative samples of children over long time spans. Robertson might think that some of his films illustrate the processes of trauma and repression at work, but this depends on whether such processes really do operate — which is in need of independent scientific confirmation. The films themselves cannot establish the existence of such mechanisms, yet there is an unfortunate shift in process from illustrating a theory — supposedly established by other means — to actually establishing it.

Journalistic and welfare circles who popularise and use Robertson's films invariably see them as directly illustrative of the long-term damage done by separation. Reviews and articles on the film *John*[7] (a boy who was very upset in a residential nursery), clearly illustrate the kinds of conclusions many draw from the more popular of these films:

At the end of the nine days he has two dominant expressions, the first withdrawn and tear-stained, a swollen little face hiding under a teddy bear; the second, a protesting howl which the camera focuses on for a second or two, long enough for the audience to feel something of his intolerable grief.[8]

This writer speaks of film 'understating the case; others go further'. But it is effective enough to prove to her that 'Of course there tends to be a high rate of delinquency and inadequacy among such children [in the nursery] when they go out into the world: in many cases they feel they have nothing to contribute to society and are capable only of attacking it'.[9]

Psychoanalysis in general is now turning more to films as a technique of conversion to its theories. The film *Family Life,* unlike Robertson's films, was no documentary, but a fictional, stage-managed drama supposedly 'proving' the truth of the notions of Ronald Laing on the causation of psychosis. It was frightening to read review after review where the writer had succumbed completely to this insidious approach, finding it all 'so true': if intelligent people are so open to this irrational, unscientific appeal, what else might they not swallow? Such an emotional approach to psychosis has quite wantonly left in its wake too many unhappy, over-burdened parents of schizophrenics weighed down with guilt, believing that they have somehow engineered their children's afflictions — that they are to blame. Since the films made for the Maternal Deprivation Theory are actual documentaries, the adverse effect on parents is probably lighter than that engendered by the Laingian material on psychosis. But, nonetheless, it was a little disquieting to hear a blind mother's letter read on the radio describing how she might have to give up the chance of a lifetime (to go on a course on handling a guide dog), because she had heard, from descriptions of Robertson's work, how near her selfishness had gone towards doing permanent mental damage to her small child.

A little knowledge of social history will tell us that during the emergency of the last war, the British Government, in an effort to get women out of the home and into the factories, utilised films of young separated children for diametrically opposite reasons to those of the Maternal Deprivation theorist. The material did not seem hard to come by. The films showed happy, well looked after, contented infants, enjoying themselves in créches while their mothers worked — not at all upset by their absence. Who is to say what is the truth? In both cases, that of the wartime government and the Maternal Deprivation theorist, films are a faithful recording of reality chosen with ulterior motives.

Now I am most certainly not arguing that pain and privation in children and adults should not be minimised whenever possible. That children's hospitals in the past completely barred visitors was utterly barbaric and typical of the traditional institutional denial of human relationships and social intercourse. But we should be able to treat each other kindly and humanely without necessarily believing that there will be actual future damage if we do not: there are basic moral considerations which apply in the treatment of human beings that are (in many circumstances) independent of causal justification. That the work of Robertson has improved the treatment of children by hospitals (for example, in the form of unrestricted visiting) is an achievement in itself, although there have been some expensive excesses such as mother-in units. It would be an even greater achievement if it were based upon an assertion of human right alone.

In summary, it does not require a long chapter to make the point that no amount of vivid emotive 'direct' observation, whether on film or not, can succeed in demonstrating the truth of a theory where objective investigation and logic has failed, any more than the Walrus could make something true by saying it three times. The point should not need to be made at all.

12 A Look at Short Separation

When presenting the Maternal Deprivation Theory in its most reasonable and unambiguous light, Bowlby, for example, refers to separation experiences of three months or more as the really damaging ones: something that would hardly be an argument against female employment, or call for any special action from sympathetic hospital or welfare authorities dealing with an everyday round of short separations for ordinary unrejected children. (Indeed, if hospitals allow daily and unrestricted visiting, separation from the mother is hardly likely to be more than a few hour's duration at a stretch anyway.) Yet it is the more excessive claims of the theorists about leaving babies for the shortest of periods that have been most eagerly accepted and acted upon. These claims have been propagated and justified largely by the appeal to the picture of the upset infant.

In their conviction that maternal deprivation is *ipso facto* harmful to children, each one of whom (it is widely assumed), shows marked distress no matter what the attendant circumstances, many have not bothered to enquire if such a response is indeed universal.

The evidence suggests that prolonged crying or other signs of distress, let alone any upset or damage afterwards, are far from being universal during short separation experiences.

We will begin with separation of a few hours' duration at a time — for example, when the mother goes out to work: nobody has produced any conclusive evidence that, other things being equal, the child will be harmed. (Some studies of working mothers have been biased by the inclusion of too many children from broken homes, poverty-stricken backgrounds, etc.) It is more a symptom of the power of dogma that while Alva Myrdal and Viola Klein themselves find no scientific evidence that young children suffer if they are adequately cared for while their mothers work, they submit to the judgement of Bowlby that it *must* be wrong for the mothers to work. In their classic study of female employment they throw their authoritative weight firmly against it: 'Obviously, mothers cannot go out to work if they are to live up to these new and exacting standards of motherhood. This has to be accepted as the consequence of the existing knowledge that love and security are essential to the growth of a harmonious personality.'[1] Consequently 'We therefore support the view that mothers should, as far as possible, take care of their children during the first years of their lives.'[2]

As we shall see below, if short stays away from home are not damaging (even in very stressful environments such as hospital), it follows that a few hours a day are not either. Children have the capacity for more than one attachment anyway. If a child is left for the first time with a stranger, he may cry, as sometimes happens at the start of school. Whether children are never meant to cry or adjust to people outside the home are questions of value which we have no room to discuss here.

As far as short separations over a day in length go Howells and Layng[3] studied the amount of separation among two groups of thirty-seven children. One was a random sample of delinquent and emotionally disturbed children attending a psychiatric clinic, and the other a control group of healthy children. About one-third of children in both groups had been separated from their mothers for more than two days under the age of two years, and by five years two-thirds had been separated for one week or more. Evidence from parents shows that sixty-one per cent of these separations were enjoyed by the children or did not give rise to any adverse comment.

In the Stacey study[4] the researchers found, on questioning the mothers about the memories of their own childhood separation experiences, that the sample did not contain a significantly larger proportion of mothers who were upset than of those who were happy or undisturbed by the experience. Those who were upset mentioned as causes loneliness (due to a complete hospital bar on visitors) and exposure to adults dying nearby, rather than missing mothers.

The Illingworth study[5] used the stringent criteria of *Emotionally normal during the day and undisturbed after the departure of their visitors during the whole of the observation period* (disturbance conveyed by looking miserable or crying). It found that 32.4 per cent of one- to four-year-olds in hospital, 56.8 per cent of five- to six-year-olds, and 72.4 per cent of seven- to fourteen-year-olds were apparently quite contented. This study is typical. The pattern over-all is for greater upset to occur the younger the children, the more total the separation, and more for boys than for girls (here the gap is usually large and corroborates the common observation that boys as a whole cope less well with all kinds of stress than girls).

The observation that the more total the break the more the distress which is initially manifest, might be taken to confirm the hypothesis that apart from pain and fear (highly significant when dealing with hospital samples), the cause of this is entirely lack of maternal contact. Actually, the evidence suggests that a major reason is the amount of change in the total environment, rather than the absence of just the mother. In the Illingworth study, out of 781 visits, 28.8 per cent of the children cried for their mother when she left them, but also 27.5 per cent cried for the father and 33.7 per cent for both together. (And, strikingly, they also showed disturbance after 61.7 per cent of the 47 visits made by grandparents. This was statistically significant and, furthermore, was unrelated to the age of the child.)

There is little indication in research that upset occurs if a separated child is left at home with father or grandparents yet Bowlby still warns against leaving a young child with grandparents.[6] Similarly, whether the child is left at home or sent away, the presence of siblings is effective in preventing upset. Hilda Lewis mentions this phenomenon in her study of deprived children consigned to full-time care away from their families;[7] and in the volume *Brief Separations*,[8] which combines a study of short-term placement in a residential nursery with a review of the literature on short separation, it is admitted that the presence of siblings always mitigates separation experience. If the child can stay in the environment that he is used to, even though a part of it (in the shape of the mother) goes away, or if he can take some of his environment with him (e.g. a sibling) distress is virtually absent.

There is also evidence for innate differences in children's reactions to new (and thus potentially anxiety-provoking) situations. Schaffer suggests that reactions to separation appear to be partly a function of organic characteristics.[9]

The completely separated child, after initial upset, usually adapts to his new environment quickly For example, the researchers in *Brief Separations*[10] found that after a few days of total separation with no visiting, resistance to nursery routine declines and the children attach themselves to the nurses. David, Ancellin and Appell,[11] investigated both the initial and the later reactions to short separation of children aged between three years ten months and six years six months, placed in a holiday centre for approximately one month. After an initial tearful reaction and confusion, all the children succeeded in emerging from their distress and showed an improvement in personality and broadening of social competence. The latter is likely to be the outcome for children from a wide variety of homes in modern society. Few children are brought up in a social environment any wider than the nuclear family, which places grave limitations even on peer-group relationships for the pre-school child, let alone relationships with adults apart from the parents. The social competence of many young children in our society is thus bound to be poor compared with those from societies that provide plentiful opportunities for social interaction from an early age. It is likely to be particularly poor in children from very inadequate homes where little consistent teaching of any basic social skills is undertaken, including even elementary use of language. The provision for a time of a broader, consistent learning environment, where there is stimulation and learning from both adults and peers can be a maturing and stabilising force. Hilda Lewis mentions how children from problem families often ceased, for example, to wet the bed during their stay in the centre, and suggests that the new routine and the relief from disturbing home influences probably brought this about.[12] Howells and Layng in their study come to the conclusion that the difficulties for the disturbed children often came from *being with their parents* and so advocate planned separation as an effective therapeutic measure when dealing with neurotic, disturbed children.[13]

Actually, where the separated child can quickly form a relationship with someone else, some observation suggests that even a total change of environment provokes a negligible to nil amount of temporary upset. Accentuated distress during a separation would therefore seem to be related also to the lack of substitute relationships and thus presents us with a further factor which complicates the study of maternal separation. It is instructive to compare the films and commentaries by Robertson on *Jane, Kate, Lucy* and *Thomas* with that on the boy *John* in the same series.[14] The first four children were given individual foster care by a sympathetic foster mother while separated. Despite expectations to the contrary; despite the fact that none of the children had been away from their mother before; despite continual attempts to keep the mother alive and important to the child by using photographs and conversation, etc. (for psychoanalytical reasons, so that her image did not undergo repression into the unconscious); despite the most minute attention to the tiniest signs of infant unhappiness which one might see in any given day in the most contented of unseparated children: despite all this, the four children showed minimal upset at separation and within a few days had developed relationships with their foster mother. Robertson's attention to detail is well illustrated by the following observations: 'She [Jane] ran down the path and tried the handle into the apartment. Then she turned and hurried back to the garden gate with a distorted expression on her face. She closed the gate very carefully, but for some minutes hovered nearby.[15] And 'Although for much of the time she [Kate] was bright and cheerful, there were some grizzling spells and tears were often near the surface.'[16]

Contrary to the expectation that the younger the child the more distress there would be, it was the two youngest children who were the least disturbed and who easily swopped their mother for a new one:

Jane and Lucy could therefore not be helped to the same

extent as the two older children to keep the absent mother in mind. Because of this and the intensity of their physical and emotional needs these two younger children accepted the mother substitute without the loyalty conflicts of the two older children. Almost immediately they related warmly and wholeheartedly to her.[17]

Indeed, one of the younger children 'was reluctant to give up her foster mother',[18] while the other, actually became better adjusted than before.

Descriptively [by the fifth day] there was a marked improvement, contrary to what is expected of young children during separation. Lucy looked bright and happy, and only occasionally withdrew. She was eating proper meals, and the dribbling had stopped. Solitary play had given way to interaction with the foster mother, who was followed about or pushed and pulled into Lucy's chosen direction.[19]

The experiences of the child *John* were different but, even here, when he first went into the residential nursery he was not distressed, but tried to get on with the nurses. It was only after his friendly approaches to several nurses failed to establish any rapport that his behaviour started to deteriorate. He then became progressively more confused and upset. He was affected by the fact that the residential nursery made no provision for stable social relationships. From the observations made of these children, Robertson is forced to agree that factors other than separation are the crucial variables involved in distress. He cannot agree with Bowlby that *all* children separated from their mothers go through protest, despair and detachment, simply because they are separated and nothing else: 'Our findings do not support Bowlby's generalisations about the responses of young children to separation from the mother *per se*; nor do they support his theory on grief and mourning in infancy and early childhood.'[20]

Yet although Robertson has to disagree with Bowlby on this point, he still feels that maternal separation *must* somehow be automatically harmful: 'But although we have shown that variables have much greater importance than Bowlby has attached to them, and that adverse factors may cumulatively overwhelm and traumatise the young child, this does not imply that separation *per se* does not threaten development.'21

Indeed, he maintains that 'even the best of substitute care is not a certain prescription for neutralising the risks.'22 The reason for still believing that separation in itself is damaging is that psychoanalytic doctrine says that it must be; and, observation or not, Robertson has gone too far in his commitment to this to be able to reject it now.

Bowlby appears to claim, as we have seen, that the child's observed tendency to make relationships rapidly with new caretakers after the initial shock of a separation experience is a bad sign (of repression). Whether the child succeeds in making relationships with others or not, it appears that his behaviour amounts to a pathological adaptation.

No healthy outcome is permitted by the theory.

This discussion of what happens to children during short separations of varying durations and completeness has reached the point where we are beginning to enter the territory of lengthy separations involving a complete break from the former environment and resulting in the formation of a new set of relationships with the abandonment of the old. At this point our discussion is entering the realm of permanent separation. If the child now returns home, this may be as foreign as the nursery or hospital originally was, and a new separation experience begins. We must now retrace our steps and look at observations of young children returned to their homes after only a brief separation, where a break of this nature has not yet completely occurred.

Douglas and Blomfield23 found that fifty-two per cent of their sample of children had been separated from their mothers before the age of six. (Only the longest separation was recorded.) Those children who stayed at home during the separation experience showed no differences when matched with controls. Again, as with the initial upset, it appears to be the total environmental change that is important, not just the presence or absence of the mother. With the children who were sent away, separations of one month and under failed to distinguish the children from controls. Howells and Layng[24] similarly found that short separations (mainly days or weeks) could not be used to differentiate a group of disturbed children from controls. Douglas and Blomfield[25] found that the mothers' reports of children sent away from home (e.g., to a hospital) for more than a month at a time, mentioned more nightmares and habits such as nail-biting on return compared with the unseparated controls. But these still did not affect the majority of those separated and away from home for over one month.

Where the literature records disturbances on the return home of a separated child (affecting greater proportions of a sample as the separations increase in length and completeness) these can roughly be grouped as follows. There are lapses in acquired habits, producing, for example, bed-wetting, and occurring mainly in younger children. Second, there may be a rise in demands for attention. Third, undesirable habits such as nail-biting thumb-sucking, over-eating, etc., increase. All can easily be explained by learning theory and none is sinister.

Learned behaviour in young children is being formed only tenuously. It requires steady reinforcement in a framework of consistent, predictable routine. On going into hospital, for example, this is likely to be broken: the particular expected and necessary reinforcements to sustain behavioural habits, e.g., bowel and bladder control, will be missing. Even if the staff provide a supportive regime, these reinforcements may be so circumstantially different as to be initially meaningless. The child's acquired habits will start breaking down (or become 'extinguished'), through the absence of the familiar reinforcements. If he stays long enough in the new environment, he naturally becomes habituated to its routine and will begin to rebuild his former habits. If he returns home, the reimposition of the old routine will stabilise his habits at their old level.

A child returning home requires consistent and intensive support for his behaviour until his expectations about the environment are re-established. He is essentially someone who has become unsettled by exposure to a novel situation, and needs reassurance that things are still the same.

Habits such as nail-biting are common reactions in both

adults and children to anxiety and apprehension (they are sometimes called 'displacement symptoms'). They are not known as symptoms of anything worse.

The reactions of aggressiveness or uncommunicativeness reported for some children during and after a separation experience represent primitive, unlearnt attempts at coping with a situation for which no learned social skills have been acquired. A new environment, incomprehensible in terms of past experience, gives rise to withdrawal or attack until behaviour to deal with it is learned. If an individual returns to his old environment, it is possible (if the break was long or complete) that the old ways of behaving in it have become virtually 'extinguished' and have to be relearnt. Lapses into crude attempts at coping are likely to occur here as well.

The institutional set-up in which John (the subject of Robertson's film and study) found himself, did not permit stable interpersonal interaction. All the boy's past expectations and behaviour were meaningless, so he reverted to primitive, unlearnt ways of coping. On returning home he was also very sensitive to being sent away again, which is understandable. After all, on the only occasion he went away, his experiences were not exactly pleasant. But this does not mean that any process has been damaged. He has merely been taught by a painful experience to be frightened of going away from home. This teaching could be reversed by exposure to pleasurable or benign separations. It is no answer to the problem to shield him from any further ones.

Studies of short separation experience show that such disturbances are no greater in separated children than in non-separated groups after six months back in the old environment. Most of the children who develop them appear to lose them within a few weeks.

If, to spare the child unpleasant experiences, we wish to minimise upset during and after a separation experience, (apart from steps that could reasonably be taken to humanise institutions), we need to know more about those children who appear adversely affected beyond the most fleeting and understandable distress. A study which investigated this difference, *Hospitals, Children and their Families*, by Stacey and colleagues[26] is a highly revealing piece of research which has repercussions for child-care and social policy well beyond the hospital ward. It demonstrates that it is precisely the cultivation of an exclusive, unbroken maternal bond that is partly productive of the very upsets utilised by the Maternal Deprivation theorists as evidence for later damage.

The study found that children who were unduly upset in the hospital had the following characteristics. They were less likely to have had experience of separation from their mothers and immediate household than those who adapted well in hospital; the latter were accustomed from an early age to benign separations in differing environments. They got on less well with strangers and were less likely to be taken visiting, or used to run messages; instead they were amused by their mothers for long periods, whereas those adapting well in hospital received less attention from their mothers. They were more likely to be indulged at home and given large amounts of pocket money, reflecting the general fact that they came from 'permissive', or 'child-oriented' homes; whereas those who coped well with hospitalisation tended to come from homes that interfered with the child's wishes and behaviour.

That it is the very absence of separation experience which leads to excessive distress at first separation, can be accounted for by the child's failure (through lack of experience) to acquire any repertoire of learnt responses that he could use to understand and manage new environments. One of the researchers in the Stacey study implicitly acknowledges this explanation when she compares the inexperienced child with the adult in the capacity to deal with novel situations:

Once a person moves into a new interpersonal setting a major problem he faces is understanding the setting and coming to terms with its demands. An adult is in a better position than a child to do this because he is likely to have undergone anticipatory socialisation in the form of the mass media and personal contact with relatives and friends. An adult will have had more experience of new interpersonal settings and greater opportunity to develop the social skills needed. Unlike a child, an adult will have accumulated an extensive repertoire of responses which can be reorganised into new combinations suitable as social behaviour in a new context.[27]

Implied in this observation is the difference between the child who has undergone 'anticipatory socialisation', had 'more experience of new interpersonal settings and greater opportunity to develop the social skills needed' — namely the child with experience of places and people outside the maternal cocoon, and the child without it. On the analogy with adults, the latter is like an unprepared inhabitant of New Guinea transported to Piccadilly Circus: all is bewildering chaos. This failure will be the greater the younger the child, owing to the smaller store of experience and the larger emphasis on exclusive maternal care. A two-year-old is less likely to be left than a four-year-old, whereas at five the start of school will force many children to acquire some social skills.

It is significant that Maternal Deprivation theorists tend to talk of five as the usual upper limit for 'damage' from separation. But the signs are that this owes itself less to the presence of some instinctual need for the mother that rapidly slackens its hold at five, than to the fact that five is the age at which the child starts school.

The problem is apparently complicated for the modern child if he comes from a 'child-oriented' or 'permissive' environment, where he is treated to lots of maternal company and attentions. For learning to take place some attentions have to be applied selectively to develop certain behaviours in the child (chosen by the adult). But the 'permissive' ethos emphasises that attentions should be given in large, steady amounts in order to feed the child's postulated requirements for love, attention, security, etc., rather than discriminately, in order to develop certain behaviour — particularly where this behaviour must to some extent subordinate and dovetail individual demands to those of others if it is to be of use. Mothers in the Stacey study who gave their children less attention than the 'child-oriented' ones, nonetheless appear to have had more effect on their behaviour, since they were better adjusted and socially more competent. Their sparing attentions at least entered discriminately into the child's behaviour to shape it to some constructive end. It is, of course, possible for attentions provided for children to get involved in learning sequences unintentionally, and help to establish certain behaviour patterns. But what will be learnt in this way are at best habits idiosyncratic to that family, meaningless or even obnoxious to outsiders. As far as social competence goes, the child might as well have learnt nothing at all.

The Stacey study also involved giving tests of maladjustment to the hospitalised group of children and a control group, before, and at periods up to six months after, the hospital experiences of the first group. This was to find out how many children showed deterioration in adjustment after return from hospitalisation compared with the controls, and if these were the same children who reacted unfavourably in the ward situation. These were to be designated children 'vulnerable' to hospitalisation, and, given knowledge of their backgrounds, it would then be possible to take special precautions over such 'vulnerable' children if hospital procedures were necessary.

The maladjustment scores of most hospitalised children rose immediately after hospitalisation (one would expect those of adults to do so also), but dropped rapidly within a few weeks. At the end of the six months the pattern of change-over time (from first test to fourth) in the number of children in different categories of maladjustment was much the same for both hospital and control groups. For instance, over the total period 14 children showed improvement compared with 11 in the control, 13 showed deterioration compared with 10 in the control, whereas 9 and 4 respectively were unchanged.

Direction of change of behaviour in successive interviews.[28]

Hospital sample	Number of cases			Number in sample
	Improved	Unchanged	Deteriorated	
Interview:				
1st to 2nd	4	2	30	36
2nd to 3rd	21	8	7	36
3rd to 4th	10	16	10	36
1st to 3rd	14	7	15	36
1st to 4th	14	9	13	36
Control Group				
1st to 4th	11	4	10	25

The researchers then examined the individual test records of each child, to see if those scoring high on maladjustment at the end of the six-month period were the same as those scoring high at the beginning (and vice versa). They particularly wished to find if any children in the hospitalised group had deteriorated in their scores between the first and fourth interview. They found that six children in the hospital group who were rated highly at the beginning were not at the end, whereas there was an increase in the category of Intermediate maladjustment from 10 to 17 (in the control group these had increased from 11 to 13).

It is most unfortunate that these researchers seem determined to find hospitalisation 'damaging', to the extent of demanding that if it is not to be demonstrated as damaging, the hospitalised children must not merely have equal rates of maladjustment to the controls, but actually lower ones. They added these children in the hospitalised group who had deteriorated to those in the same group who were just as maladjusted at the beginning of the survey as the end, and called all these the children 'vulnerable' to hospitalisation. (Such grouping implies, fallaciously, that hospitalisation should be automatically seen as detrimental to those already disturbed.)

This grouping overlapped the one for children showing most upset in hospital. However, it does not show that the hospital experience was harmful, since control group children deteriorated as well, and some in the hospital group improved. All it shows is that certain children with certain patterns of maladjustment scores are among the ones to make a great deal of fuss in hospital. The backgrounds of the 'vulnerable' children were found to be the same as those most upset in hospital — namely, a permissive home regime with little experience of separation from mother.

The rating indices for maladjustment used in this study (and similar to those widely found to differentiate normal from maladjusted children), are particularly concerned with the presence of aggressiveness and withdrawn, dependent behaviour. Now these are usually primitive and chaotic responses to interpersonal situations and demands that the child cannot interpret, and fails to cope with. Maladjustment has typically been associated with poor organic and genetic endowment (see Prechtl,[29] Stott[30] and Drillien).[31] These give rise to maladjustment symptoms because they interfere with the learning capacities of the human organism, making difficult the acquisition of sequences of learnt behaviour that enable the person to deal with his environment.

This being so, it can be postulated that symptoms of what has been traditionally termed maladjustment will arise not only when the organism, due to inherent faults, cannot learn, but also when no attempt has been made to teach. Social competence is not an instinct which simply matures spontaneously in a given natural environment, maternal or otherwise. It is something taught and learnt, and its absence is not due to any pathological warping of a natural tendency, nor any 'sickness' brought about by 'unnatural' behaviour on the part of parents. There is no natural impulse towards social ability which is thwarted by misguided interference: on the contrary, this ability is the result of interference in the form of teaching.

The parallel with criminality is obvious. Criminality does not arise as a sickness which could have been avoided by the provision of some postulated natural environment, discoverable by science, which feeds the child's true 'needs'. It arises because certain rules, considerations, social skills, have not been taught to the child; and they will not be taught unless the mother (or other adults) deliberately set themselves the task of imparting them.

Criminality used to be largely confined to families that showed other forms of neglect besides the failure to impart rules for socially responsible behaviour, but is now more widespread in families who do not otherwise deprive their offspring. The same probably holds for other socialisation, for the imparting of other cultural norms. Harriette Wilson[32] found that children from problem families (characterised by a marked isolation from community and kin), often coped easily with the interpersonal relationships of their own families — the only place where they were not confused and inadequate. But outside they were either 'unruly, noisy and anti-social', or 'quiet, uncommunicative, detached, unresponsive to overtures from children and teachers', appearing to be 'overcome' by any new environment. Even their language may be limited to their own sib group. But for all that the modern 'permissive' home is better furnished and equipped, for all that the child is better fed and clothed, has more toys, love, understanding, patient and continuous adult attention, it is possible that much of his social behaviour could easily be idiosyncratic to that particular home, thus making him as lost outside it as any child from a problem family.

On the evidence that 'vulnerability' to hospitalisation is associated with 'indulgent' and 'permissive' homes, Stacey and colleagues[33] predict that 'there is no reason to suppose that a ceiling has been reached in this process: one may well expect increasing numbers of children to come from such homes', children who in going into hospital will 'experience some "culture shock" on admission'. In the light of these facts, the authors are right to conclude that 'If, therefore, our suspicions that there may be an association between the permissive home and disturbance are confirmed, it may have important consequences for future policy.'

Consequences that obviously spring to mind are encouragement and facilities for parents to accustom their children from an early age to benign separation, so that the world is less of a shock later. Clearly, there could be more provision for the socialisation of the child outside the nuclear family, so that he could develop social skills useful in a wider world than his home, intelligible to more than one or two adults. While it may not be the best way, why not make use of unavoidable extrafamilial experiences (such as hospitalisation) as appropriately managed circumstances for the child to acquire some of the learning he has missed through his sheltered home experience? After all, it has been widely commented upon how, after initial upset, a separation experience can have great therapeutic value, leading to maturation and social responsiveness.

But, puzzlingly, Stacey's study advocates that since the child cannot deal with social interaction outside his family and the wide world clearly upsets him, he needs to be helped by being 'cushioned by the continual presence of parents and/or play leaders'.[34]

Of course, admirable though this study was in investigating the actual differences between children upset by hospitalisation and those not upset (instead of assuming

universal trauma due to mother's absence), its over-all
impartiality was greatly undermined by having from the
outset the extra task of finding out why mothers will not go
into hospital with their children. To this extent the issue was
prejudged. And this assumption (along with many others
about childrearing) is not modified in the light of the data.
The authors are clearly committed to the childrearing
practices which, they recognise, produce those children who
need to be continually cushioned by mother and play. They
come down hard on mothers, doctors and nurses who believe
in 'independence', that is, that a child (particularly one over
four) should have some wider social competence and not
require its mother twenty-four hours of the day as interpreter
and crutch. Those who hold such views are seen as a
reactionary rearguard, resisting the truth of modern theory.
Indeed, the very discovery that children from non-permissive
homes cope well in hospital appears to be taken as a sign that
all is not quite well. (One is strongly reminded of Bowlby's
assertion that a child's ability to 'get on easily with strangers'
was 'ominous'.) A drawback to getting all mothers to go into
hospital with their children is described by Stacey *et al.*: 'The
situation is further aggravated if the child appears to be quite
happy and occupies himself playing on his own or with other
children. One then hears the comment "I might as well not
be here" '.[35]

Since empirical findings such as these can be given such
unusual and surprising interpretations, it is time we turned to
that body of very special knowledge lying behind Bowlby's
claims that, all appearances to the contrary, maternal
deprivation does produce Affectionless Thieves. That body of
knowledge is Kleinian psychoanalysis and its assumptions, if
not its explicit teachings, underlie much of modern thought
and recommendations on childrearing.

13   The Fantasies of Infant Thieves (and Adult Theorists)

For the lay public and the less sophisticated researcher the manifestation of infant distress is often in itself sufficient evidence that damage must be taking place (since it is now assumed, without further reflection, that all stress is automatically detrimental to the human young). However, it should be clear that sophisticated theorists see the behaviour of an upset, separated child as a means to corroborate truths which have been confirmed elsewhere — but not necessarily in empirical studies. Indeed, the results of research are seen as relatively unimportant in supporting the theory in comparison with the superior force of 'clinical insight'. Spitz has claimed that his research was 'not introduced by me to *prove* my point', it was merely to illustrate 'clinical data', and was therefore 'subordinated' to this.[1]

Robertson found to his surprise that the four separated but fostered children did not react adversely, but we must still be careful not to infer from the evidence of our senses that they were not therefore damaged, for there are hidden internal processes that might be going all wrong:

> ... even if Jane and Lucy had changed mothers without extreme upset, what might have been the consequences for their subsequent development ... ? From birth internal structures including precursors to object relationships are in the process of increasingly refined development, and these are endangered by interference with or interruptions of the affective interactions unique to the particular mother—infant couple.[2]

At the beginning of his 1956 sanatorium study Bowlby outlines succinctly the relevant psychoanalytic theory which governed the interpretation of its findings. Like Spitz, he sees research as essentially illustrative of already well-established theories:

> This hypothesis . . . is, of course, a special case of certain
> well-known psychoanalytic hypotheses regarding
> personality development. These state in effect that the
> core of healthy adult personality is the ability to make
> continuous stable and cooperative relationships with other
> persons, especially love objects, and that the satisfactory
> development of this ability in the adult is dependent on its
> healthy development in childhood, especially during the
> first five years of life, when the child is making his first
> social relationships — those with his parents. These
> psychoanalytic hypotheses state further that the majority
> of personality disturbances, and of neurotic and even
> psychotic symptoms, are the end results of dysfunctioning
> of the personality in the field of object relations. It was
> this general theoretical orientation which led Bowlby and
> others to pay special attention to early mother–child
> relations in their inquiries. Bowlby (1944) suggested that
> the frustration engendered by the separation was likely to
> cause, on the one hand, increased libidinal and aggressive
> impulses and, on the other, a lack of the usual inhibitory
> superego function, the development of which is dependent
> on satisfactory relationships with love objects.[3]

It is clear that if the findings of research and the deliverances of clinical insight clash, it is held to be right and proper that the experimental findings must be the ones to go. Clinical insight tells us that maternal deprivation is disastrously damaging despite appearances to the contrary from public procedures of observation. What is the nature and authority of this clinical insight, that it can decide that an experience of maternal deprivation must, *ipso facto*, permanently warp?

It needs to be emphasised that 'clinical' theory underlies much of the modern child-care advice and theory about the first five years of life, and this extends well beyond the specific Maternal Deprivation Theory. This theoretical source is rarely made clear to the public to whom advice is addressed. Books, films and reports often give the impression that a specific recommendation about child upbringing is the result of more or less self-sufficient experiments and observations. But this is frequently not so. Even in those cases where experiments or surveys or careful observations have taken place, they often presuppose the validity of quite obscure and elaborate theories of infant mentality and are interpreted in terms of these theories. Researchers and childcare advisers do not always make these explicit, partly because they themselves unquestioningly accept the theoretical groundwork. It is also for this reason that they are ready to accept some new discovery or observation which is in line with the theoretical model. It is accepted, for example, that the dynamic system of infantile ideas and the precise techniques for discerning these have been firmly established by the pioneers in the field many years ago.

In the Maternal Deprivation Theory, as in all clinical theory, the basics were laid by Freud, whose general theoretical model is by now very familiar.[4] The area of concern of clinical theory, or psychoanalysis, is the unconscious mind. The latter consists of thoughts which can become conscious through the use of special procedures by a trained analyst. The unconscious is quite distinct from the conscious mind, which comprises all the thoughts that we are currently aware of, and distinct also from the pre-conscious, whose thoughts can be brought into consciousness with more or less difficulty via the mental efforts of recollection, by reminders, or by stimulation from an associated idea. The structural basis of the mind is the id, an impersonal mass of mental energies or instincts — an undifferentiated foundation for mental life that lies behind and determines the processes of conscious life in the individual's psychology while remaining itself impersonal. (It can be construed simply as the human organism.) Early in life a portion of the id becomes separated as a result of contact with the world outside the body. This is the ego. However, we are given to understand that this does not imply that the ego is wholly conscious: important parts of it remain unconscious.

The ego can become critical of the demands of the parent id; it may accept some while rejecting others. Those rejected become repressed, and form another part of the primitive id. The ego does this repressing of id demands at the command of the superego. This is the last compartment of the mind to form, and it results from unconscious sexual interactions between parents and child. The superego acts as a kind of censor, warning the ego to be on its guard against any repressed wishes in the id finding a way into consciousness. Herein lies the genesis of mental ill-health. Many things that undergo repression do so because were they permitted to enter consciousness they would afford the individual acute displeasure. Repression is thus a protective device to shield the mental personality. This process whereby certain impulses are thrust back into the unconscious — dissociated from conscious life — is often referred to as mental splitting. The ego's use of repression to get rid of intolerable ideas is usually a failure in the sense that the repressed notion cannot be completely expelled from the mind but exists in the unconscious and is on the lookout for ways and means to become activated. It is a partial success in that the repressed idea can send into the consciousness only a disguised and unrecognised substitute for what has been repressed. This substitute is proof against further attacks from the defences of the ego, but it unfortunately attaches to itself the feelings of displeasure which it was hoped could be avoided by repression. The substitute is a symptom. Symptoms cover the range of mental ailments and illnesses and can only be eradicated by tracing back from the symptom to the original repressed ideas. The bringing of the idea back into consciousness is very difficult because the same mechanism that repressed it in the first place now offers resistance to the probings of the analyst.

Let us look closer at the formation of this superego which gives the instructions for repression. The baby comes into the world supplied with a certain store of libido — which is, roughly speaking, sexual energy. Early in babyhood the infant derives its sexual pleasures from its own body and extraneous objects are ignored. This is the auto-erotic phase. First he derives his pleasures from his mouth (his oral stage), and next from his anus. During the latter phase some of the manifestations of sexual pleasure, or part of the libido force or stream, start seeking their satisfactions via an extraneous person. They are said to be directed via an object. Next, the child begins to make an object choice, that is, one person towards whom he can direct his libidinal force. This pushes

auto-eroticism into the background as he chooses one of his
parents as his object of sexual desire. The boy's desire to have
intercourse with and impregnate his mother is cut short
(almost literally) by the horrific discovery that little girls do
not have penises. He infers that they must have been cut off,
and fears that his father's jealous rivalry will lead him to be
castrated too. Worry about the future of his penis leads him
to give up coveting his mother, identify with his father,
differentiate himself from women, for whom he develops an
overwhelming contempt, and take in his father's system of
norms and values which equips him for civilisation and
society. So the process of socialisation is facilitated by the
libidinal charges of energy from the id directed towards an
external object — in this case the mother, being transformed
by identification with the father who is introduced into the
personal ego of the boy, becoming his superego or, in a sense,
his conscience. The term however covers more than just
moral discriminations. It implies the capacities for tasks of
civilisation beyond simple morality — for example, cultural
achievement in the widest sense, and the formation of later
interpersonal relationships.

If it happens that auto-eroticism is not properly
conquered, if attachment to the original objects of libidinal
energy are not renounced, then the person remains fixated at
infant stages, develops perversions or disguises, such as
neuroses. All defects of mental functioning in later life (and a
great deal of physical defects also) are thus due to a faulty
passage through the Oedipal stage. The repressed wishes of
the id that give rise to incapacitating symptoms are invariably
those for sexual relations with the parents.

The main change in this classical Freudian picture of
human mental and social development, which is highly
important in the understanding of the Maternal Deprivation
Theory, was undertaken by Melanie Klein. She postulated
that the superego forms far earlier in life than Freud thought,
and that it comes about through the introjection by the baby
of the mother — not the father.

In fact, the seeds of her theory were already present in the
later works of Freud. Here Freud postulated that object
relationships probably begin to develop well before the
Oedipal lusts for the parent of the opposite sex become

apparent. This is so because the baby cannot tell which is the breast and which is his own body, so that some of his libido is discharged via the mother's breast instead of being used up in auto-eroticism. This discharge of libido via an external object is a catharsis. If the baby wishes for the presence of the mother and is afraid of losing her, it is because she provides a channel for the release of libido, which otherwise will build up inside him, causing an 'economic disturbance'. His fears that this might happen therefore centre on the person who can both cause it and relieve it.

The early Freudian workers on Maternal Deprivation, particularly Spitz, were concerned with how a baby without a mother (for long or short periods) can deal with the libido that builds up inside it. It was because of this theoretical background that Spitz held that the poor physical and mental condition and the deaths of the babies in the institution he investigated were due, not to diet, disease, heredity, or other more obvious causes, but to the absence of a 'mother figure' to drain away the libido:

> Now the drives hang in mid-air, so to speak. If we follow the fate of the aggressive drive, we find the infant turning aggression back onto himself, onto the only object remaining. Clinically [but presumably not nutritionally? – P.M.] these infants become incapable of assimilating food; they become insomniac; later these infants may actively attack themselves, banging their heads against the side of the cot, hitting their heads with their fists, tearing out their hair by the fistful. If their deprivation becomes total, the condition turns into hospitalism; deterioration progresses inexorably, leading to marasmus and death.[5]

It also appears that the infant requires nutrients for his primitive libidinal force, which come from physical intimacy with the mother. Indeed, he has to have nutrition for his libido before he can utilise ordinary protein and vitamins from food and drink. The fact that the libido building up inside the baby is also starving makes it an awful destructive force, so that maternal loss leads to

> ... the infant's instinctual drive elements remaining

relatively undifferentiated and unneutralised. These archaic drive elements are retained by the body where . . . one might say that they have the effect of a catabolic force. Rather than being discharged in a health-giving interaction toward the mother and other figures in the environment the deprived convalescing child's interests and energies are withdrawn from the outside world. This withdrawal further weakened the child's libidinal nutrients that were available.[6]

The direction of the child's libido through an object would also, of course, wean the child away from its isolated narcissistic auto-eroticism towards the outside world (i.e., people outside its body). Other people come into existence as the libido seeks satisfaction through them. It can thus be seen that, in the light of this theory, lack of interaction with a mother in early life, and thus lack of libidinal outlets, renders impossible the development of later object relationships. The libido fails to find a bridge to the world in early life via the mother, and so can never establish any contact with other people in later life.

The mother is also the bridge whereby energy is focused upon the inanimate objects of the material world, so that in her absence the infant cannot achieve any sensory stimulation from these, and they are meaningless to him. On this argument, Spitz repudiates any suggestion that the poor development of his institutionalised infants might be due to sensory deprivation, restrictions on almost all physical movement, and absence of learning situations. Instead:

At this age (under twelve months) the child is not yet capable of distinguishing the real purpose of an object. He is only able to use it in a manner adequate to his own functional needs. Our thesis is that perception is a function of libidinal cathexis [*sic*] and therefore the result of the intervention of an emotion of one kind or another. Emotions are provided for the child through the intervention of a human partner, i.e., by the mother or her substitute . . . He learns to distinguish inanimate objects from animate ones by the spectacle provided by his mother's face in situations fraught with emotional satisfaction.[7]

Also 'in these emotional relations with the mother the child is introduced to learning, and later to imitation . . . the emotional bait offered by the mother calling her child teaches him to walk.'[8]

More recently, Bowlby has used a similar explanation for the postulated defects arising from separation. His explanatory analogy to describe libido is no longer the classical Freudian mechanistic one of torrents of water seeking outlets which can get dammed up and diverted; instead, we have 'chemical organisers'.[9] To these the tissues of the body must be exposed at critical times for growth to proceed smoothly. And as with the physical, so with psychic. The mother provides 'spiritual nourishment' for her baby's soul, so being his 'psychic organiser'. She is 'his personality and his conscience' and she can fulfil this function 'by her mere presence and tenderness'.[10] Those who do not have a mother to stand in for their personality and conscience (or ego and superego) do not acquire the abilities to learn and abstract later: 'It may be that these grossly deprived infants never having been the continuous objects of care of a single human being, had never had the opportunity to learn the processes of abstraction and of their organisation of behaviour in time and space'.[11]

The influence of psychoanalytic libido theory has been enormous, so much so that it is now automatic in discussion of social and personal relationships to refer to them as 'object relationships', and to assume, however vaguely, that they came about originally from one unique bond involving a purposive, directed energy, distinct from anything involved in other environmental interactions. Since 'object relationships' are different from other more mundane environmental involvements and interests, and must be based upon a piece of crucial and obscure early 'experience', it follows that deprivation of this experience in early life will make it impossible for the person ever to be capable of personal and social relationships and responsibility.

Even if the child is not destroyed by the build-up of undischarged libido, it is also inherent in psychoanalytic theory from Freud onwards, that a child deprived of his mother, particularly if, for his first few years, he is in an institution — or anyway not in a nuclear family — will grow up devoid of moral sense. Morality is derived from the renunciation of sexual desire for the mother. If there is no mother there can clearly be no desire for her, and thus none to give up in the face of the father's threats. If there is not a family structure with one male having exclusive possession of wife and children, then no morality can develop, as there will be no Oedipal father to warn the son off his property: 'Without parents there cannot arise a situation of the "Oedipus Complex" type: and if this complex is an essential feature of human society, no true society will develop without it . . . the nursery group cannot, in any way, be a substitute for the influence of the family on the development of personality'.[12]

This is, therefore, a reason to shun any alternative to the nuclear family during childhood: other arrangements will result in moral imbecility in the race. Because of the dictates of this theory Anna Freud finds that although the orphaned children from the camp (who, while being cared for and supervised by the adult inmates, knew nothing 'of private life, or of the meaning of "father" and "mother"') showed the most tender care and concern for each other, they were nonetheless socially and morally abnormal — not being able to form a superego out of sexual jealousy:

> Children who do not live with their parents, or with satisfactory substitutes, do not make the usual identification, and so do not develop the usual moral agency — the Superego. The Superego may develop incompletely, or with less strength, and so lead later to very serious trouble in social adaptation. Further, children who have experienced no early love life are unprepared for the storms of adolescence.[13]

Melanie Klein's innovations in psychoanalytical theory make the mother the exclusive source of morality, so that there is no need for the father to seize the son away from the seducer [14] in the interest of civilisation and morality — these can now be found exclusively in mother's arms.

To Klein, the ego exists from birth onwards and the infant

comes into the world with 'an innate unconscious awareness
of the existence of the mother', from which he 'not only
expects food' but 'also desires love and understanding'.[15] The
projections for the infant's ego consist of fantasies about the
behaviour and intentions of external reality, namely the
mother. He feels that the activities of the world that involve
any discomfort or frustration are deliberately contrived to
hurt him. Indeed, he has a deep sense of persecution: 'the
new born baby experiences both in the process of birth and
in the adjustment to the post-natal situation, anxiety of a
persecutory nature.'
As a result he

> . . . feels unconsciously every discomfort as though it were
> inflicted on him by hostile forces. If comfort is given to
> him soon − in particular warmth, the loving way in which
> he is held, and the gratification of being fed − this gives
> rise to happier emotions. Such comfort is felt to come
> from good forces and, I believe, makes possible the infant's
> first loving relationship to a person . . . to an object.[16]

He feels persecuted also because he has violent emotions of
his own towards the external object − his mother. His
awareness of his own strong destructive emotions towards the
one who nurtures him again intensifies his feeling that
punishment will ensue. That he realises his mother nurtures
him, makes her a 'love object' for him, whereas in his
destructive moments she is an 'object of hate'. His destructive
moments are incredibly intense:

> He has certain oral-sadistic phantasies of a quite definite
> character, seeming to form a link between the oral-sucking
> and oral-biting stages, in which he gets possession of his
> mother's breast by sucking and scooping it out. This desire
> to suck and scoop out, first directed to her breast, soon
> extends to the inside of her body . . . its predominant wish
> is to rob her body of its contents and destroy it.[17]

After fantasies such as this, any frustration of his needs,
any absence of the satisfactions given by his mother when he
requires them, leads to the fear that he has not merely lost

his 'good object' but is responsible for her destruction because of his own greed.

The terror that he has destroyed his mother when she does not instantly satisfy any of his needs is further exacerbated by another factor. For, quite early in babyhood, the mother ceases to be just an 'external object' on to which the infant projects his desires and ideas. She now becomes introjected (in the manner that father became introjected in classical Freudian psychoanalysis). Furthermore, she is introjected in her different aspects. A 'good' mother is introjected — the one who satisfies his needs and does not frustrate him; and a 'bad' mother — one who inevitably must thwart him at some time or another, and cause him such anguish because he feels he has destroyed her with his sadistic lusts: 'The mother in her good aspects — loving, helping, and feeding the child — is the first good object that the infant makes part of his inner world'. [18]

Because of the intensity of the infant's persecutory fears arising either from his belief about destroying his mother, or his belief that discomfort is deliberately sent by her to destroy him, the truth that the 'good' and the 'bad' mothers he has introjected are one and the same person, is too much for the infant to stand:

> In my experience this fear of the total loss of the good object (internalised and externalised) is interwoven with feelings of guilt at having destroyed her (eaten her up) and then the child feels that her loss is a punishment for this dreadful deed: thus the most distressing and conflicting feelings become associated with frustration and it is these which make the pain of what seems like a simple thwarting so poignant.[19]

The beginnings of the realisation of what his destructiveness and greed might do to these external and internalised love objects is the beginning of the superego formation. His superego is usually fully formed by three years of age. Social morality, like the capacity for interpersonal relationships in general, is thus formed not by learning process or social experience, but purely from these secret, unseen fantasies arising from the isolated interaction between mother and infant. In the later stages of superego formation the young child in his play makes restitution to the mother for his former destructiveness — he rebuilds his external and internal love objects: 'In games of building houses and villages, for instance, he will symbolise the restoration of his mother's body and his own', and instead of regarding his penis as a weapon for sadistic attacks on his parents, 'he will, in his period of making restitution regard it as a fire-extinguisher, a scrubbing brush or a container of healing medicines'.[20]

The 'capacity for love and devotion, first of all to the mother',[21] that develops from the unconscious fantasies of the infant — which accompany his every impulse and every external event impinging on him — is the process of socialisation and the acquisition of morality. It 'develops into devotion to various causes that are felt to be good and valuable'. All of which are 'symbols of the good and protective mother'.[22]

We have seen that the bad mother the infant introjects results from the infant's sense of frustration. He will interpret in fantasy all her failures to afford his limitless satisfaction, and indeed any thwarting of his will, as the work of hostile agencies. It is impossible, of course, to satisfy absolutely all infant demands, but at least for the sake of his future introjections it is necessary for the good mother to balance or outweigh the bad.

This she can do by a regime of minimal frustration, and hence it can be easily seen that one of the most important things to avoid is absence from her baby. That she is not present to satisfy his needs (for he knows that he will die without her), gives rise to the most dreadful fantasies of all — of hostile and malicious mother figures:

> For a child to hate his mother is for him to picture her as not merely frustrating but filled with emotions of animosity and revenge. Phantasy, born of rage, thus distorts the picture of the real mother. A kindly mother who has to put her child into hospital, a frustrating yet well-meaning mother and a really unkind mother can, by this process, alike come to be regarded as malicious and hostile figures . . . The child thus becomes haunted by bad

objects, with the familiar result that he comes to regard himself also as a bad object.[23]

So, not only does the child's world become peopled with bad objects who are untrustworthy and unloveworthy, but because these bad objects are also internalised, he 'comes to see himself as a bad, unloveworthy child and interprets circumstances accordingly'.[24] There is also the self-reproach of thinking that one is responsible for the destruction of the love object because of one's excessive demands, so that when the mother separates herself from the child his worst fears are thus confirmed.

The fantasies of hostile and frightening objects, the self-reproach that exists for every child (since none can be completely satisfied by the mother), are usually brought to an end by renewal of contact with her. If the child is really physically separated from her, the horrifying fantasies continue unabated. And so horrifying are the products of infant fantasy that no mother could be as bad as the ones he invents:

> Normally when such fantasies arise in children they are soon corrected to some degree by contact with the real mother, who, whatever her shortcomings, is never so bad as the bad mother which the child pictures to himself when he is in a rage. The mere presence of the real mother, therefore, almost irrespective of what she does, will go to offset the fantasy figures and so will reassure the child as both regards her and himself. But when a child does not see his mother for many months there is no opportunity for this correction of fantasy by reality testing to operate.[25]

This consideration would appear to be the one behind the cryptic remarks of Bowlby concerning the removal of children from intolerable homes. No mother, no matter how cruel, violent or neglectful, could be as bad as the child's fantasies. There really does seem to exist a fate worse than death, for children anyway. We can now understand how, if we take a visibly starved and battered child away from his family, we are inflicting a far worse form of stress upon him.

If he fattens and smiles, we can now see that this is no evidence that he is healthy, for his unconscious fantasies might be destroying him.

Thus there seems just no way of saving a child from the tragedy of an intolerable family. Welfare services have taken the message very seriously. Based partly on this the aim over the last two decades has been largely to keep the neglected or ill-treated child at home, if at all possible, and to return with all speed those who have to go into care or hospital. Seriously injured children have been medically treated only to be sent back again and again to violent homes — in some cases till death ensues from the multiplying injuries. Those whose ills are not so severe or apparent to warrant hospital care may not even have this brief respite from fear and pain. Conversely, the child with a more than transitory stay in care, who — sometimes for the first time — appears well fed, smiles and is apparently happy, is regarded as dangerously vulnerable and deprived — until he can be sent home.

In the rare examples of other human groups where childrearing is held to be quite indivisible in the manner of the Maternal Deprivation theorists, it is apparently usual to destroy the infant,[26] there being no substitute form of care such as exists in the overwhelming majority of human societies. If separation really does have the inevitable appalling consequences these theorists maintain, then are they suggesting this as the only solution in the tragic cases (such as maternal death, insanity, or downright abandonment) which will occur no matter what social precautions are taken? James Robertson[27] is reported as saying that children are better off gassed than taken into care, which he likens to post-natal abortion — the child being an inseparable part of the mother, like the foetus.

Tony Calaman[28] of Protection Prevention (an anti-care organisation) maintains that a child is better beaten than bored and that even the best foster home is no substitute for the worst natural one. Apparently only 'well-brought-up' middle-class matrons are shocked, for example, at the thought of a child being forced to have sex with a male relative.

Let us look at the case of child abuse mentioned by two researchers in the field of battered children, Selwyn Smith

and Sheila Noble.[29] This concerns a nine-month-old girl
admitted to hospital with an extensively fractured skull
several weeks after her brother had been discharged after
investigations for a number of 'unexplained' burns, fractures
and bruises. Two weeks after being sent home on the
recommendation of social workers, she reappeared in the
hospital with multiple abdominal injuries and peritonitus,
from which she died. Better than being bored?

Middle-class matrons have been mentioned, but one
wonders if it is not the people who make light of such
terrible events who have been over-protected. There seems a
basic failure to grasp what violence is really about and what it
does. It is comprehended almost as a kind of horseplay, a
rough wooing, since no one is envisaged as really basically
unkind or lacking in affection, particularly in families.

If, unfortunately, the child suffers separation but remains
alive, Kleinian theory maintains that the separation will
inexorably smash any chance of development into a normal
human being. 'The progressive modification of phantasy by
contact with reality is thus stultified and the child doomed to
see himself and the world of people as reflections of his own
angry and horrifying conceptions of them'.[30]

The inhibition of love by rage blights his ability to make
any relationships with other human beings, since the
affection felt for others is an extension of the affection in the
original mother–child relationship. This

... provides a useful model also for other libidinal
relationships, for example sexual (genital) and parental ones.
Such relationships are conceived as built on the same general
pattern and incorporating many of the same instinctual
response systems as that tying mother to infant, though it is
evident that each contains also certain systems which are
characteristic of itself.[31]

No affection for others can develop if this is not
established in a satisfactory way first; affective relationships
with others can develop in no other way than via the
unbroken mother–child relationship. People outside the
family cannot place the child on the road to healthy
interpersonal adjustment, nor can close relatives. We see now

why Bowlby uses the term 'affectionless' to characterise those children who do not get on with their mothers, no matter who else they may love or like. For, given the theory, a child who does not develop a loving relationship with his mother is *ipso facto* incapable of other loving relationships, no matter how appearances may contradict this. As he claims, some of these appearances are 'known clinically as an ominous combination of features'.[32]

It can also be seen why the theory makes it imperative that the child develop this capacity for personal relationships by unbroken interaction with his mother early in life. As with the schema of Freud, that of the Kleinians is bound by fixed time schedules in which events must occur. If the correct development does not unfold at the biologically determined time in the infant's life, the chance is permanently missed.

This is why mothering in later life is ineffective for one who missed it in his first few years; why there is no cure for the deprivation of early maternal care. This consequence of the theory is contrary to the observed fact that many people deprived for long years of close human relationships, or unable to make them for a variety of reasons, often do learn later to feel and care for others. However, the theory would insist that these relationships are more apparent than real.

As the capacity for morality and law-abiding behaviour is also regarded as an extension of the initial love relationship developed with the single mother figure, then those without this relationship during the first few years of life will, as well as being *ipso facto* affectionless, be automatically delinquent. There is no other way for the superego or conscience to form, but via love for the mother. Disobedience to the law and immoral behaviour generally is due to (fantasied) loss of love at a critical early age. Those so deprived cannot but be anti-social, and any later training in social virtues at five, ten, or twenty is futile, for the future course of development has already been laid down and cannot be remade.

We have arrived at the theoretical origins of the Affectionless Thief. The teachings of Kleinian psychoanalysis on the origins of the capacities for interpersonal relationships and social responsibility, entail that, given a certain early background, he must come into being. Although the concepts and terminology of Kleinian psychoanalysis might at first glance appear alien and remote from the language and assumptions of the layman, it is remarkable how easily they can be translated into these. Served up in an everyday guise, they are eminently acceptable as child-care advice at a wide spectrum of levels, from the text book to the woman's magazine and 'Family Doctor' booklet.[33]

Where libidinal supplies can become spiritual nourishment and catharsis a cuddle, introjection of 'good objects' (through the mother alleviating the baby's fear of hostile forces by providing plentiful libidinal nutrients and channels) is easily converted into popular concepts. It becomes, for example, the familiar hypothesis, that love is stored up by the baby to be given out later as social morality. On the other hand, the mother who is unsatisfying, who 'frustrates' the infant and makes him angry, provides him with stored spite to unleash on others. Later psychoanalytical theorists have used this ease of convertibility into the vernacular as further proof. (It is 'what every mother knows', ignored by cold laboratory science.) Thus, ironically, we can now find psychoanalysis — which took at first the stern pose of the dissecting investigator — coming round to the certainties of a mother's heart, of which pale, chill reason knows nothing. This appeal to the consensus of uneducated sentiment provides both the cheap appearance of vindication and an extra, emotional redoubt against critical attacks. The feeling is put about that criticism of such sacred verities is almost indecent. This attitude owes a great deal to the work of Margaret Ribble, an analyst who wrote of mother—infant relations in maudlin fashion (or according to her successors, 'humanized' the discipline).

In his more recent work Bowlby has added extra refinements to the Kleinian conception of what happens when a child loses its libidinal 'object' in early life (this is connected with his use of ethological material). He seeks to explain in greater detail how the speculated 'damage' is done by 'object loss'. He holds that it takes place because the child undergoes a period of pathological mourning.

He explains that, in adults, mourning goes through three stages. When the loved object is first lost there is a stage of anxiety and anger during which 'the bereaved person is striving . . . to recover the lost object and is reproaching it for its desertion',[34] so that, although there is irremedial loss, 'thought, feeling and behaviour are nonetheless organised to achieve reunion'.[35] The next phase of adult mourning is one of despair: here patterns of behaviour that are based on the assumption that the other person is still present or can be regained, drop away, and the behaviour instead becomes organised on the basis of the permanent absence of the object. It is during this second phase that the process which Bowlby refers to as disorganisation takes place. Disorganisation is necessary to break down old patterns of thought and behaviour that are orientated towards the lost object, so that new ones can be assembled and the person can go on to make another object relationship. This phase successfully completed, the third phase of hope ensues.

Now in the pathological mourning, the essential difference is that the person remains orientated towards the lost object so that he lives in the past. He does not accomplish the process of disorganisation. He still angrily strives for reunion, and is reproachful towards the object for its desertion. Because of this, the object itself becomes a distorted source of wish-fulfilling fantasy and relationships with others in the real world are impossible. Why cannot he achieve this disorganisation, why cannot he disentangle himself from this old relationship to free himself for others?

Apparently disorganisation is avoided by *'an abrupt cleavage of the psychic apparatus'*[36] or, in original Freudian language, the splitting of the psyche. And, as with all mental splitting, the parts which split are consigned to the unconscious. In Freud's theory it was unpermitted sexual wishes and their objects that were thrust into the unconscious, where they were then unknowable to the conscious mind except via a therapist who overcame the ego's resistances. Nonetheless they caused trouble by giving the person untoward symptoms. In Bowlby's theory it is the person's anger towards the lost object, his reproaches towards it, which are split off and consigned to the unconscious. This is not, of course, apparent to his conscious mind: the person is not aware that he is pining for his lost object and reproaching it, and therein lies his trouble. For all the 'instinctual response systems with their related phantasy' which the person directs towards his lost object are 'split off from the main structure of psychic organisation' and become 'almost wholly unknown to the conscious world of the individual concerned'.[37] They will appear instead as symptoms, as neurotic disorders and behavioural deviations.

Bowlby explains that the main characteristic of pathological mourning is

> . . . an inability to express overtly these urges to recover and scold the lost object, with all the yearning for and anger with the deserting object that they entail. Instead of its overt expression, which though stormy and fruitless leads on to a healthy outcome, the urges to recover and reproach with all their ambivalence of feeling have become split off and repressed. Thenceforward, they continue as active systems within the personality but, unable to find overt and direct expression, come to influence feeling and behaviour in strange and distorted ways. Hence many forms of character disturbance and neurotic illness.[38]

Those who will suffer this pathological mourning, who will be blighted by this yearning and anger becoming locked inside them, potentially active but incapable of release, will be young children when they are bereaved or separated.[39] It can be seen, in Bowlby's embellishments of Klein's ideas on object loss, that if children cannot achieve the disorganisation necessary for new relationships after they have undergone separation and bereavement, they will not be able to make new relationships if their mothers leave them during the early years of life. They will be left with symptoms of the forces still operating in their unconscious minds. These symptoms, Bowlby assumes, will take the form of stealing, for example — a disguised attempt to win back the mother.

Now the question needs to be asked: Why is it that children undergo pathological and not normal mourning? Bowlby suggests that in children, the phases of mourning tend to be telescoped, so that the child, in detaching himself from the missing lost object, has not yet shaken off his anger and yearning for it. The incompatible forces are only reconcilable by the mental splitting, the yearning and anger being consigned to the unconscious, whereas in the adult, this first phase would have been completed and there would be no incompatible anger and yearning left over to push into unconsciousness. This does not appear very satisfactory, for elsewhere Bowlby talks as if the three stages of mourning are not distinct, but rather are mixed in the adult also. He talks of behaviour and feelings oscillating wildly between rage, yearning, protest and despair.[40] His main source of explanation for childhood mourning being pathological is Freud's doctrine that neurosis must form in the first five years of life because the ego then is 'feeble, immature and incapable of resistance' so that it 'fails to deal with tests which it could cope with later on with utmost ease, and instead resorts to repression or splitting'.[41]

Bowlby's conception of the infantile mechanisms associated with separation represents a further modification of the Kleinian standpoint, which in turn derives in all essentials from Freud's basic schema. Though there have been considerable differences of interpretation within this schema, it is clear that the classical dynamic conceptions originating from Freud have been taken for granted in working out these new suggestions. The tradition of psychoanalytic thought provides a very rich fund of ideas from which interesting and stimulating theories can be continually constructed. But sooner or later the simple question has to be asked: are they true? In the next chapters I will examine the claims of these various theories to describe reality.

II   The Psychoanalytic Basis

14 The Status of Kleinian Theory

If Bowlby's evidence that adults go through a proper sequence of mourning after losing their love object is that they are observed to make other relationships, then, presumably, his confirmation for his notions about children going through pathological mourning is their inability to make other relationships when their first one is broken. Yet reality would seem to refute Bowlby here, for enough observations show that children separated from their mothers do make subsidiary or alternative relationships (depending on their length of separation) and do not go into social hibernation. The only time anything like the latter happens is where children are confused by the contradictory behaviour of (one or more) transitory caretakers, which can equally happen at home if the mother is neglectful or arbitrary. Withdrawal is then an understandable reaction, and it ceases when the environment becomes more constant, friendly and predictable. The postulated consequences of pathological mourning thus cannot be derived from any observation of a child's social behaviour.

We are told that the reason we cannot derive the pathological mourning account from observed reality, is because it is actually operating unconsciously. Things are consigned to the unconscious when the conscious mind refuses to admit to them and pretends that they do not exist. The ordinary capacity to make relationships would therefore in the psychoanalytic term have to become a defence, a pretence, since really the person cannot make them. But this is a travesty of logic and could equally be used to prove that anything in the real world of experience is actually the opposite of something in another, unseen world – which is the 'real' one. The everyday world of our senses therefore becomes an illusion as if we exist in an unreal dream. To this we are entitled to reply that Bowlby's theory too may be an illusion, a disguise for something in another realm (his own unconscious or whatever).

However, he claims he found that a pseudo capacity to make relationships and the more straightforward symptom of stealing, were due to pining for the mother, as a result of 'evidence [that] came first from the psycho-analytic treatment of adults and then from that of children'.[1] In *Forty-four Juvenile Thieves* he describes how (in reference to case histories) he obtained this evidence during psychoanalytic treatment: 'No.34, Derrick O'C., whom I was able to see regularly, reluctantly admitted (after interpretation) that much of his stealing had been done out of revenge.'[2]

The child was reluctant in admitting this — perhaps because he thought it was false? Had Derrick eagerly admitted that it was revenge, would Bowlby then have held this to be evidence against his supposition? One very much doubts it. Bowlby had to 'interpret' Derrick's stealing to achieve the conclusion that it was due to his feelings of revenge towards his mother, dating from the separation experience. Interpreted according to what code? That of Kleinian psychoanalysis: 'the lack of inhibition [against stealing and other anti-social conduct] is the necessary result of the lack of a love-relationship, a result which is explained by a theory of the origin of the superego and the development of object-love.'[3]

One is therefore entitled to ask where Klein derived her knowledge about the fantasy-ridden libidinal interchange between mother and baby that gives rise to 'object love' and the superego (the postulated agent of social responsibility). Babies obviously have no linguistic ability to communicate to Klein or anyone else what is in their minds. Nonetheless, Kleinian pyschoanalysts claim that clinical techniques employed on young children, emerging from infancy and able to talk, confirm the theories.[4] As well as via speech, the mental life of young children is studied using their play, some analysts specialising in certain aspects of this (for example, Winnicott makes use of their drawings and squiggles). Klein explains:

The child expresses its fantasies, its wishes, and its actual experiences in a symbolic way through play and games. In doing so it makes use of the same language, as it were, that we are familiar with in dreams, and we can only fully understand this language if we approach it in the way Freud has taught us to approach the language of dreams. Symbolism is only a part of it. If we wish to understand the child's play correctly in relation to its whole behaviour during the analytical hour we must not be content to pick out the meaning of the different symbols, striking as they often are, but must take into consideration all the mechanism and methods of representation employed by the dream-work, never losing sight of the relation of each factor to the situation as a whole. Analysis of children has shown again and again how many different meanings a single toy or a single bit of play can have, and that we can only completely comprehend their meaning when we know their future connections and the general analytic situation in which they are set.[5]

But, unfortunately for the non-Kleinian, there is still nothing directly observable in children's play or communicated in their speech that supports Klein's theories unless it too is 'interpreted' in terms of these. There is nothing to suggest that anyone unconversant with Kleinian theory would independently reach these conclusions by looking at child behaviour.

No unambiguous features in child play or communication favour a Kleinian interpretation rather than any other. It seems that it would be equally possible, for example, to interpret a child's play in terms of the political and economic destinies of their nation or race, as Joseph interpreted the dreams of Pharoah, or, if one believes in reincarnation, in terms of ancestral memories of former lives. How does one get interpretations such as the following, if one is not already a dedicated Kleinian: 'Trude, aged three and a half years, would lift up the rug on the sofa and say she was doing "Po-Kaki-Kuki". This it turned out meant she wanted to look inside her mother's bottom for the "Kakis" (faeces) which signified children to her.'[6]

Such interpreted meanings, derived from the play or utterances of small children, are no more empirically based

than those the Egyptians derived from dreams. Even those
ancient methods of divination did usually follow some rules
of interpretation which the divinator had to abide by. To this
extent the process was reduced in arbitrariness. In Kleinian
analysis there are no avowed rules whatsoever for how a piece
of play is to be interpreted, except that it should fit the
'situation as a whole' — that is, the Kleinian account of infant
mentality. Anything can be used to this end, and the analyst
is unlikely to have to admit that the signs conflict or that
interpretation is unclear. Klein finds in the case of little
Trude that: 'her wetting and dirtying herself were attacks
upon her parents' copulation with each other' and these in
turn symbolise her wish 'to rob her pregnant mother of her
children, to kill her and take her place in coitus with her
father'.[7]

In this particular case, even an incident when Trude hit her
head against a pillow symbolised her father's role in coitus
and the child's wish to usurp her mother's place. Apart from
such compellingly persuasive 'evidence', I know of no other
empirical observation offered by the Kleinians.

According to Klein and many of her followers (such as
Winnicott) infants who have not yet even begun to talk
experience a detailed fantasy life. They are capable of
complex emotions, ideas and memories, and can make
predictions about the future. They feel emotions such as
'resentment about frustration, hate stirred up by it'[8] they can
feel acutely persecuted and have a dread of 'what is going on
inside' as a result of 'crude frustration rage', which changes to
a 'feeling of total bliss'[9] when the mother allays this
frustration. According to Winnicott (in *The Child, the Family
and the Outside World*) the infant can have the fantasy of
'magically annihilating the world'. He has 'a point of view'[10]
that must be considered. Babies are born with innate ideas of,
among other things, mothers, breasts, penises, poisoned
mousetraps and unique goodness.[11] (The notion of such
innate ideas in the human young, although more prominent
in Klein than Freud, is nonetheless present in his work; for
example, in the study of Little Hans he refers to 'instinctual
premonitions'[12] possessed by the boy of the existence of the
vagina and copulation.) It is, frankly, surprising that
an   educated   public,   brought   up   in   a   broad

ethos of science and experimental knowledge, should have accepted notions of this kind with so little scepticism. After all, traditional religious doctrines describing the actual nature and wishes of God are usually met with the very proper questions: How do we know such things? How are such claims to knowledge to be distinguished from fancy and invention?

Controlled observational studies of babies, our present neuro-physiological knowledge, plus the extensive cultural experience which (in the absence of innate social concepts), must be presumed for Kleinian thoughts, suggest that the basis for such a sophisticated, elaborate mental life is simply not present in young infants. This is not to suggest that the infant, in default of being a homunculus, is, from the sensory viewpoint, little but an inert, unresponsive, vegetable-like being. This is a fault which some empiricists may have fallen into (although to nothing like the extent that psychoanalysts and the lay public have anthropomorphised infant mentality). Recent research suggests that the sensory apparatus of the newborn child is very well developed and the human infant perceptually surprisingly active. However, the brain, compared with that of the adult, is still very immature (humans are among those mammals that show marked extra-uterine brain growth and maturation). There is still disagreement over whether it is possible to set up simple conditioned reflexes in the young infant, although the extensive research now being carried out on babies should clarify this question soon. But much infant activity is controlled by the spinal cord and the lower part of the brain stem,[13] and is thus largely reflexive. For example, a most common and striking behaviour of young babies − crying (apart from the crying due to pain and hunger) − is maintained by a simple feedback process unconnected with cortical activity, and resembles more than anything else, an attack of hiccups.[14] Techniques that stop crying and induce rest inhibit diffuse activity and thereby cut out peripheral self-stimulation. A baby who is muscularly active will not sleep; the diffuse thrashing maintains itself through feedback, and the high arousal level promotes crying. Binding up a baby, or swaddling, a technique widely used, has been historically a most effective way to arrest and discourage crying (a poorly swaddled baby who can move in its bonds, screams, probably because its movements against them heighten the feedback and have a marked arousal effect). Also effective are pacifiers and constant or rhythmical non-painful stimulation such as rocking, providing a background of white light or noise, and tapping the spine. These all bring about rhythmical or constant stimulation that gives rhythmical or constant feedback and lowers the state of arousal. Nothing in research on infant vocalisations and movements suggests that these are manifestations of anger, rage or aggression, or that an infant wishes to be 'destructive', the solution to which is 'a maximum of parental reassurance'.[15]

For a baby to come into the world feeling persecuted presupposes an innate social concept of persecution — the knowledge of other people, of human motives, the ability to interpret intentions as revealed in behaviour (hostility, for example), and this would require the genetic inheritance of a vast amount of very precise social discriminatory capacities. No evidence has emerged that these kinds of specific discriminatory abilities are transmitted genetically. The same is true of other social concepts such as trust, or what it is to be 'unaccepted'.

A weaker assertion of the Kleinian case for the state of the newborn might be that the infant is basically fearful when he comes into the world, so that he must be made to feel less anxious, more secure in this alien place. There has been a certain amount of research on infant emotional development, particularly on the emotion of fear.[16] But none of it suggests that any emotion of this nature is present at birth. An infant does not appear to respond with anxiety towards his environment before the end of six months. Attempts to frighten babies before this age with monster masks, contorted faces, ugly grimaces and so forth, provoke only indifference, smiling, vocalisation unconnected with discomfort. At six months of age, distortions of familiar configurations (for example, a clear plastic mask that distorts the normal facial features) produces crying in some babies. But there is no definite pattern exhibited by all babies.[17]

Again, study of infant reactions to unfamiliar people, so-called 'stranger anxiety', shows that there is no anxiety before six months.[18] Indeed, below this age infants are likely to reach out to strangers.[19] It is not until twelve months of age that infants exhibit more negative than positive responses towards strangers, and few negative responses have been seen before eight months.

It is possible that the capacity of the human infant for discriminatory behaviour is partly governed by the process of *myelination* — the insulation of the nerve cells. Before this takes place on a significant scale (usually between four and six months), impulses are transmitted between nerve cells at a slow rate. The cells have to undergo a cumbersome electrochemical change in order to do this, and furthermore have to have time to regenerate chemically before another impulse can be carried. The operation roughly resembles the ignition of a trail of slow-burning powder. Myelination involves the appearance of insulating sheaths for the cells and nodes, that allow impulses to jump from one to another instead of having to change the walls of the cells chemically as they travel. A very small myelinated nerve-fibre can carry messages and signals at high speeds, and regenerate quickly to carry the next impulse.

With myelination complex behaviour becomes possible: for example, myelination of the motor control areas of the brain means that a baby can control and direct his musculature, for example, to manipulate objects and to walk. (Those unfortunate individuals who do not experience myelination, or in whom it is incomplete, retain all their lives the mental and behavioural characteristics of a young baby.)

The process of brain growth and myelination proceeds at different rates for different brain centres. At birth the most undeveloped areas of the brain are those thought to be most important in the control of emotional behaviour and the acquisition of memories. The sensory apparatus is comparatively well developed, but the corresponding association areas of the brain are not. Thus the infant's eyes may be able to see, but what they see is probably largely 'meaningless'. During the first few months of life it is still doubtful if any of the neurones in the cerebral cortex are capable of transmitting nerve impulses, or if there is any communication between one area of the cortex and another. As events are likely to be meaningless at this age, it is misleading to talk of any stable, learned and remembered likes and dislikes apart from the actual responses themselves. For these would involve a complex ability to understand and relate phenomena to each other in causal sequences, requiring good communication between, as well as within, different brain areas. Complex concepts require sequences of experiences to have meaning over long time spans, which involves an ability to make predictions about the future behaviour of the environment as well as relating it to the past. Claims that someone can remember his birth or earlier infancy must be ruled out; such remembering is virtually as impossible as messages from the dead.

The first areas of the cortex to become myelinated in the young infant are the motor control areas. Here the first linkages are between the visual and motor areas, so that a child under six months can both converge his eyes on an object and make limited movements towards it. At six months the sensory areas of the brain are more developed than at birth, but the sensory association areas of the brain still remain undeveloped at this age, so that the infant's capacity to interpret his sensations is probably limited or non-existent. That he could envisage his discomfort as 'due to hostile agencies' inside or outside himself, and feel threatened by 'bad objects', is questionable.

During the first three years of life this sequence of development continues in the brain with the motor area always ahead, reaching full maturation with the development of the leg control area late in the third year (which accounts for the difficulty young children have with stumbling when they walk, compared with their great dexterity in arm and trunk). Next the sensory and visual areas develop. But lagging behind these are the sensory and visual association areas, so that, whereas at fifteen months the sense of touch is probably well developed, the immaturity of the sensory association area implies that the child still cannot interpret his tactile sensations very well. Similarly his ability to understand what he sees is also still limited. It takes past the second year for myelination of the association centres to enable the infant to interpret sensations and relate them one to another in something resembling an adult fashion — particularly if this is over long time sequences. Development of long-term memory in the way that adults understand this (that is, the ability to remember an experience for a period of years or even the remainder of life) does not usually come about until around the third or fourth year. Much of the experience of the younger child is simply not recorded as long-term memory in this sense.

The fact that the memory span is shorter the younger the child, would better and more economically account for the phenomena observed in separated children who appear to forget their mothers after a certain amount of time has elapsed since last seeing her, than the story that they have 'repressed' the mother's image. Children who can still remember their mothers after lengthy separation tend to be older children or adolescents. (Hilda Lewis mentions in *Deprived Children* that, whereas younger children soon forgot their parents and played as if nothing had happened, it was the adolescents who were sad and apprehensive.)

Our knowledge of physiology not only contradicts the Kleinian theory of the infant fantasy world, but also undermines the more general psychoanalytic concept of libido, which is so integral to it. Although the stockpiling hypothesis of maternal love and attention seems a sufficient causal explanation to many who believe the indulgences of infancy to lie at the basis of social capacities and morality, those who require more detail of this miraculous transformation have to rely on the analytical accounts of libidinal *cathexis* and the introjection of the 'good mothers'. Apart from learning theory, the latter has been the only causal explanation widely subscribed to to explain the long-term effects of environment on the human organism. In the learning model, the parental behaviours that constitute 'love' or 'mothering' would have to acquire (if they do not already possess) reinforcer value, and be applied selectively to certain behaviour shown by the child in order to have any effect on his social conduct. Whereas, in comparison, the libido theory posits a sort of psychic energy – a force for good, being transferred to and from the child like an electric current when the mother cuddles it or is in its vicinity. It then forms a sort of umbilical bridge to the world along which the 'objects' which are to be introjected can move (the father in Freudianism, the 'good' mother objects in Kleinianism).

In psychoanalysis this psychic energy (libido) has been closely connected with sexual satisfaction, and used to denote sexual energy. The first activities of the infant, it is said, are sexual and in some of these he cannot help but involve a second person, as, for example, when he sucks the mother's breast. So his libido gets carried to the outside world via his sexual activities. Since any activity which involves a human interacting with or orientating himself to another comes from an early direction of this psychic sexual energy, all human endeavour and motivation, and the constructions of civilisation, culture and morality are, fundamentally, redirected sexuality. Thus, libidinal sexual energy is identical with all living experience and becomes an utterly general life-energy. This is hardly illuminating if one wants to make distinctions about components of the world of human experience. Libido is presented as a magical substance capable of infinite transformation, yet remaining in some metaphysical manner the same. It is anything and everything at any particular moment. As it stands, such a concept has no proper explanatory value and is scientifically worthless.

One more concrete interpretation that has been given to libido is that it is bodily energy (whether we continue to call it sexual is beside the point, as long as some more restricted, usable definition can be arrived at). But the energy used in the body is burnt from nutritional intake as it is required; if the person is inactive the sources go unutilised and no energy is manufactured from them. We do not produce energy that behaves like the analyst's libido, namely, a fixed amount which must either be dissipated or else build up inside us as in an unregulated pressure system. If we do not utilise all our food intake, it becomes glyconel stored in the liver (if protein) or deposited as fat if not. Is this fatty tissue libido? Hardly. Nor is there any evidence that physical energy can be stored for a lifetime, so that we have libido bottled up inside us from babyhood. This raises the question whether we produce amounts of libido throughout life or whether we are born with a fixed amount. If the latter, could we run out? What if we used it too quickly? It is postulated (for example, in the work of Spitz) that the baby requires supplies of libidinal nutrients from maternal contact. At other times such writers postulate the baby as having excess libido, which, furthermore, it cannot discharge into the atmosphere, but must do so via another. If the bottled-up libido remains in the baby it will destroy it – like a time-bomb. No medical researcher has, to my knowledge, come across an infant death due to accumulations of libido, or energy, which it could not dissipate.

Obviously the physical energy model of libido will not do. Actually the nearest analogy that we have with the analyst's libido is the primitive's *mana*. The baby appears to be conceived of as full of magic, almost like the shaman, the returning warrior or menstruating woman. In fact, the libido concept is a survival of the speculations of nineteenth-century amateurs, and has its place among other postulated forces, such as animal magnetism. It cannot compete empirically with learning theory in accounting for long-term behaviour. Here the mechanisms are experimentally definable and their operations observable.

The bankruptcy of the concept of libido has been recently recognised by Bowlby.[20] This is, of course, threatening for psychoanalysis since it is so central to its tenets. It provided the whole causal explanation in the theories about critical set stages in infant development, the basis of civilisation and morality in early parent–child sexual interactions, and so forth. Learning theory would postulate that, given an intact neural apparatus, there is no inherent reason why learning (of anything) should take place at one age rather than another. And, of course, learning theory is fully conversant with the process of 'extinction' whereby learnt behaviours can be eradicated and/or replaced by other alternative behaviours. Indeed, our knowledge of neural development and observations of the learning process in young children suggest that young children, if anything, learn with much greater difficulty and less retention than do those who are neurologically more developed and sensitive – that is, the adolescent and young adult.

The adoption of learning theory would also dispense with the idea that later behaviour, skills and social attitudes are based on the emotional experiences of infancy and early childhood — love, hate, rage, trust, etc. — involved in the interaction with the parent. It would insist that these would have no effect on the young unless they became involved deliberately or accidentally as reinforcers or elicitors of behaviour in learnt sequences. It would also deny the notion that this highly-charged emotional interchange must be with certain prescribed 'figures' (for example, the mother) or against a certain social backcloth (such as monogamous marriage where there is exclusive sexual possession). Anyone who interacted with the young sufficiently to shape behaviour, mother, father, aunt, teacher, and so on would be in a position to bring about long-term changes in skills and conduct. And most crucially (and indeed paradoxically when one considers the poor scientific status of psychoanalysis) the promise of discovering scientifically the one proper, super-cultural way in which we were 'naturally' intended to bring up children would be undermined. If the attributes that make humans skilful, civilised, responsible and moral beings do not emerge spontaneously from untaught processes of emotional interchange but have to be actually taught, then by *whom* they are taught, *what* is taught and the *aims* behind the teaching are all matters of cultural choice.

It is clear, then, that those theories which depend upon the necessity for a certain relationship at a certain time of life, vital in itself, quite apart from any learning that takes place within it, would be sunk by a surrender to the learning model. To provide a more plausible explanation for the operation of its processes than the libidinal energy model, Bowlby has now put forward a different explanation, based upon elaborate postulated instinctual systems. In his *Attachment and Loss* a somewhat strained case is presented for such instinctual patterns controlling our behaviour and development, which makes use of cybernetic (control systems) theory. This is combined with a mass of ethological material of varying quality. The use of these two sources to postulate an elaborate instinctual endowment in humans, with fixed critical periods of operation, would, if successful, rescue the Kleinian postulates of the Maternal Deprivation Theory from the sinking libido ship. The need for one mother 'figure', for the relationship with her to be unbroken, and this relationship is the origin of all later capacity for human relationships, moral conduct, etc., is relocated by Bowlby in human instinct. The examination of this wholly new case — principally, an examination of the ethological evidence of genuine relevance to human child-rearing — can be found in the final section of this book.

It would be possible to extend the basic objections to libido theory to other key concepts in psychoanalysis, such as the id, the unconscious, etc., the objections, that is, that they are so vague and all-embracing as to have no real explanatory power, and that where they have been pinned down to more precise meanings, these have had no support in experimental knowledge.

If the theories of Melanie Klein are without foundation, what about the epoch-making discoveries of Freud himself, about infantile sexuality and the stages through which the child's psyche must pass? Klein's modification of Freudian theory — particularly her location of the processes at a much earlier age — may have been mistaken, but did not that theory, at least, embody an important gain in our knowledge of child development? Freud claimed that child analysis provided him with: '. . . unambiguous information on problems which remain unsolved in the analyses of adults; and they thus protect the analyst from errors that might have momentous consequences for him. One surprises the factors that work in the formation of neurosis while they are actually at work and one cannot then mistake them.'[21] Is it here, at last, that we shall find the foundations of psychoanalysis, and see its concepts substantiated? This expectation is slightly deflated by Freud going on to say that the evidence from child analysis did not actually play a part in the formulation of his theories: it was only useful in confirming them:

We had begun by inferring the content of sexual childhood from the analyses of adults — that is to say, some twenty or forty years later. Afterwards, we undertook analysis on children themselves, and it was no small triumph when we were thus able to confirm in them everything that we had been able to divine, in spite of the amount to which it had been overlaid and distorted in the interval.[22]

Freud's work with children consists of one case:[23] hardly an adequate sample to test any hypothesis. Nonetheless, his devotees have long talked of it as *the* classic case of child analysis, the paradigm that provided the basis for procedure as well as illustrating the truth of all the main standpoints of the theory of infantile sexuality and the formation of neurosis.[24]

In its time the analysis of Little Hans was a remarkable achievement and the story of the analysis constitutes one of the most valued records in psychoanalytical archives. Our concepts of phobia formation, of the positive Oedipus complex, of ambivalence, castration anxiety and repression, to mention but a few, were greatly reinforced as a result of this analysis.[25]

During this analysis[26] Freud saw this four-year-old boy only once. He was kept informed by the father, himself an ardent believer in Freud's theories, who sent him written reports. The child's neurotic disorder consisted of a phobia that a horse would bite him; he was frightened of going out in the streets and was depressed in the evenings. His father decided that the fear of the horse somehow resulted from Hans having been frightened by a large penis and that the ground for this had been prepared by sexual excitation due to his mother's affection. Freud told the father to enlighten the child by telling him that he wished to sleep with his mother, and that his fear of horse was due to his being too interested in their penises. To bring this Oedipal complex to a close the father told Hans that females did not have penises, intending thereby to increase his castration anxiety and stop his coveting his mother and wishing to destroy his father. But despite his father's eager attempts to convince Hans, the boy would not believe him and did not improve.

In this analysis the boy himself talked of his phobia, admitting that he was most scared of horses with a 'thing' on their mouths and frightened in case they fell down, particularly if they were drawing a horse-bus. When his father asked why, Hans replied that he had seen an incident when a horse pulling a bus fell. The father told Hans that he already had his 'nonsense' then, which the boy denied: 'No I only got it then. When the horse in the bus fell down, it gave me such a fright really . . . ' The father found that the actual incident was confirmed by his wife, as well as the fact that the anxiety broke out immediately afterwards.

An analysis of the data hardly supports the ideas of Freud or the boy's father. Before the child saw a horse fall, he had already been sensitised to the dangers from horses by seeing fairground horses beaten, which upset him; by hearing his playmate warned not to touch a horse in case it bit him, and by his friend cutting himself while they were playing horses. That the 'nonsense' was a scheme to be alone with his mother is made more unlikely by the fact that the phobia was as bad when he was out with her. How this child (indeed, every male child) could have such strong wishes to sleep with his mother that they have to be resisted with the threat of castration from the father, when he is physically quite incapable of intercourse, even if he conceives of it, strains credulity.

Freud admits that 'It is true that during the analysis Hans had to be told many things which he could not say himself, that he had to be presented with thoughts which he showed no sign of possessing and that his attention had to be turned in the direction from which his father was expecting something to come'.[27] This is a poor showing for an investigation of a boy supposed to be at the most important, most dramatic period of his life, when the crucial Oedipus complex is operating. Yet this single case is the only piece of observation on which the whole grand edifice of Freudian doctrine on infantile sexuality rests.

Hans's phobia can be perfectly adequately explained by learning theory. The point is that such an alternative requires no comparable distortion or 'interpretation' of what the child said, and is by far the simplest explanation with the minimum of conjectures. In learning theory phobias are regarded as conditioned anxiety (fear) reactions. Any neutral stimulus that happens to make an impact upon the person at the time the fear is evoked, itself acquires the ability to evoke fear, particularly if the situation is many times repeated. There is, further, a tendency to generalise the fear to similar objects. It is invariably people of introverted temperament

(Hans was said to be a very sensitive child) who develop neurotic fears. Hans eventually lost his phobia, and this appears to be unrelated to the analysis. Neurotic phobias, particularly those of children, extinguish themselves in the great majority of cases if they are left untreated.

15   The Scientific Credentials
      of Psychoanalysis

What of psychoanalysis as a whole, this authoritative and
influential movement in psychology for the last sixty years?
In most quarters it enjoys the status of a science; its
practitioners occupy eminent positions, and are treated as
experts by, for example, government departments,
commissions of enquiry, courts of law and education
authorities. We must briefly clarify what it is for a discipline
to be truly scientific, and then see how psychoanalysis
measures up to the requirements.

What qualifies a body of study as scientific is not its
subject-matter, but its use of a particular method. It is not
that it studies only 'material' things (gravity is wholly
immaterial); nor that it recognises only directly observable
entities (the entities of subatomic physics are essentially
unobservable); nor simply that it appeals to evidence
(astrology, alchemy and Rosicrucianism have hoarded
enormous masses of facts and observations). Very briefly, the
peculiarity of the scientific method, and its one claim to
superiority over all other schemes for understanding the
world, is that it is inherently self-correcting. It formulates its
theories so that they are clearly capable of being tested by
public observation. For convenience, these conditions may be
condensed into five basic requirements: (1) falsifiability; (2)
precise definition of terms; (3) independence of variables; (4)
repeatability of results and (5) publicity of results.*

The scientific explanation of an event consists of showing
it to be an instance of a universal law: it must happen, in the

---

*These headings have been adopted for simplicity; it is not pretended
that they represent totally independent conditions, or that the schema
could not be presented a different way. For example, (2) and (3) could
be expressed as part of (1), and (4) and (5) could form a single
condition.

sense that there is a law which states that whenever certain kinds of conditions hold, this type of event occurs. But, precisely because such covering laws are universal, they can never be more than highly probable: even though every case so far has conformed to them, it is always logically possible that others will not. They cannot therefore be confirmed with certainty. But they can be falsified with certainty: for discovering only one genuine kind of instance where the predicted event fails to occur, *prima facie* contradicts the law, at least in its original form. Thus it is the potentially falsifying observations which constitute the crucial area of test for a proposed law, or theory. If, in spite of an active search for them, no falsifying facts can be found, the theory is greatly strengthened. On the other hand, if we only look for 'confirming' facts — that is, relevant facts which are consistent with the theory — we shall easily find them. There are plenty of facts consistent with just about every theory that has ever been proposed, which is obviously why it was ever proposed. But it is the facts which are inconsistent with it, which must be sought by a worthwhile empirical test.

But for this to be possible, the theory must be so formulated that it is clear what kind of possible observations would falsify it. To say anything substantial at all about reality, any factual statement must forbid certain possible states of affairs, which, if they did occur, would render it false. This is clearly seen if we consider the statements of newspaper horoscopes and the prophecies of soothsayers: they are so vague and ambiguous as to forbid nothing, and to be compatible with any possible state of affairs; nothing that happens, or could happen, definitely contradicts them. And this is the very reason why they are uninformative, scientifically worthless.

This aspect of the need for falsifiability in a theory naturally illustrates the requirement of precise definition of terms. Otherwise we shall always be in danger of finding whatever we are looking for, by unwittingly bending our terms out of all recognisable shape. Clearly we can 'discover' anything we like if we are allowed to decide as we go along what is to be included in the scope of our terms. Theories which mention such things as vital forces, or abnormal tendencies, or historical necessity, or a death-wish, without defining these terms any more precisely, have a built-in vagueness which makes them empirically almost worthless. For the same reason, they usually have the appearance of enormous scope and profundity, of explaining everything. Like the newspaper horoscope, they are compatible with every possible state of affairs. Their true logical model is not the grand universal laws of classical physics, but the irrefutable, because empty, prediction that it will either rain tomorrow or it will not.

Not only must the criteria for identifying the variables of a theory be clearly specified, they must also be genuinely independent. If a theory says, for example, that fever is caused by weak bodily humours, then we must know something more about weak bodily humours, must have some way of identifying them, other than simply that they will be present when a person has fever. Without such independent criteria, a theory is not even in principle testable.

Again, just anything cannot count as evidence by which a theory is to be testable. We have already seen that the observations must represent genuine falsifying risks for all or part of the theory. They must also be repeatable in similarly constructed circumstances. Some random effect which appears for no apparent reason, and for the production of which no experimental instructions whatever can be given, is not yet eligible as a scientifically significant observation. Further, the effect must be publicly repeatable. Anyone following the appropriate procedures should be able to reproduce it, regardless of their beliefs or wishes concerning it. Now, there are some theories which offer as 'evidence' results which are not open to general inspection, but have to be interpreted by practitioners who already believe the theory supposedly being tested. It is important to realise here that the objection to this is not that the observations have to be interpreted: for so do most, if not all, scientific observations of any sophistication. It is that no public criteria, no rules, are given for the interpretation. Only those with the eye of faith can interpret the signs, and they cannot explain how they do it.

We have seen that an initial supposition, idea or hypothesis, can only achieve the status of probable

knowledge by public empirical testing, aand that it is only
amenable to testing if it is formulated in a certain way. A
factual statement or hypothesis which is such that we cannot
conceive, even in principle how it could be tested, may not
be wholly meaningless:[1] but it could not be part of scientific
knowledge. For if no conceivable observations could support
it, it is likewise inconceivable how anyone comes to know it.
Now, it is important to stress that these very general
conditions apply to any scientific discipline, whatever its
subject-matter: the study of the human mind is no exception.
The fact that a great deal of the interesting phenomena of
psychology may be private (dreams, for example), in the
sense that only one person can observe them directly, does
not mean that they cannot be the subject of publicly testable
theories. Science is concerned not with particulars, but with
general regularities, because particulars themselves can only
be explained by such regularities. If, for example, a
significantly large number of subjects, unknown to one
another, report strikingly similar contents of their dreams
after they have all been exposed to the same special
experience, then here is a promising lawlike connection,
which may suggest or support some theory, and is obviously
open to testing with further samples. A subject may, of
course, be lying, but sufficiently large, controlled samples
will make it progressively less probable that all are lying in
the same way at the same time. The important difference
from the study of simple laboratory phenomena is, of course,
that in normal circumstances the subject himself is the final
authority on what he does or does not dream.

In other words, while each science must evolve its own
appropriate instruments of investigation, these must operate
within the same overall methodological framework. Now
psychoanalysis, as everyone knows, developed the new
technique of free association to study the contents of the
subject's unconscious. This involves getting the person simply
to say whatever comes into his head, so that the ideas
occurring to him reveal the forgotten continuations of a
conscious memory. But very early on in the history of
analysis, unusual features of this technique began to appear.
The situation was said to occur frequently where 'ideas kept
on emerging which could not be the right ones . . . '.[2] One

assumed originally that there could not be right and wrong ideas, since the whole point of free association appears to be discover, without preconceptions, the contents of a person's unconscious mind. But accounts of analyses clearly show, and the analysts themselves do not deny, that in free association the analyst already knows what he is looking for, and is prepared to ignore the patient's claims about the relative importance of mental data.[3]

Very well. It is clear that free association is not purely an observational technique, but an interpretative one. The analyst presumably bases his selection of the raw free-association data on some prior knowledge of the general mechanisms of the human unconscious. What is this knowledge, and how was it obtained? By what rules are the outpourings of patients interpreted, and how are these rules justified?

First of all, what basic training does the analyst undergo? He equips himself for practice by actually being analysed, the analysis ideally following the lines of a successful patient analysis. Now, for an analysis to be successful, the subject must come to recognise and accept his unconscious wishes for what they are — their nature being uncovered by the analyst's interpretation of the raw free-association data. In other words the central training of an analyst consists of being successfully analysed, which itself requires that he acknowledge and believe the theory as it applies to himself. But in that case, does the student receive any independent assurances of the truth of the basic theories themselves? Does he, for example, repeat for himself the classic experiments of his science, which originally established the general nature of the unconscious? Unfortunately, it appears that he does not. And it also appears that there are no classic experiments in the scientific sense. Successful analysis of the student has to be sufficient: and independent questioning of the theoretical groundwork is not encouraged — indeed, it may constitute an indication that the analysis was not successful after all.

But what about the cures of neurotic patients themselves? Unlike an ordinary medical cure, a successful psychoanalysis requires the patient to be convinced of the truth of psychoanalytical interpretations: otherwise, it will not work. This means that a successful cure alone cannot, without circularity, be sufficient evidence for the truth of the theory on which it is based. In point of fact, Freud himself declined to use the rates of cure of psychoanalysis as its justification, when he admitted that Lourdes probably has a better rate of cures, since more people believed in the existence of the Blessed Virgin than in the unconscious.[4]

Certainly, some neurotic patients recover after analysis. But, as analysts themselves have now been forced to admit, the numbers recovering after analysis are not significantly greater than those recovering spontaneously with no treatment at all.

With the appearance of mounting evidence that psychoanalysis and other analytically-based therapies are ineffective in curing neurosis (let alone psychosis, the hard core of mental illness), Rachman[5] undertook a detailed survey of all available evidence on rates of cure for different psychiatric therapies, including psychoanalysis. For a therapy to be considered effective Rachman held that it would have to show success rates in excess of the sixty-six per cent spontaneous recovery rate over two years shown by the completely untreated. Before such comparisons can even get under way it is rapidly made apparent that as well as complete lack of controlled experiments on psychoanalytic treatment, its mode of operation renders it virtually inaccessible to scientific examination. First of all, the analyst claims the right to select those neurotic patients who he thinks might benefit from the treatment, thus ruling out random allocation of cases to different therapies to see how the results compare. This selection is made on criteria of type of neurosis, the educational and intelligence level of the prospective patient (since understanding of the analyst's interpretations is important to cure) the time he has available (psychoanalysis involves several sessions a week for many years) and the money he can afford to pay (psychoanalytic treatment is very expensive). The criteria for successful analysis have never been agreed; where the patient's symptoms do improve (or where analysts have not had their faith shaken in the efficacy of their treatment to accomplish this), it is held that the aim of the analysis is the removal of neurotic symptoms. Where psychoanalysis appears not to be very successful at this task, it is held that the aim is to change the 'character structure' of the patient, not to cure his neurosis. Again there will be little or no idea of what constitutes a change or improvement of the 'character structure'. Even if criteria of success are agreed, the span of time allowed for recovery allocated to the different therapies is not. Psychoanalysis holds that the only successful analysis is a completed one, and the only completed one is a successful one. Thus the tremendous drop out of uncured or dissatisfied patients from analysis are not recorded as cases where the method has failed, but frequently as cases of 'incomplete analysis', often put down to the patient's 'resistance' to the interpretations of the analyst. It is thus the only therapy outside various types of religion where failure is blamed on the patient. The Greek physician Galen long ago commented on this type of therapy: 'All who drink this remedy recover in a short time except those whom it does not help, who all die and have no relief from any other medicine. Therefore, it is obvious that it fails only in incurable cases.'

Making the best he could of studies that compare psychoanalysis with other therapies, Rachman found that its recovery rates were no better than those found in untreated samples. Indeed, if one considers the time and money which a person has to spend to undergo analysis, it is pointlessly wasteful. (If those who had dropped out of their analysis are listed as failures then we get a depressing recovery rate of only thirty per cent, far below the rates of recovery for untreated samples.) There is also the consideration that a certain amount of tentative evidence suggests that sensitive patients may make their phobic conditions worse, or give themselves additional obsessive worries from exposure to psychoanalysis.[6] It cultivates an excessive introspection which, combined with its notions about human motivation and unconscious forces and desires, is not the best mental stimulation for the introverted neurotic.

Analysts, however, remain firmly convinced that the founder of their movement made discoveries of enormous significance which clearly established the fundamental principles of their discipline beyond serious doubt. By what methods did Freud make these discoveries?

Legend has it that Freud sat astounded beside the couches

of neurotic patients as they poured out quite unsolicited memories of incestuous desires and adventures in early childhood. The truth, however, is not quite like that. We have already seen that the data of free association yields evidence only under certain theoretical interpretations, and this is true even of Freud's earliest investigations with patients. The original elements of the theory, which provide the starting-point for interpretation, Freud derived from his own 'self-analysis'. Jones, Freud's official, approved biographer, tells us that Freud's specific method of investigation was unsuitable for setting up boundaries and strict definitions. Instead, 'through insight into himself, he came to understand a psychological phenomenon, and from the beginning his discoveries carried a strong inner conviction of certitude'.[7]

How did this feeling of certitude stand up to empirical test? Jones tells us that Freud tried three times to use the experimental method and failed, so that he finally abandoned it. He wrote copiously at very high pressure for short intervals at the end of a tiring day. The work was not a careful recording of clinical data, nor a more theoretical examination of current scholarship in the field of mental medicine, but (as one critic puts it) a kind of chirographic rumination.[8] There was little time for correction or revision.

This ruminative method of 'self-analysis' not only yielded an insight into the general structure of the human unconscious: more important, it supposedly provided a key whereby the initially incoherent, trivial, and unconnected material of patients' free associations and dreams can be selected, edited and interpreted to make a kind of sense — which, if accepted, strikingly supports the original theories. But what are the rules for interpreting, and how do we know this interpretation to be the correct one? Unfortunately no rules can be specified, no procedures can be set out for others to repeat, modify or criticise. The ostensible reason for this is that the unconscious itself consists of a great flux of illogical, uncoordinated ideas in which all kinds of contradictions are tolerated: it simply will not yield to any straightforward logical interpretation. Instead, Freud had to guess at the real meanings of the reported material, by assuming that its various elements were distortions and disguises of the true unconscious contents. He proceeded piecemeal, gradually perfecting a special kind of insight which led him to what he was looking for, but whose method could not be explicitly communicated, beyond saying that it consisted of picking out those possible symbols and interpretations which his theory of infantile sexuality suggested to him.

In fact, Freud considered virtually everything in dreams or free association to be 'significant' — to have a hidden meaning, and sometimes several meanings. The most trivial events — slips of the tongue, lapses of memory, random numbering, doodling, fidgeting, fiddling with objects, mislaying things, elementary, everyday errors of all kinds — all can be considered symptoms of some unconscious motive. Even language itself for Freud has latent meanings: each word has several hidden meanings in addition to its overt one (though not, unfortunately, in anything like a one-one or one-many correspondence which might enable us to reconstruct the vocabulary). In addition, the manifest content of dreams was 'over-determined', that is, several latent meanings could be assigned equally to any one overt dream symbol: which one, the analyst could choose according to the clues in the rest of the analysis. The latent meaning of a word could be discovered by assuming it to imply its opposite, or to be a disguise in the form of a pun on speech, or even just a similarity, which could on occasion straddle different languages. Freud's analysis of Leonardo da Vinci rested essentially on a dream where Leonardo saw a kite on his cradle. Kite was mistranslated into German as *vulture*. Freud noted that the Ancient Egyptian for vulture was *mut*. Being similar to the German for mother it was helpful for reconstructing Leonardo's Oedipal relationship with his mother — the presumed motivation behind his artistic and inventive achievements.

The material is potentially limitless, given that just about everything is 'significant', without there being any restrictive language whereby the items signify. Moreover, the necessary lack of a systematic, procedure formulated for interpreting patients' material, protected Freud's method and results from public appraisal. He insisted that only those who had mastered the technique and repeated it for themselves on patients were in a position to make any judgement about the doctrines of psychoanalysis.[9] This is not just mastery of a specialised tool, such as exists in other sciences: it is an esoteric form of 'observation' which is not even in principle public.

A rudimentary starting-point in testing Freud's original hypothesis might have been, say, to have a number of subjects under free association, unacquainted with Freudian theory, observed independently by different judges, themselves non-converts, who then compared the results of their impressions. If, among all the other disconnected deliverances, there were recognisably Freudian themes (for example, unusual emphasis on childhood, ambiguous relationships to parents, or some generally recognisable, though oblique, preoccupation with incest, castration, etc.) in a significant number of cases, then the first tentative connection would be established, making the theory a serious candidate for further research.

The outside enquirer cannot have his doubts satisfied. But once he does make the leap of faith, accepts the theory and is psychoanalysed, all becomes clear. He also has a means of dealing with any lingering doubts he might feel: these doubts, he now sees, are merely symptoms of his own unconscious resistance to recognising the truth. Likewise he can now see his way through the more impenetrable thickets of a patient's ramblings, and this way gives surprising support to the theory. Thus, if a patient actually admits to thoughts, dreams or wishes clearly in line with Freudian theory, this is taken as a piece of confirming evidence for the theory. But when the patient does not admit to the right thoughts or wishes, this is taken as a symbolic disguise of his real unconscious wishes, and so it still confirms the theory. And if he expressly denies having had any such dream or thought or desire, this is taken as resistance to the analyst's suggestions due to effective repression of his real unconscious wishes — and hence it still confirms the theory.

In other words, nothing the patient could say is allowed to count as possible counter-evidence. The theory is compatible with any possible test result, any possible state of affairs: not being even in principle falsifiable, it is empirically vacuous. It is a sad but unavoidable fact that analysts, including Freud himself, not only considered this built-in irrefutability to be legitimate to their discipline, but actually elevated it into a great scientific strength:

> It was accordingly plausible to suppose that the greater the resistance against what we were in search of becoming conscious, the greater would be its distortion. The idea which occurred to the patient in place of what we were in search of had thus itself, originated like a symptom: it was a new, artificial, and ephemeral substitute for what had been repressed, and was dissimilar to it in proportion to the degree of distortion it had undergone under the influence of the resistance.[10]

Elsewhere Freud wrote: 'If this "No", instead of being registered as the expression of an impartial judgement (of which, indeed the patient is incapable), is ignored, and if the work is continued, the first evidence soon begins to appear that in such a case "No" signifies the desired "Yes".'[11]

Just as patients' objections and disavowals could be subverted into support for the theory by the simple device of detecting unconscious resistance, so could the disagreements of critics. Psychoanalysts thus equipped themselves with a handy and seemingly invincible weapon against any rational or scientific criticisms of their system. They did not need to argue with academic colleagues: they merely discovered that the hidden motives for their opponents' disagreement were a quasi-pathological, unconscious, unacknowledged, resistance to recognising the truth. Freud himself used this stratagem frequently in dealing with critics:

> Psycho-analysis is seeking to bring to conscious recognition the things in mental life which are repressed; and everyone who forms a judgement on it is himself a human being, who possesses similar repressions and may be maintaining them with difficulty. They are therefore in him, as in our patients; and that resistance finds it easy to disguise itself as intellectual rejection . . . We often become aware in our opponents, just as we do in our patients, that their power of judgement is very noticeably influenced affectively in the sense of being diminished.[12]

In fact, it should not need to be pointed out that this

whole kind of stratagem is fatally self-defeating. If any
dissenting argument or alternative theory is invalidated,
simply by showing it to be the product of ulterior
motivations or determining causes — whether of the Freudian
kind or any other — then so, too, is the very theory which is
being defended, and which demonstrates these influences.
Either rationality is acknowledged all round, or it disappears
from under everyone's feet, including the theorist who thinks
his arguments have undermined it.

We have seen how training in psychoanalysis consists in the
initiation of being psychoanalysed by another qualified
analyst — and so on, in apostolic succession back to the
Master, who was the only person who did not need to be
analysed, since he analysed himself. This remark is not mere
rhetorical metaphor: the history of the psychoanalytic
movement strongly suggests that it derived its remarkable
strength and persistence, not from the open, self-correcting
nature of a science, but from the esoteric, dedicated
character of religious faith and a priesthood.

Most important here is the inescapably personal, prophetic
character of Freud's 'discoveries'. Prophecy involves not just
the personal revelation of a message to one chosen individual;
it also involves that the message is given once only: after that
deliverance the heavens close. The original self-analysis of
Freud was such that 'Once done, it is done for ever. For no
one again can be the first to explore those depths.'[13] Thus all
authority, all justification and validation for psychoanalysis
ever since derives from these utterly unique, particular
unrepeatable happenings to one special person.

The character of science proper is just the opposite of this;
its theories are repeatable, and therefore public and
impersonal. Certainly it has its historical legends and heroes,
like Archimedes in the bath, Newton in the orchard, or
Kekulé who dozed by the fire and suddenly intuited the
benzene ring from the dancing flames. But these are a luxury:
everyone knows that the soundness of the theory of gravity,
for example, would not suffer one iota if it were somehow
established that Newton had never sat in an orchard in his
life, or even that the discovery was made by some wholly
different person in a quite different way. But suppose the
same for Freud's once-only insights, and what becomes of

psychoanalysis?

Again, many great discoverers have undoubtedly been arrogant or eccentric, or displayed similar failings: but in these cases it has gradually become possible to separate the valuable — because repeatable — discovery from the personal fads and quirks of the man, and indeed to recognise just where and why these hindered the genuine scientific achievement. But after nearly seventy years this is still impossible with Freud. There has been no lack of able attempts, but the net result has been that the later theorists who have undertaken this task have either reluctantly abandoned the central tenets of psychoanalysis, or have had to fall back inexorably on the sole authority of Freud's 'original genius', his profound personal insight which no one has equalled or repeated. The external trappings of his movement mimicked science sufficiently skilfully for the literary intelligentsia and many of the medical men to be taken in; in due course Freud was receiving the accolade of a great scientist, and in many quarters still is: he was simply a Scientific Genius[14] and so, like another Midas, everything he touched became scientific. His bold pronouncements in fields of which he knew nothing or next to nothing — anthropology, aesthetics and even archaeology — were taken as fundamental contributions.

There are, however, current arguments, very different from those of Freud and his immediate followers, which one sometimes hears in favour of psychoanalysis, and which deserve mention.

The undeniable fact that the notion of unconscious mental activity has passed into our language and become part of our ordinary view of things, is often cited as demonstrating that Freud discovered something very substantial about our mental processes. It is true that we do use this and other terms borrowed from psychoanalysis to describe everyday realities, but a little examination shows that we certainly do not use them in the Freudian sense. We generally use the term 'unconscious' to describe four broad categories of things: (1) dreaming, daydreaming, mental wandering, etc.; (2) the material stored in memory which is not currently present in consciousness; (3) conditioned reflexes, automatic or physiological processes ('instincts'), acquired habits, irrational phobias, etc.; and (4) purposive self-deception, convenient blindness, motives which we do not want to recognise.

The first three of these have little or no resemblance to Freud's special concept of the unconscious. He was not entirely clear or consistent in his use of the concept, but he did definitely distinguish it from what he called the pre-conscious, to which memory and overt dream contents belong. The contents of the Freudian unconscious are wholly beyond the reach of consciousness, and can only be deduced from clues derived by the analyst from the pre-conscious. At most, the subject may be unable to recall an item of memory because the item (psychically innocuous in itself) has become associated, usually by long chains, with something in the unconscious; or the elements of a dream will similarly resemble or symbolise something in the unconscious, which likewise needs to be deduced through analysis. Thus, contrary to what popular usage might suggest, the contents of memory are not the Freudian unconscious, nor are unusual lapses of memory themselves repressions, nor are we getting a glimpse of the unconscious when we dream.

The Freudian unconscious, though totally inaccessible to the subject, nonetheless consists of purposive, intelligible (though unacceptable) wishes and desires analogous to conscious wishes and desires – Oedipal jealousy, castration fear, rivalry with the father, etc. And not by the remotest stretch of imagination can these be equated with the mechanisms of learning, conditioning and habit as now understood. The latter are not conceived as caused by an intelligent, but hidden agency, but completely mechanistic processes of association. Now it is, of course, always possible to regard automatic habit or indeed all behaviour beyond conscious control, as the working of an 'unconscious mind' if we are determined to do so. It does not matter finally what words we use, so long as our concepts are clear. But if we make this step, we should also have to extend the term to all self-regulating mechanisms, and say that perspiration and goose pimples are due to an unconscious wish to maintain a constant body temperature, and that a guided missile keeps on course because of an unconscious wish to hit its target. It is always regarded as a retrograde step in science to choose explanations in terms of animistic agencies rather than in terms of laws.

In the fourth case, we have known for a long time that rationalisation, wilful self-deception, convenient failure to recognise one's own motives, go on in people. These are purposive in the sense that they are intelligibly goal-directed and clearly akin to the normal kinds of wishes and intentions which the agent acknowledges. But they do not need to be considered as preconceived plans located in a second, rival consciousness utterly hidden from the ordinary one. The point is that most of a person's mental attitudes — his beliefs, wishes, fears, etc. — are revealed, not just by what he sincerely says, but also by what he does. In the cases of self-deception and rationalisation, one of these criteria conflicts with the other. For example, I may sincerely declare that I do not believe in God, yet if on several occasions of danger or trouble I am seen to fall on may knees and pray, other people will conclude, rightly, that I really do believe, however much I may try to explain away these momentary lapses. Since these mental attitudes are all partly public in character, there is no reason why I should have infallible knowledge about myself. I can be mistaken about my own motives in basically the same way that I can be mistaken about the motives of others. And when such errors are so convenient to my self-esteem that they become reinforced and repeated, they take on a quasi-deliberate appearance. Such self-deception consists, not of one half of the mind deliberately plotting to deceive the other, but of others clearly seeing that I wish something, whereas I blatantly and very conveniently fail to see it. The wish is 'unconscious', not in the sense of existing in an unconscious mind, but in the sense of operating publicly, yet the agent having too much vanity or too little self-knowledge to recognise it for what it is.

Some recent supporters of psychoanalysis, faced with its negligible rate of cure for neurosis, have argued that analysis is justified not as a cure, but as a means of gaining insight into oneself. It is a kind of educative therapy whereby the patient comes to understand himself. Quite apart from the obvious observation that patients normally want to be cured if possible, rather than educated to see why they cannot be cured, this claim begs the whole question very badly. Since, as we have seen, a successful psychoanalysis requires that the patient becomes convinced of some, or all psychoanalytic theory in order to 'understand themselves , the value of such 'understanding' depends entirely on the truth or falsity of that theory. If it is false, the patient is not understanding himself but deluding himself, even though he may get some emotional satisfaction. Faith-healing evangelists can offer this — and they sometimes have better rates of cure as well.

This line of argument is, however, paralleled by others. It is sometimes admitted that psychoanalysis is not scientific, but also insisted that, anyway, there cannot be a science of human beings. This usually goes with a great deal of disparaging talk about the limitations, artificiality and inhumanity of 'laboratory' science, with its attempts to quantify everything, to manipulate the world and people, the indignity and dehumanisation of viewing humans as 'mere' intelligent rats, which paves the way for 1984, and much else in that vein. It is strongly implied that psychoanalysis (or 'dynamic psychology', or whatever its current label) on the other hand, recognises the uniqueness of people and circumstances, and respects their individuality and dignity. This is a far cry from the tough, even brutal attitudes of Freud, who compared himself with Copernicus and Darwin as a great debunker of rational idealist pretensions, by laying bare the unsavoury but decisively powerful elemental sources of our most sublime motivations.

From proudly proclaiming that psychoanalysis was the one discipline that made psychology scientific as opposed to speculative and literary, representatives of the movement have come full circle, and are fervently attacking science. This kind of polemic, not just against experimental psychology but often against the scientific method *in toto,* which is seen as a manipulative conceptual tool of the powers-that-be, inseparable from destructive technology, has come strongly into vogue in the last few years, and obviously goes well beyond the scope of this book. But a few relevant observations might be made.

Of course, there is a way in which we understand each other, as persons, which is not expressible as a series of scientific hypotheses. It involves our ethical values, and our imagination, and is based on a fundamental reciprocity which could never govern our understanding of things. But why should psychoanalysis have any special claim to this? One of the distinctive features of this understanding is surely that it is informal: it does not consist of any doctrines or developed theories, but rather, of an ability which is shown by experienced and mature people: it can be acquired through experience, but not taught in the way factual knowledge is taught. Some psychoanalysts undoubtedly have this ability, but so do many other people untrained in psychoanalysis or any other discipline. Psychoanalysis, on the other hand, is based on certain definite doctrines about human behaviour which claim general validity, and thus stand in need of justification. As a movement it aspired to be a science and failed. Were this not so, analysts would not, as they do, interpret what patients tell them according to a theoretical model, despite (or even because of) repeated and coherent disavowal. They would have to treat people just as any other lay person does who is habitually asked for advice − by accepting their reports about themselves at face value until some inconsistency appears. And in doing so they would lose any privileged status as analysts.

To the question, 'can there really be a scientific psychology?' the answer is yes, because there is one. Experimental psychology has produced a modest body of knowledge, which does stand up to, or at least is open to empirical test. Undoubtedly, there may be many things it will fail to explain and areas where it is wrong, but this is no argument for not pursuing it until it does come up against such obstacles, and absolutely no argument for throwing it over in favour of a pseudo-science. To argue that its theories 'dehumanise' us, is simply not enough. What must be shown is that the theories are incoherent, or untrue or improbable. Certainly it is important to examine the theoretical assumptions and understand what the experiments do and do not indicate. But this can only be done by searching continually for the most economical theories which manage to entail all the known facts, including, ultimately, the full facts of our ordinary experience, which must be satisfactorily accounted for by any truly comprehensive psychology. It cannot be right to reject a theory which seems to be true, just because it appears offensive to our values: no values can be genuine if they necessarily depend on falsehood. Perhaps the greatest single liberating development in Western medicine was achieved when educated people finally overcame that deep sense of spiritual outrage which was expressed in the Church's ban on the dissection of human bodies. But modern medicine has not, I think, thereby dehumanised us or robbed us of our dignity.

III Instinct and Culture

16 Motherhood and Monkeys

It has recently been widely publicised that, unlike some aspects of psychoanalytical theory, the vital formative importance of the one-to-one relationship of an infant with its mother has been demonstrated in the laboratory—on monkeys. These observations have been used to illustrate a causal theory for the basis of later personal and social incapacities in the early mother—infant tie, that depends upon instinctual mechanisms rather than the increasingly defunct infant libidinal energy model.

The laboratory experiments are on Rhesus monkeys, the best known being carried out by Harlow *et al.*. The shocking effects of maternal separation are widely held to be demonstrated by the later behaviour of monkeys reared without a proper mother.[1] These monkeys were reared from birth in cages where some were provided with a cloth dummy mother, some with a wire dummy mother; others were in empty cages.[2] When mature they were introduced to other monkeys but were incapable of sexual behaviour. Some of the females later became mothers (see below) but were unable to care for their offspring, repudiating them and treating them with violence: '. . . the mother sits staring into space—while the infant makes a desperate attempt to get to her. The mother puts her hand on the infant and crushes its body into the floor of the cage. All four of these animals in their original contacts were either completely indifferent or violently abusive to their infants.'[3]

This is frequently held to be supporting evidence for the notion that bad marital and parental behaviour in particular owe their origins to a separation experience. But there is a consideration which seems to have been overlooked. These monkeys have not only been reared without a mother, they have also been reared in total isolation from their own species from birth to maturity: they have been reared literally without a society, not only without mother. The corresponding form of rearing for a human would be to bring someone up from birth until about fifteen years of age in a bare wire cage, without seeing or hearing another human. Released into the company of other humans, of whose existence he has up to then been ignorant, and without the slightest learnt behaviour, it would hardly be surprising if his responses appeared bizarre. It seems to be insinuated by many that this monkey isolation is actually comparable with leaving a child with grandmother, father or relatives for a period, sending him into hospital, or perhaps having institutional or customary arrangements where child-care is shared. The extrapolation from society-less (not 'motherless', as Harlow calls the deprivation) monkeys to children separated for periods from their mothers and looked after by others, is quite invalid.

Other work of Harlow demonstrates how wrong were the naive conclusions about maternal deprivation drawn from this highly publicised part of his work. The other work, involves monkeys brought up without a mother but with peers. Those brought up with peers only were no more maladjusted in later life than monkeys brought up with peers and a mother.[4] They demonstrated quite normal adult social and sexual behaviour. Whereas in contrast, monkeys brought up with a mother only but without peers, were less well adjusted.

Concerning monkeys brought up with peers but without a mother, Harlow makes the following comments:

> Our predictions concerning the eventual social capabilities of these unmothered, 'together-together' infants were gloomy, but the infants' long-term social adjustments have been far better than expected. Interactive play did develop, aggression within groups was low, and normal heterosexual adjustments were the rule, not the exception. One female has thus far become a mother, and her behaviour towards her infant has been normal in every respect.[5]

The availability of peers also made for good social adjustment in those monkeys who had indifferent or hostile mothers. On the other hand monkeys reared with a mother but deprived of peer relationships showed impaired social behaviour towards age mates when united with them, this was worse the longer the deprivation: particularly noticeable was hyper-aggressiveness. Some individuals are affected more than others, showing no ability for social interaction after peer deprivation, while other milder cases, quickly improve with exposure to age-mates.

Analogous extrapolations have also been drawn from experiments where infant monkeys have been separated from their mothers. The infant separated first shows increased locomotion, vocalisation and exploration of its environment; it then becomes withdrawn, huddles up and remains passive. Attention needs to be drawn again to the crucial fact that by virtue of experimental isolation these infants are not merely being deserted by their mothers, but often by all society. One cannot compare many of these experiments with maternal separation in humans, unless the child is placed in solitary confinement when separated. That the withdrawal phenomena in experimental monkeys is due to social, not maternal, desertion, tends to be confirmed by other observations of monkeys living with peers to whom they had become attached; when they were separated, they showed exactly the same behaviour as the maternally deprived.[6] Whether separation involves isolation or not, its effects in monkeys tend to be shortlived; after reunion behaviour is normal within a few weeks.[7]

We thus have a picture of monkey development where the maternal relationship has no importance *per se* for the social, sexual and later maternal development of infant monkeys over and above other early relationships. The monkey studies have certainly not proved any fundamental necessity for the mother—infant relationship. Indeed, if there has to be a choice between rearing monkeys alone except for a mother, or alone except for peers — the latter seems the most beneficial. After their experience with various types of deprived monkeys the Harlows conclude that it is the age-mate or peer affectional system, developed through the interchange of play and grooming that is the primary socialisation mechanism in macaque monkeys. Maternal presence only partly compensates for this.[8]

However, given that there is no absolute necessity for a maternal relationship, does not this evidence still point to a critical phase in monkey infancy for the development of interpersonal relationships — a sort of period in early life during which an imprinting on one's own species occurs which is vital for the capacity for later relationships and which cannot be made good later? Monkeys brought up until maturity in isolation from their own species clearly cannot form social relationships. Does this mean that they never will? An early experience, fixed-stage story of infant development, would strongly suggest that the time has been missed. Whether or not Harlow shared this assumption, it is striking that his work threw up evidence suggesting the contrary, even though this was not part of the original design of his experiments.

We saw how, in his experiments, the monkeys reared in social isolation did not demonstrate normal adult sexual behaviour; when placed with other monkeys of the opposite sex they were unable to mate. However, Harlow's determination to see how these socially-deprived females would treat their offspring led him to many subterfuges to try and get the isolated females pregnant.[9] The successful strategy was to put the females with older experienced males, noted for their breeding success; after a while several conceived. But it so happened that one female thus successfully mated was infertile, and was kept with the males for a far longer time than the others. Her sexual behaviour improved progressively and within a few months was quite normal. A similar observation of postponed adaptation occurred with the maternal behaviour of the other socially isolated females. Often an infant's continual attempts to make physical contact with its mother wore down the mother's original resistance, and afterwards her behaviour with subsequent offspring was normal.

These accidental observations of the reversibility of the effects of total social isolation from birth led to further deliberate experiments with this factor. Harlow thus began to use normal socialised monkeys as 'therapists' on those reared in social isolation. He used younger monkeys because they were less likely to be upset or aggressive when faced with an isolate's lack of response; they were also more likely to approach and play on an elementary rather than sophisticated level. He found that after five or six months, the behaviour of a social isolate was virtually indistinguishable from that of any normal monkey. The results, he claimed, exceeded his highest expectations.[10]

On the other hand, some work,[11][12] with chimpanzees has shown that behavioural abnormalities due to early isolation were less modifiable. There is no reason to suspect that evidence from animals with rigid developmental patterns is more applicable to humans than evidence demonstrating the primary importance of flexibility and learning. Human beings are cultural creatures with an extraordinary lack of instinctual behaviours; they have also developed language, which dramatically extends the scope, flexibility and modifiability of learning at any age.

But even here other work has shown that the effects of deprivation and isolation may be partly attributable to the nature of the transition from the rearing environment. Chimpanzees reared in isolation and then gradually introduced to social and other stimulation were as normal at five to six years of age in their responses as African born animals of comparable age.

If the effects of rearing in social isolation are reversible in later life (in some monkeys anyway), this has obvious repercussions for those who are attempting to find in ethology a basis for the vital importance of early critical times in the development of later capacities. They are, furthermore, basing the origin of these capacities in the instinctual interchange of an indivisible biological relationship rather than in social learning—which would be transmissible by any other members of the same species with the requisite skills.

The Harlow observations, as well as many more from other primate and human studies, tend to demonstrate that the capacities for social, sexual and maternal behaviours do not result from an instinctual relationship with 'the mother' in very early life. They suggest that they are learnt, that they are social capacities and skills which are not acquired by some natural sort of emotional or sensual interchange (instinctual or libidinal) between a biological pair.[13] Given these skills are learnt, it does not necessarily require the mother to impart them. Also, if they are learnt, there is no 'critical' period for their acquisition. Learning depends upon flexibility, the capacity for extinction (of old learnings) and continual readiness to acquire new. Learning capacity is indeed dependant on neurological differences between individuals which certainly vary with age, but these are in no way comparable with 'critical periods'. It is also, of course, true that more complex learning depends on prior simpler learning, and the organism with this will have an initial advantage over the one with next to none. The greater one's pre-existent repertoire of learnt responses, the easier and quicker it is to acquire each subsequent piece of learning and the greater the advantage acquired thereby (so that in many competitive social circumstances the gap will increase). Nevertheless, there is still no warrant for identifying these facts with 'critical periods'. It is both possible and probable that, given the relevant opportunities, an organism which lags behind others of its kind in its learnt repertoire of adaptive behaviour, could catch up and throw off its initial disadvantages. Some evidence for primates which we will examine below shows that, if anything, the mother—infant bond can militate against the acquisition of social learning and render the young 'backward' compared with more independent age-mates, and that this can be compared with both traditonal and recent observational evidence from human children.

17 Instinct and Human Attachment

We must now consider Bowlby's new theoretical alternative to libido theory, which, he considers, gives a more adequate explanation of the mother–infant bond and its crucial importance for all later development. The discussion will illuminate some important and currently popular issues about the role of instinct in animal and human development.

It should be pointed out that Bowlby's theory of instinctual mechanisms has not been stimulated by the emergence of any new scientific evidence about separation damage which calls for explanation. Bowlby explains that he considers the separation of an infant from its mother to be a traumatic, pathological event — as given datum — and is concerned to suggest hypotheses concerning what the underlying mechanisms might be. To locate these he looks at the promising fields of cybernetics and ethological studies. In *Attachment and Loss* there is a wealth of material about control mechanisms and lengthy descriptions of animal studies, all of which makes fascinating reading and is full of interesting and provocative suggestions. But it must be borne in mind that this cannot be a substitute for the one thing which could really strengthen Bowlby's contentions — namely, some independent bioligical or physiological evidence that such instinctual mechanisms as he proposes really do exist in human infants.

Bowlby postulates (as with libido theory) that the capacity for social and moral behaviour results not from social learning, but from crucial interaction with a 'mother figure' or 'attachment figure'. Instead of this arising because she acts as an outlet for accumulated libido, it is now because in the child there are innate instinctual mechanisms that have attachment to mother as the 'goal'. These are, mainly, sucking, clinging, crying and smiling, all of which have the effect of keeping the infant close to its mother.

But later, all these discrete instinctual responses are
incorporated into a far more sophisticated and integrated
system of behaviour which unfolds automatically between
nine and eighteen months. The infant can now vary its
behaviour in far more complex ways to keep the mother near
it. The new structure of instinctual systems is described as
'goal-corrected' (as a predictor-controlled anti-aircraft gun
automatically tracks the evasive tactics of an aircraft), and
the 'set-goal' of the whole system (the condition or behaviour
which is maintained by negative feedback) is proximity to
the mother. As he grows up, the development of the child's
cognitive apparatus relates him to his mother over greater
time and space intervals, so that he can maintain proximity
over greater periods and distances. His adult relationships are
copies of this infant—mother tie and have the same tendency
to 'monotropy' – this is, one-to-one pairing. All man's
important capacities have their origins in this instinctive tie
to the mother, and his ills in frustration of these instinctual
systems which seek the maternal presence.

Bowlby also postulates that there may be something akin
to the 'maternal instinct' in the natural mother which makes
it easier for her to respond to her baby than a non-parturant
substitute:

> Though there is no doubt that a substitute mother can
> behave in a completely mothering way to a child, and that
> many do so, it may well be less easy for a substitute
> mother than for a natural mother to do so. For example,
> knowledge of what elicits mothering behaviour in other
> species suggests that hormonal levels following parturation
> and stimuli emanating from the newborn baby himself
> may both be of great importance. If this is so for human
> mothers also, a substitute mother must be at a
> disadvantage compared with a natural mother . . . a
> substitute's mothering responses may well be less strong
> and less consistently elicited than those of a natural
> mother.[1]

When Bowlby postulates that the original discrete
instinctual mechanisms – sucking, crying. etc – are incorporated in a complex system seeking a higher-order goal

(proximity to the mother), it must be emphasised that he is not proposing a theory that supposes that the child becomes attached to the mother because she happens to satisfy his discrete biological needs for food, comfort, protection, etc. This would imply a learning theory explanation for human attachments, and it would likewise imply that anyone else, male and female, who did all these things for a child would for that reason acquire importance in his life. The whole point of Bowlby's book is to avoid resorting to such theories, which are termed 'secondary drive' theories (they suppose attachment to the mother is based originally on other satisfactions which later generalise to her) and to reassert attachment to the mother as a unique and independent instinctual goal in itself. Bowlby claims that these other satisfactions are largely irrelevant, and neither compose nor account for attachment behaviour. The evolutionary function of sucking, he argues, is not to get nourishment, out of which attachment to the mother might arise as a secondary consequence. Nothing so contingent is permitted in his theory: for if that were the only connection, the child would become attached to anyone who fed him (and similarly anyone who responded to his crying), and furthermore these need not be the same person. On the contrary, says Bowlby, the evolutionary function of these initial instinctual responses such as sucking is simply as basic components which later integrate into the overall mother-seeking, goal-corrected system. Thus, quite apart from the satisfactions and necessities she provides for the infant, the mother is instinctually homed-in upon, is a goal in and for herself to which innate, unfolding automatic behavioural mechanisms are set.

Now the use of a control systems model to account for 'instinctual' behaviour (roughly, that which is environmentally stable, unlearnt, yet apparently purposive and goal-directed) is obviously superior to teleological accounts, using libido or 'drives'. It is superior because it offers causal law explanations, which alone are scientifically acceptable. But it is not at all clear that it yields Bowlby what he wants, which is an explanation not just of the initial sucking, clinging, etc., but of the later, more discriminating and organised behaviour towards the mother. Bowlby starts by stating the need for a theory of instinctual mechanisms; and, indeed, cybernetic models of negative feedback, etc., for example, are probably the most promising direction to look. Accordingly, Bowlby defines the 'set-goal' of a feedback system in terms of the output which it is (genetically or technologically) 'set' to maintain. This may be a stable condition, or continuous variation according to changing instructions: thus, the set-goal of a thermostat is just that heat output which maintains the temperature for which it has been set, and the set-goal of the anti-aircraft gun is continual realignment in the way dictated by the instructions of the predictor.

Before long, however, Bowlby is using 'set-goal' in connection with quite other arrangements of human behaviour which are clearly not instinctual but learnt, and which are not examples of negative feedback control systems, or even elaborate combinations of such systems. He argues that, since both instinctive and learnt behaviour are likely to be present in varying combinations in most of the behaviour we are considering, it is not very useful to expect exclusive explanations in either category. Henceforth he talks not of instinctual mechanisms but far more vaguely and generally of 'behavioural systems', which do not only comprise automatic behaviour but also include sophisticated and conscious plans of people organised in discernible structures. After such generous concessions, it is difficult to disagree with his thesis as formulated (that attachment results from behavioural systems developing in the infant as a result of his interaction with his environment of evolutionary adaptedness) since it is now sufficiently general and loose not to preclude learning processes. In other words, his use of control systems theory, whose principal merit here is to account for automatic, instinctual mechanisms of behaviour, does not seem to be of any notable help in getting him over the crucial gap from the undeniably automatic bits of behaviour—sucking, crying, clinging, etc.—to the not at all obviously automatic behaviour of later discriminating and sophisticated attachment to the mother (or anyone else).

Still, the vital point is that Bowlby sees this later 'behavioural system' goal-corrected on to proximity with mother, as innately programmed and unfolding autonomously in each biologically normal infant, much like the unfolding of sensorimotor behaviour. To the question *why* we have such genetic programming, Bowlby explains that it can be understood in terms of our 'environment of evolutionary adaptedness',[2] that is, the usefulness of such mechanisms in the world in which our species actually evolved. Those carrying such mechanisms would increase their number and supplant the others by Natural Selection. The use of these instincts that gave the young proximity to mother is posited as protection from predators, which would explain why they are so strong, and why such disturbance is caused by thwarting them.

There are two basic questions here. Would these instincts confer great survival potential on man in his primeval environment, compared with others? And, do human infants in fact show this instinctual attachment behaviour towards their natural mothers? The answers to these questions also help us to understand some of the broader issues involved in describing and explaining the basis of human personal and social relationships.

Cultural man has been on this planet for approximately five million years. For all but the last few thousand — during which agriculture has been practised (the Neolithic period) — *Australopithecu* and his descendant species have been hunters and food gatherers. This existence, particularly for species prior to *homo-sapiens* (the most recent variant) has been largely nomadic. Archaic man was essentially a creature of the river valleys, coasts and plains (savannah land) during much of his evolution. A vast evolutionary gap separates man from his nearest surviving relatives, gorilla and chimpanzee. If we seek to use ethological knowledge in our study of human behaviour we must not only look at biological relatedness, but also to those species who have occupied similiar habitats to man, and have thus had to cope during their evolution with the same essential problems. The differences in their behaviour compared with those other related species who have not been faced with such problems, gives us some idea of the distinctive differences that have come about in adapting to a certain environment (for example, the open savannah), and it is to these that we should give our attention. What may be adaptive to forest-dwelling apes may be highly disadvantageous to the creatures of the open plains, faced with problems that may require radically different solutions. Those biologically closest to man who have also shared, and competed for the same environment, are the plains-dwelling monkeys, principally baboons.

Bowlby rightly emphasises the role of predator protection in primate evolution; for the plains-dwelling primate, this must constitute his most pressing problem. The forest-dwelling ape is hardly faced with the dangers that exposure on the open ground can bring, particularly at night. Tree cover provides camouflage and easy escape from predators — both gorilla[3] and chimpanzee build nests in the trees. African cats usually shun forests as sources of food, preferring the easier pickings from the exposed plains species. To the heightened vulnerability of plains dwellers is added the important fact that the primate generally is poorly equipped with natural defence: he lacks the claws, teeth, strength and speed of the cat; he has no armoured or spiny covering, etc. Indeed, in comparison even with the baboon, who possesses a heavy jaw of tearing teeth, man is physically very defenceless, particularly considering his dangerous environment.

For many forest dwellers (such as the gibbon) the most adaptive form of protection for the young is the mechanism of clinging to the mother that leaves her arms free to make an escape by moving away through the branches of trees. There are many primate young who do indeed possess the ability to seek out the nearest creature (obviously the mother) directly or very soon after birth, and to cling tenaciously without assistance, particularly in response to fear. But the means of avoiding predation in this manner are not open to man or baboon. For the land-dwelling primate such a mechanism by itself would be ineffective: mother and infant clinging together would be mincemeat for any passing leopard.

In baboon and man the protection of the individual, including the infant, is afforded largely by the social group. It is significant that the social groups of land-dwelling primates are far larger than those of forest dwellers, whose groups diminish in size the more exclusively life is lived in the branches of the dense forest. For example, the gibbon and orang-utan have little social group to speak of, often living alone or in pairs. Group solidarity in the face of threat means that in the case of the savannah baboon, other females and males help the mother to protect her infant, not simply through the organisation of the group, but individually too, by carrying it away from danger.[4] In no plains-dwellers that we know of is the female left alone to provide protection for her infant.

The responsibility for the welfare of the individual revolving so much on an enlarged group gives rise to other aspects of baboon life (and that of other land-dwelling primates), again comparable with those in human societies. There are complexities of social organisation which involve patterns of authority and status, and procedures to stabilise these. The latter are also important because in large, land-dwelling groups, aggression, as well as being an external threat, becomes also an internal problem for the group. Internal regulation of behaviour to prevent clashes is an important task of the authority and status system. The viability of the young individual being so dependent on the group, and not just on its biological mother, involves other individuals in care and concern for the young, going beyond simple physical protection. As biological ties become increasingly irrelevant to survival, this involvement includes males as well as females, who begin to take part in the social process on a wide scale; whereas in species more dependent on biological ties, males tend to be peripheral to any social groupings that might emerge. The former aspect is most highly developed in Man, where cultural evolution has enormously overshadowed and overwhelmed instinctual, biological capacities.

Even in laboratory studies of small groups of Rhesus monkeys, considerable interaction between non-maternal females and young has been observed, which includes the adoption of orphans on the death of a mother.[5] From what we know of monkey groups it is unusual for an orphaned youngster to have to die because its mother does.

In the wild species,[6] although males play no part in child-care, the young Langur are accustomed from just after birth to being looked after for periods by other females who act as aunts to a number of young. Among baboons, males dominant in the hierarchy take an active interest in all infants, a mother with an infant getting special attentions, a privileged position (involving the safest place in the middle of the group) and protection from all the threats and attacks of fellow baboons. Her infant will be groomed, nursed and carried by males (this is particularly developed among the Hamadryas), which are able to provide virtually everything except suckling, and will automatically go to the defence of any infant in distress. Among the Japanse macaque, centrally-placed males select and nurse particular infants during the birth season, the relationship persisting or reappearing the following year. When an infant macaque is orphaned, substitute care is provided by centrally-placed males. The most extreme form of male care is provided by the Barbary macaque, where infants are passed between the males for nursing and grooming, riding on their backs, etc.; this parallels the female group-care provided in the Langur monkey troops.

Compared with other land-dwelling monkeys, humans also make use of their own special aptitude for protection—that of intelligence and culture, so that artificial weapons (including fire), are manufactured, or ready-shaped objects employed to compensate for the poor natural endowment. Weapons have probably been in use since the days of *Australopithecus,* even if they were not actually being shaped from flint. Cultural instead of natural weapon-development in humans has obviously opened up an extravagant and wide use of violence far beyond the powers of those species possessing biological weapons.

Certainly, it is absolutely essential for the human young to be drawn towards members of its own species, and they to him. But this is very different from postulating the existing of a biological orientation to one individual. Bowlby has made the statement that Man has not been a social and cultural animal during the great proportion of his existence but that, in fact, his relationships were purely biological: parent-to-young and mate-to-mate. He writes, 'It is only about six thousand years ago that man attempted the task of going beyond these basic, biological, family relationships to form larger societies.'[7] Such a view presumably is unacquainted with archaeological, anthropological and palaeontological evidence, and can only derive from the prejudice that the nuclear family is an eternal institution seen now as something alternative or even opposed to, society. The existence of widespread cultures of flint-tool making alone points to elaborate and stable organisations for cultural transmission and dispersion operating for probably over a million years. It seems unlikely that thousands of isolated families each individually invented flint tools, fire, shelter-building, stock-rearing, agriculture and metalworking, and passed them on to their individual offspring at much the same time.

A simple, isolated, biological relationship could hardly form the basis of continuity necessary for transmission and accumulation of these skills. (If we consider almost any pre-industrial human society, the mortality rates are so high that any single biological family—except large polygamous groups—rarely perpetuates itself for more than a few generations. Most families die out or are assimilated without trace into others. Where one name or house or line does retain a continuous identity, this always depends on the regular adoption or inclusion of outsiders.) There is ample indirect evidence for the operation of human language—which itself presupposes a reasonably wide social group—in the upper and middle Paleolithic, over 100,000 years ago. Neanderthal Man, associated with the Mousterian tool culture, did not merely make tools but had forms of (possibly totemistic) cults, and elaborate rituals connected with burial of the dead; that indicates at least the operation of some characteristically human beliefs and ideas which would hardly have been expressible without fairly rich linguistic resources. Cromagnon Man exhibited considerable artistic, ritual and belief systems which are manifested in the art, cult-objects and rudimentary inscriptions dating from about 35,000 years ago. It is preposterous to suppose that these could be the product of basic biological pairs who had not constituted a wider society; or, indeed, that the mammoth could possibly be hunted, decoyed, trapped and brought home without considerable skilful cooperation by a number of people. The first settlements we know that could qualify as cities (involving walled defences, planned buildings and streets, a complex division of labour and a class structure) were already in existence 6,000 years ago, and at the time

Egypt (not then a city civilisation) was on the way to becoming the first (known) large-scale political kingdom, unified by the Pharoah Narmer, probably in 3064 BC.

In his *Attachment and Loss* Bowlby is at first aware that there were archaic societies of men and apes. But these soon drop out of the picture, leaving the mother and baby in splendid isolation. The source of such faith lies in the fundamental tenet shared by all variants of psychoanalysis that 'child's first human relationship [is] the foundation stone of his personality'.[8]

We come to the next consideration: do we have reason to believe that intensely strong instinctual mechanisms tying the young to mother alone, exist in man during his vulnerable early life? Is there a 'focusing on a figure'[9] (i.e. the mother), shown by human infants in the way Bowlby describes? And is this the basis of later relationships and social responsibility? We will examine these claims apart from the consideration that, even if these did exist in humans in the way in which Bowlby says, it is doubtful that they would be any use as predator-protection without group solidarity.

Sucking, crying, smiling, clinging, babbling and following etc., are all supposed to be the components of a behavioural system having attachment to mother as its goal. As will be apparent from further discussion, only babbling, smiling and perhaps crying, seem to be directly implicated as foundations for human relationships. Both, compared with sucking and clinging, have clear social utility from the beginning and have developmental potential, particularly babbling. Following would seem to imply a pre-existent attachment which itself needs explaining.

Sucking

What evidence is there that the mother must be the one towards whom this is directed, either at birth or well afterwards? Suckling can be done by a wet-nurse, a bottle, an animal. In many tribal societies, group feeding is practised by women, so that those with little milk do not lose their infants and those engaged in agriculture, food gathering, hunting, fishing, or away at a market, are freed from this tie.

Bowlby points to non-nutritional sucking as evidence for sucking having reasons other than nourishment for its existence. But again, non-nutritional sucking is practised on the nipples of men and children, on thumbs, fingers, blankets and dummies. Sucking in young children is accentuated by the provision of plentiful opportunity for its indulgence, so that its frequency is partly due to reinforcement. The aim of sucking would therefore appear to be little else but sucking, and there is nothing that suggests that it has attachment to anyone as an initial or later goal. Is dummy-sucking part of maternal attachment? Will the baby with a dummy only be able to make relationships with dummies later? Wolff[10] showed that attention to other stimuli was low when an infant was hungry or otherwise viscerally excited, so it is difficult to see how sucking can generalise to something as complex as a personal relationship.

In societies where children are allowed plentiful sucking (for example, by breast feeding continuing late into infancy) there is often a problem over breaking the child's well-entrenched habit. It is not observable that the sucking gets transformed into anything else: rather, after a struggle with the child it undergoes extinction, as must any habit faced with continual negative reinforcement. Both cross-cultural and experimental evidence demonstrates the connection between the length of sucking that a child is permitted and weaning difficulties. For example, see Arnold Bernstein 'Some Relations between Techniques of Feeding and Training during Infancy and Certain Behaviour in Childhood', *Genetic Psychology Monographs*, 1955. Here the hypothesis that reinforcement increases the strength of sucking drive was supported by the findings, also that thumb-sucking is encouraged by reinforcing sucking.

Sucking hardly provides any basis for a relationship for the Manu child, when someone else offers more exciting, complex stimulating activities:

Father is obviously the most important person in the house; he orders mother about, and hits her if she doesn't 'hear his talk'. Father is even more indulgent than mother. It is a frequent picture to see a little minx of three leave her father's arms, quench her thirst at her mother's breast,

and then swagger back to her father's arms, grinning
overbearingly at her mother. The mother sees the child
drawn further and further away from her. At night the
child sleeps with her father, by day she rides on his back.
He takes her to the shady island which serves as a sort of
men's club house where all the canoes are built and large
fish traps made ... Father is always in the centre of
interest, he is never too busy to play. Mother is often busy.
She must stay in the smoky interior of the house. She is
forbidden the canoe islands. It is small wonder that the
father always wins the competiton: the dice are loaded
from the start.[11]

And they are clearly not loaded in favour of the sucking
relationship. Ironically (as Margaret Mead pointed out in her
criticism of the Maternal Deprivation Theory[12]), if a society
insists on an indivisible mother-and-infant bond (which
would involve that only the natural mother feed the child),
this would lead to an enormous wastage of children, which in
some circumstances could seriously undermine population
replacement. Whatever the Natural Motherhood people may
say, it is a common observation that the human female is
often not very adept at adequate breast-feeding. The
precariousness of infant life has often been bad enough
without undermining it further by insisting on feeding by the
biological mother; it would usually be quite pointless to let
healthy infants die like this when there are other females
available in human groups to carry out the task. The
insistence of ruling classes on the wet-nurse had the crucial
purpose of guaranteeing the survival of heirs, and was not
necessarily connected with female vanity or laziness. It is
only in modern Western society that the advent of the
sterilised feeding bottle has made the unique inseparable
one-to-one pair a reality for many of the population. (The
tragi-comedy of the situation is that whereas this indivisible
relationship is often only possible with the feeding bottle, the
modern child-care expert often also insists on breast feeding,
upbraiding vast numbers of women for their 'unnaturalness'.
If he were to accept very high infant mortality rates as part
of natural childrearing, then we might be some way along the
road to consistency.)

It is also a very recent aspect of Western society that women have actually had the time available to provide anything like the prescribed unbroken infant—mother bond, with all its recommended ramifications. Women no longer have to grow or gather food, hunt or fish, tend animals, fetch water, grind corn, make pottery or baskets, spin, weave, dye and make up cloth, no longer even have to bake bread, brew beer, preserve meat and fruit and heat water, to name a few of the tasks of the past. Many jobs which women are left with — shopping, washing dishes, dusting, tidying (or their equivalents) — were usually those given to children. Only in the twentieth-century West has a woman's time been freed for constant child-care.

The notion is unfortunately very widespread that the female is economically unproductive out of the natural necessity to devote her time to child-care, and that this has been the pattern since time immemorial. Influences ranging from Desmond Morris to children's reading-books paint a cosy picture of the dependent, immobile, secluded female, being protected and provided for by the productive, active male—whether he leaves home in bearskin or bowler; bringing back woolly mammoth or wages to his cave or semi-detached. If anything, it is the pattern of known primitive and historical societies for female work to be heavy, laborious and virtually unending: once the fields are tilled there is still grain to grind for the evening meal and spinning or mending to fill the spare moments before sleep. Male labours, on the other hand, are often intermittent and short in duration — for example, seasonal hunting of herd animals or fishing trips. It is therefore hardly surprising that in many primitive societies it is usually the men who fill their idle hours with the decorative arts (utility items being made by the women), personal adornment and gossip, with its elaborations into politics, plotting and war. In some societies the latter activities comprise almost the totality of male exertions. This means that in some societies children may be left in the settlements under male supervision when the women go to the fields or markets or gathering food. It is also very common for siblings to bring up the younger children, answering for their behaviour to the adults, as in Samoa;[13] or very common for older women, to mind children when their

mothers are engaged elsewhere, as in the West Indies. A
mixture of sibling and grandmother care was the norm in the
large families of the British industrial working class in the not
too distant past.

In Britain the concept of the secluded, economically
parasitic female confined to child-care and attendant
domestic work is historically very recent indeed, dating from
about the turn of the nineteenth century. With it has gone a
prescribed female personality, a 'femininity', emphasising
physical and mental inferiority and more or less emotional
instability. This personality is then held to make women
unfit for participation in the wider world with all its
demands, stresses and strains, but nonetheless to fit them
very particularly for intuiting and answering the sensitive
needs of small children. It has been the ideal of social
reformers and commentators since the Industrial Revolution
to 'free' all women from the onerous burdens of external
concerns for this devotional attendance in the home.
(Except, of course, in wartime when women are rapidly
mobilised to do almost every job formerly filled by men —
only to be dismissed when peace returns, with the former
insistence that they are really incapable of doing the jobs
they have been doing or do not really want to do them, or
that they will damage their children's personalities if they
do.)

It can scarcely be emphasised too much that all this is a
reversal of the state of affairs pertaining even in the Middle
Ages and after, when both men and women were expected to
be in some form of productive labour. Reproduction was
viewed as something incidental to life, and not as a 'career'
that enabled a withdrawal from the world's work.

Crying

Crying in the very young infant is either a response to pain,
hunger or cold or is maintained simply as a reflexive habit. It
is certainly a powerful signalling mechanism, but it could be
responded to by a variety of individuals, as it frequently can
be throughout life. But at an early age mere proximity to the
mother has no effect on the child's crying, unless followed by
feeding or some other definite comfort. Many cultures have

immobilised infants by swaddling or strapping them to cradleboards, thereby restricting crying.

As the infant gets older his crying can be terminated (at first temporarily, then for longer periods) by auditory and visual stimulations.[14] The attentions of human infants are increasingly caught by 'interesting spectacles' and sounds, particularly those made by the human voice. The infant himself shows a phenomenon known as 'fake' crying before breaking into ordinary crying; vocalisations are made during this (which spectogram analysis has shown to be related to human speech), and once they appear they are likely to be repeated in contexts other than that of crying, often when the infant is alone, but alert. Later, of course, when these sounds become more distinct, parents mimic, reinforce and thus stabilise those necessary for correct speech.

The sensitivity of the infant to objects in the visual field is demonstrated not merely by the way in which sensory experiences can arrest crying, but also, conversely, by how the removal of stimulating objects from the visual field will initiate crying, that is, when a person or attractive toy moves out of range. This tends to illustrate that infants have a sensory sensitivity to complex shapes and sounds before these can be understood by them or used in learning, or before there is much memory capacity. (If a person or toy absent themselves during the infant's sleep, they are not missed on waking, and no distinction is made until the second half of the first year between a stranger or familiar person re-entering the visual field; an infant can remain oriented towards an absent person for hours and sometimes days after his departure.) The older infant also, of course, learns to use crying to get adult attention if he finds that this works to bring him any satisfactions which he may want. These need not all come from, or via, the mother.

Clinging

The presence of clinging in the primate young has lately received considerable prominence in any discussion of basic infant behaviour, and has been widely employed to 'prove' how very tenacious is the mother—infant bond in monkeys (and, by implication, in humans also). This is probably partly because, in clinging, there is positive action on the part of the young to secure closeness to the mother, which can be used as evidence for infant preferences. Clinging in primate young has thus been used to draw attention to the vital importance of bodily contact for future mental health and social capacities, human mothers being accordingly urged to provide plentiful 'mothering', cuddling, holding, etc. This clinging itself is frequently referred to as 'love' or 'affection'.

As clinging (i.e., climbing on to the mother by grasping her fur) is activated by fear in primate young and provides for easy transportation, leaving the mother's arms free, its presence or absence and its usefulness in providing predator-protection ought to clarify some of the claims about its evolutionary advantage for man.

Harlow's[15] experiments with Rhesus monkeys showed that infant monkeys preferred comfortable 'cloth mothers' to cold, uncomfortable wire ones that nevertheless provided food — the conclusion being that the importance of 'mother' lies more in her ability to provide this 'contact comfort' than nourishment. We need not dispute such 'contact comfort' in the Rhesus monkeys. But it has been further inferred by so many people that because it is a source of satisfaction in infancy it must *ipso facto* be important for the future development of Rhesus monkeys — and of humans. Actually Harlow's experiments (quoted above) on monkeys reared in social isolation revealed that, whether they had cloth mothers or wire ones, they were all incompetent sexually and maternally, indicating that comfortable clinging has nothing to do with the monkey's later social abilities. Unfortunately the popularisation of the Harlow experiments has led to the widespread assumption that the two are causally connected.

The capacity of Harlow's Rhesus monkeys for social life appeared to be related to their social learning. If monkeys are reared alone with a real monkey mother rather than a dummy one, they are not so socially incompetent. This is because the mother obviously provides her offspring with some social skills.

That the human infant could be endowed with later personal and social advantages by giving it plenty of what the Rhesus infant likes (bodily contact), is a far-fetched supposition, not only because there is not evidence that this even benefits the Rhesus, but also because newborn human infants do not even cling to the mother, and the human mother herself has nothing for them to grasp, such as fur. Humans have thus lost both the ability and the means to cling in the monkey's manner. The only thing approaching clinging to be found in humans is not seen until the end of the first year of life. At that age, the infant, when frightened, may tend to cling to or hug the nearest familiar person. Thus, during the infant's earliest and most vulnerable period, a most vital aspect of the postulated evolutionary necessity for maintaining maternal proximity for predator-protection, is absent in humans. Surely clinging in the monkey fashion could hardly have had such evolutionary importance if this is the case. On Bowlby's claim, if it had been so drastically necessary, those not carrying the genetic clinging instructions in the first vulnerable year of life should have died out in favour of those who did. Instead, they now constitute normality.

Ironically, Bowlby admits himself that the beginning of attachment behaviour in the human young (that is, the definite appearance of his postulated attachment instincts towards 'the mother') is very difficult to discern: 'Because the human infant is born so very immature and is so slow to develop, there is no species in which attachment behaviour take so long to appear. This is probably one reason why until recent years, the behaviour of the human child towards his mother seems not to have been recognised as belonging to the same general category of behaviour that is seen in so many animal species.' (*Attachment and Loss, p.228*) Even the clinging to a familiar person in response to fear is quite inadequate to enable the child to climb on to its mother by its own efforts. It is also quite common that, despite the presence of familiar people with whom the child has personal relationships, clinging may be to inanimate objects; a toy, a piece of blanket, etc. The futility from a survival point of view of the human infant clinging to the mother's legs or a toy for protection, needs no emphasis.

One reason why we have not died out as a species could be that such instincts as clinging were so long ago rendered redundant for human protection by cultural arrangements. The human young, compared with the young of other primates, is born in a very embryonic condition because of the unusual size of the brain pan which must be delivered. This embryonic condition makes the individual infant extremely helpless; but it is compensated by the far wider cultural possibilities — organisation and artifact — which the large brain opens up among the adult members of the surrounding society. The transport problems posed by the human infant's inability to cling and the disappearance of the furry coat have been solved by various cultural inventions such as slings and cradleboards. The pattern for many cultures has been a lack of maternal and infant physical contact, (except with the nipple), since the practice of swaddling or cradle board strapping prevents it. Mobile and busy mothers and confined, primitive dwellings where most objects, dangerous or precious, are on the floor, all add to the convenience of making a tight bundle of an infant.[16]

Clinging in monkeys and humans is often discussed as part of the behaviour pattern where the older infant likes to keep the mother within sight when he explores the environment, running and clinging if he is frightened. How close the infant stays and how much he clings appears to be related to the attractiveness of other stimuli and to his anxiety about novelty. This behaviour can be manipulated with drugs. Those drugs which raise arousal thresholds (that is, increase indices of extraversion),[17] produce more exploratory behaviour and less worry about the mother's whereabouts, and vice versa for those which increase indices of introversion. Thus the amount of clinging versus exploratory behaviour appears to be partly related to innate personality factors. New environments and experiences (and most of the world *is* new to infants) alert the individual's attention with a mixture of interest and caution until they can be assimilated. Introverts err on the side of caution, while extraverts whose stimulation requirements are so much greater, will be more adventurous (or rash). Caution will obviously encourage proximity to the familiar. It is possible that the clinging has arousal-reducing properties.[18] If the mother is not present monkeys and apes will hug themselves or try to escape from the source of overpowering, frightening stimulation: children hug inanimate objects. If clinging does have arousal-reducing properties, its function is close to that of the deliberate use of swaddling on young human babies.

In the light of these observations, I do not think that the pattern of exploration-clinging requires the rather elaborate, loaded explanation that some have put forward: that the infant is too young to have a proper internal picture, or 'representation' of 'the mother' and thus has to keep running back to her to remind himself. This behaviour seems related to the perceived nature of the general environment, rather than internal to the mother—child relationship.

In some respects, rather than being the basis of primate and human relationships, the clinging response, if too frequently activated, would appear to be antagonistic to their development. Although it helps the animal to stick to the familiar if there is any intimation of danger, the blindly automatic nature of this reaction suggests that it is an instinct with very poor adaptability. For example, the source of fear can be mother herself if she attacks her infant,[19] the infant in turn intensifying its attempts to cling to her—its most disastrous course of action. This is observed experimentally with Rhesus infants of socially deprived mothers who rejected and abused them. Similarly, cases of abusive human mothers tend to suggest that children will sometimes behave in this fashion also. Given that this is so, it is really not permissible to speak of this clinging as mother—infant 'love'.

It would probably be best to try and iron out some of the confusion by postulating a distinction between automatic, arousal-reducing clinging activated by anxiety, and more positive, voluntary forms of physical contact which operate in a safer, more confident atmosphere, for example, social grooming, fondling, cuddling, etc. But whether this has any major or minor importance in the actual formation of the relationships in which it occurs is a complex question. In monkeys social grooming is an important part of social interaction. But for humans, auditory and visual satisfactions and communication overshadow direct physical contacts, which in turn are extensively governed by cultural convention and frequently require learning and practice.

In human cases where child ill-treatment or neglect is suspected, the child's readiness to cling to the mother should be regarded with suspicion rather than with a sentimental response that 'she may be bad but look how the child loves

her.' The mother's abuse, and the child's experience that only
misery is associated with adults, is likely to activate the fear
and blind clinging if anyone tries to take him away. Yet if he
is prised away, subsequent experience is likely to lead to a
radical adjustment to a better situation, and an unwillingness
to return to his former torments.

The less they are in fear and the less they cling, the more
the young of both humans and primates are willing to
explore their environment and, importantly, to take part in
social interaction with peers and other adults. Among wild
monkeys it has often been observed how the offspring of
dominant females are themselves more likely to adopt
leadership roles in later life.[20] It has been suggested that one
of the paramount reasons for this is that mothers whose
status is low and who are near the group periphery are
constantly being frightened by the threats and attacks of
other monkeys, and accordingly emit more alarm calls. This
will cause the infant in turn to spend far more time clinging
to its mother and will restrict its opportunities to learn social
behaviour useful in acquiring a better social position, that is,
the infant becomes socially 'deprived' or backward.
Offspring of low status females remain strongly attached to
their mothers long after their peers are showing more
advanced patterns of social behaviour. Harlow himself
observed how 'too prolonged and intimate contact with the
mother inhibits all types of play responses, even play
responses to the mother.'[21]

Harlow[22] in his studies of the maternal behaviour of
Rhesus monkeys, records that after an initial early phase of
strong protectiveness towards the very young infant (where
the mother dislikes it leaving her immediate proximity and
encourages it to cling), she begins deliberately to break down
this attachment. She threatens, punishes and withdraws from
her infant, often in a most harsh manner, hitting it and
twisting its arms to stop it making contact. At first this will
intensify the infant's attempts to cling, but then the
punishment begins to have its desired effect and the infant
keeps a safe distance. If another infant is born 'this physical
separation is quite traumatic'.[23] But as the infant's attentions
are shifted from the mother they become more involved with
other juveniles and they join the pre-adolescent play groups.

The latter are very important in the socialisation of the Rhesus macaque.

As so many other parallels and recommendations have been drawn and made for human mothers from these monkey studies, it is significant that little attention has been paid to this observation. On the contrary, even those child-care experts who resort to ethology always emphasise the necessity for human parents to make their child feel one hundred per cent wanted. He must never be given the least suspicion that he is rejected, never be made to feel insecure, never be separated from mother or given any reason to fear that separation will ever occur.[24] Indeed, Bowlby emphasises in *Attachment and Loss* the need for mothers to understand the strength of the attachment instinct, and accordingly never to thwart it — a failing to which he attributes all human ills. Yet what the Rhesus mother does is to force her infant to acquire social experience and competence for his later personal and social adequacy, and this is just what the human mother is warned is the very worst course.

Protective clinging observed in primates and residually in older human infants is hardly a basis for relationships. It is largely a crude, atavistic instinct that often has to be weakened in order for social learning to be acquired.

It is, of course, highly likely that the human infant will build a relationship with its own mother, but on a different model from that postulated by this instinct theory. And furthermore this need not be the only early relationship, nor need it form the foundation for later ones unless behaviour has been acquired within it such as can be generalised to these.

The confusion that results from theoretical attempts to make clinging the basis of relationship-building is illustrated by the difficulties of Ainsworth, confronted with the observations that the less attached (that is, children who clung less to mother and appeared to be independent of her) were more capable and advanced than those strongly attached. Somehow she has to square this with Bowlby's theory of the origins of human relationships and personal competence which would predict the opposite. She makes the move of holding detachment to be really a manifestation of deep attachment:

... some of the infants in this study who seemed most solidly attached to their mothers displayed little protest behaviour or separation anxiety, but rather showed the strength of their attachment to the mother through their readiness to use her as a secure base from which they could both explore the world and expand their horizons to include other attachments. The anxious, insecure child may appear more strongly attached to his mother than does the happy, secure child who seems to take her more for granted. But is the child who clings to his mother — who is afraid of the world and the people in it, and who will not move off to explore other things or other people — more strongly attached, or merely more insecure?[25]

Similarly, Bowlby is faced with the problem of the obvious decline of 'attachment behaviour', as the child grows older. If this version of attachment behaviour were not posited as the basis of human relationships it would present no problem; but it is, and so it does. Bowlby admits the decline of attachment behaviour with age; but how is it that as it declines, the capacity to make social relationships apparently increases? Or are adults supposed to be less capable of relationships since they have lost the sucking and clinging reflexes? Bowlby tries to deal with the problem by talking of the ability of the infant to maintain 'proximity' to mother over greater distance and time spans as it matures. And this, Bowlby feels shows that it is still really attached. But what is it doing while it maintains this proximity over distance? If it is engaged in interaction with other humans — as it frequently is — where did this behaviour come from? What has this relationship-building behaviour to do with these attachment instincts? Bowlby's theory does not even begin to explain how this early relationship generalises to any other later ones, just as it cannot adequately account for the existence of more than one relationship in early life.

18   Early Relationships

Although the particular instinct theory I have considered appears inadequate to explain the foundations and growth of social relationships, we cannot fall back upon a 'secondary drive' hypothesis that the child's first relationship emerges out of physical dependence on the person who undertakes his basic care. Too much evidence now tells against this superficially obvious explanation. A more likely one is that attachment to any given individual emerges initially out of the infant's sensitivity, principally, to auditory and visual stimulation. Furthermore, not only is he sensitive, but as stimulus objects, other human beings would be far more likely than inanimate objects to attract an infant's attention. They emit stimulation of a highly complex varied nature, they move, they make noises, and touch the infant. Of the total human person obviously the face is the most mobile, detailed part. Observations show that, for example, young infants pay more attention to a disc with human features[1] painted on it than to other stimuli of similar shape and size. 'Faces' which move are preferred to those that do not,[2] as are three-dimensional heads to flat faces.[3] This is not to say that there is an in-built genetic mechanism in the infant that recognises the human face. Young infants respond equally to real and 'scrambled' representations of the face (where the features are mixed up, multiplied or missing). Where one representation is more complex than the other, this will provoke the stronger response, independent of its authenticity.[4]

It is in the third to sixth months that preference for real faces rather than just any equally complex pattern, starts to appear,[5] [6] so that the infant must be beginning to relate the features visually. At six months two-dimensional faces are no longer sufficient to elicit the automatic smile. These distinctions are made because other human beings are not just an interesting bundle of stimulus attributes, but are also responsive and adaptable, altering their behaviour to comply with that of another, reciprocating and reinforcing many of his responses. Due to this interaction, restrictions begin to take place on the infant's wide stimuli preferences in favour of those which have proved responsive, and these now become increasingly tightly organised.

This narrowing of the range of stimuli required to elicit response is of course made possible by the growth of the infant's perceptual abilities. Infants under two months generally show no habituation, meaning that they cannot differentiate between novel and familiar stimuli, no matter how often and closely presented.[7] The latter are always treated as new events. There is thus no capacity to be affected by previous experience. At around three months infants begin to show the habituation response, after a series of exposures to a given stimulus, alertness declines. This ability to carry forward information increases steadily with age. (But it must be emphasised that this ability to differentiate the familiar from the unfamiliar refers to time spans which are exceedingly short by adult reckoning, matters of seconds and minutes rather than weeks or months, so that if he is to make stimulus distinctions in his everyday life there must be continual reinforcement by plentiful presentations of these.) A baby is in the vicinity of other human beings much of the time, so not surprisingly, the stimulus configurations he responds to begin increasingly to resemble a real person. At the age (three to four months) when perceptual discrimination is beginning, some experiments have shown differential responsiveness to familiar and unfamiliar adults, for example, mother compared with stranger.[8] [9] But in her absence there seems to be no awareness of her; this does not happen until about the age of eight months when proper memory or recall is beginning, in contrast to temporary recognition when in the presence of an object or stimulus.

Having first experienced the stimulating qualities of other people, the infant thus comes gradually to learn to distinguish them as a class of entities in their own right and will come not only to react differently to them compared with inanimate objects, but will also seek their proximity so that he can experience their accommodating attributes. The latter begins to occur in the last half of the first year of life.

A couple of months or more after this, sharper distinctions between the familiar and unfamiliar mean that the infant ceases to smile readily and accept attention from strangers. The appearance of proximity-seeking to familiar people and avoidance of the unknown is again tied to the infant's maturation. Hitherto there has been no tie-up between perceptual faculties and motor control.

The onset of both proximity seeking and so-called 'stranger anxiety' have often been seen as part of a critical period for relationship formation, so that if an infant's attachment is broken afterwards, he cannot form another. An instinctive barrier of fear has been thrown up against strangers, forbidding contact. The period of promiscuous socialising is past and his fate rests with his 'object' choice — for better or worse. Actually, as we have seen, preferences for familiar individuals are unmistakably manifest before 'stranger anxiety' appears. What experimental evidence there is suggests that there is little or no anxiety towards strangers *per se*, but only towards ones that actively, sharply, impinge upon the infant.[10] Obviously strange inanimate objects do not behave in such an aggressively mobile manner and can be explored more at leisure. If a child is given time to examine a more passive stranger before any interaction occurs it is far from axiomatic that fear will be shown.

Even active behaviour on the part of a stranger does not lead to fear reactions in a sizable proportion of infants. (This may be due to innate differences in anxiety levels.) In Schaffer's sample between thirty and fifty per cent of the infants at some point in the study failed to show signs of fear. The early formation of relationships would appear to be more a matter of positive orientation to one or more persons than a repudiation of all others.

In insisting that the outcome of mother–child separation can only be morbid and damaging, the proponents of the Maternal Deprivation Theory do not seem to have considered how very disadvantageous such a response is on the part of the organism in terms of a species' evolution—particularly a social species. If no one else can take the place of a missing mother, this is a grave hazard to physical survival and would result in a great wastage of otherwise healthy young. There is also room for doubt whether creatures with such rigid developmental requirements could ever be capable of social behaviour of the flexibility and diversity shown by *homo sapiens*. (And this when proponents of the Theory are now trying to justify it in ethological terms!) Very rigid attachments, or 'imprinting' of the young on one mother, occurs more commonly the more the species in question is non-social and the young mobile from birth (e.g. ducks). With no one else to protect the young from predators and little or nothing in the way of cultural behaviours to acquire, the advantages of such strong, inflexible ties to keep the young close to the mother outweigh the accompanying disadvantage: that they perish if she does. In human groups, by contrast, the social unit affords protection and is available for substantial substitute care, so that a strong single bond with the natural mother is irrelevant to survival. It would indeed militate against the building and transmission of a culture to possess such a rigid preference for a relationship restricted to one individual, with an incapacity for any others should this be broken. It could be postulated that the more adaptive, inventive and successful a social species, the less it has need for the tight one-to-one bonds and the more the capacity for diverse relationships becomes an asset.

The capacity of the human child quickly to build up alternative or complementary relationships to that with the mother is emphatically not a pathological condition, but a demonstration of the great adaptability, survival potential and cultural possibilities of the human species. We have come to a very sad state of affairs where such natural talents are regarded as symptoms of a sick incapacitated condition, in a species that owes so very much to them.

Obviously the longer and more completely a child is separated, the more he will develop and rely upon other attachments than the maternal one. In the here and now, others are looking after him and providing the environment in which he operates and learns: it is their responses that come increasingly to sustain his behaviour which in turn has become modified to comply with their expectations. The life of the organism, its on-going interaction with its immediate environment, cannot simply be suspended. If the mother is out of sight, she becomes increasingly out of mind, unable to fill his horizons and shape his actions. If she is remembered at all by the child or referred to by his new caretakers, it is, as Bodman suggests in his work on institutionalisation, as 'a mythical figure bearing no more significance than the King or Prime Minister, as far as his personal life is concerned'.[11]

If, at the end of a protracted period of separation, a child no longer recognises his mother, on whose behalf are we pleading when we insist on the need to avoid this? Is it for the child's benefit that he must not be put in danger of 'finally forgetting her and thus breaking the mother–child relationship, the strongest tie in his young life'?[12] If he forgets so quickly and now has alternative ties, then it is most palpably not the strongest tie in his life. It is for the child's benefit indirectly, in that cultural child-care arrangements usually involve legal complexities and in modern times the physical separation of living units; as a consequence, the growth of completely new ties between adults and children which displace the former ones, yet cannot have more than temporary existence, may have to be discouraged. But this view of the child's future welfare is one perceived by far-sighted adults in the light of their society's child-care arrangements, not necessarily as perceived by the primitive opportunism of the adaptive child.

Environmental factors other than the obvious necessity for repeated exposure to another person also influence the onset of specific attachments. Schaffer found in one of his studies[13] that a large amount of social stimulation, independent of who or how many provided it, was more important in the early formation of specific attachments than long exposure to simply a one-to-one relationship. The explanation is that the former provides more experience of the stimulating properties of other humans and leads the infant to seek them earlier in life. One of his groups of infants of eight to ten months had spent much of their previous life in hospital, receiving visits from their mothers but little attention from the nurses; another group of the same age had spent similar periods in a baby-home (because of contact with tuberculosis), where there was no contact with mother, but considerable social interaction with a large number of nurses. On return home, the baby-home group of infants formed attachments far sooner (the result was statistically significant) than those who had been in hospital and in contact only with their mothers.

With whom is the infant likely to form his early relationships? And is this attachment indivisible? Considering that in our culture most children are likely to be with their mothers, and their mothers alone for most of the time, observations show that single attachments are surprisingly rare, and primary attachments need not be directed only to the mother. Referring to his research on infant attachment behaviour Schaffer has this to say:

> In the first place, we have encountered very few instances where the mother is the *only* person to whom the infant under twelve months shows attachment behaviour. From the very beginning of this particular phase of development it appears to be the rule rather that the exception that several individuals are selected as the objects of the infant's attachment responses, that protest at being left in one or another of separation situations investigated by us is evoked by a number of persons and not just by one.[14]

The attachment behaviour can be more frequently and intensely shown to the father (very common), a sibling, or an outsider; no less than one-fifth of the persons selected by the infants in this study for principle attachments did not participate even in the most minor way in child-care:

> One of our most striking examples is provided by the infant who showed far more intense attachment behaviour towards the ten-year-old girl living next door than towards the members of his own family — despite the greater availability of his parents, and despite the fact that the neighbours' daughter never fed him and rarely cuddled him (but she did carry him around a great deal).[15]

'Despite the greater availability of the parents': this observation is common in the studies. Again, this would work against the notions that attachment behaviour exists to keep 'proximity to mother' which is a 'predator-protection', since it is so often shown to other people who are not there most of the time, such as the father. What, then, is it that causes an infant to attach to one person rather than another, or render one attachment stronger than another?

The studies of attachment behaviour point to the conclusion that it is not bodily care or satisfactions that are relevant, but rather the amount of social interaction a person is willing to take part in with an infant. People not only are and do interesting things themselves, they are also a source of all manner of novelties and can provide a variety of pleasurable and exciting experiences. The girl next door in Schaffer's study was willing to carry the baby around, which would particularly have provided him with varied visual stimulation; the Manu father wins the child's attention by providing a variety of experiences which the mother cannot. Learning involves the ability to discriminate, and those who do not reciprocate the infant's attentions and provide him with stimulating experiences will come to be ignored or avoided in favour of those who do.

The child's specific attachments will obviously also depend upon his personality and the personalities of those who surround him. Yarrow[16] has drawn attention to the role played by the personality of the child in forming relationships. For example, he compared two children occupying the same foster home: one a passive baby with a very low level of responsiveness to his environment who showed no initiative in social interaction, and the other an active, forward, highly responsive infant, who took the initiative in interpersonal contact. Despite the fact that these two shared the same environment, as time wore on the first child was increasingly isolated, negatively evaluated and provided with no stimulation, whereas the second was related to as an individual and family member, extensively played with and pleased by all the household who made plans for his future.

Freedman[17] has claimed that a genetic component in basic sociability is in evidence from earliest infancy. In his study, correlation between the age when visual orientation to others, such as smiling, appeared, was higher for identical than for fraternal twins.

A similar experiment by Scarr[18] involving personality ratings of identical and fraternal twin girls revealed that sociability was probably a strongly inherited trait. Apart from this general sociability, there are, of course, a multitude of other individual differences which determine the attractiveness or otherwise of contact with certain people. The importance of these will increase with age, not only because of maturation, but also because of the complexities of each person's experience and education. Even in infancy change or multiplication of initial attachments are common. Three months after the onset of specific attachments only forty-one per cent of Schaffer and Emerson's[19] sample had one relationship. A year and a half later this percentage had decreased to thirteen! And this is in the urbanised West with largely nuclear households. The capacity of the infant and the child for a number and a variety of relationships has been (rather dogmatically) under-estimated. The attraction of individuals other than the mother may partly be accounted for by the fact that the activities which comprise the mother—wife role in our society may be soon seen as rather limited. Fathers, for example, have access to a far more varied, exciting world. Similarly, many children on starting school quickly find that they have more interest in the teacher than in their parents — particularly where there is a big gap between parent and child in intelligence and/or personality.

At several points in *Attachment and Loss* Bowlby emphasises the great virtue of generality in scientific theories, and claims that his theory exhibits this. But it is difficult to avoid the conclusion that the kind of generality he has in mind is only achieved by extending definitions in a way that empties them of informative content. Thus, he finds some children who are undoubtedly attached to their mothers, and takes these cases as confirming his thesis. He then, say, finds children who are attached quite happily to fathers, grandparents, and so on. These other individuals are dubbed 'surrogate mothers', or 'mother figures' or 'attachment figures', and so still confirm his thesis. This kind of procedure is illustrated in his discussion of Schaffer and Emerson's study of Scottish infants,[20] most of whom showed multiple attachments at the age of eighteen months. Instead of taking this as a serious *prima facie* counter-example of the 'single attachment figure' thesis, Bowlby (endorsing Ainsworth's procedure) looks more closely at this plurality of attachments; notes that they are not entirely equal in 'intensity'; arranges them in hierarchical order of 'intensity'; and then in effect strikes all off the list except the top one — the 'primary attachment figure' — and considers the thesis not at all disturbed. Given such laborious *post hoc* defensive work, there is, as Ainsworth says, nothing in these observations strictly inconsistent with the theory that the infant will seek attachment with 'one' figure. But good scientific theories are simply not those which, by heavy qualifications and appendages after the event, can be somehow arranged not to contradict experimental data. They are those which retain tightly restrictive definitions and concepts, yet still find the predictions from these corroborated by such data.

Together with the assertion of the importance of the child's relationship with his mother, comes the information that the first relationship(s) is/are vital for all later ones. But is the assertion correct? And if so, what is it in this early relationship which generalises to others? In contradiction of accepted ideas, one can point to a number of dramatic examples where an early, very satisfactory relationship (in terms of the individuals concerned), led to little or no later abilities for building other relationships.

Among the Manus, for example, the young child's highly enjoyable relationship with its father must be contrasted with the observation that Manu adults are hostile and suspicious towards each other. Unable to express affection or sympathy, at worst violent and at best pathetically clumsy in interpersonal behaviour, the Manus society keeps together largely on the basis of ritualised property transactions.[21]

Nearer home, a detailed study of 'problem families' by Harriette Wilson[22] is illustrative of the argument that early relationships are not necessarily the basis of social competence or responsible moral behaviour. The study, which appeared in 1962, was designed to establish the relations between parental neglect and delinquency in a sample of extreme multi-problem families. Wilson studied fifty-two families who had been referred to the Medical Officer of Health (Chairman of the local Coordinating Committee) as showing evidence of child neglect. Her selection of these fifty-two was on the basis of a set of symptoms of inadequate performance within the areas being provided for by the machinery of the welfare state. All symptoms were of social performance (as opposed to personality traits, for example), all were such as could be properly ascertained and corroborated, and all were observed over a number of years. The symptoms were headed solvency, health, education, and whether or not a formal case had been opened with the NSPCC. Each of the first three symptoms broke down into various indices. These were carefully checked and cross-checked, and only those which had been observed for a lengthy period — that is, well over a year — were included; all temporary difficulties were dismissed. For inclusion in the study of these fifty-two families, the score for inadequacy had to be consistently high.

The total number of children in these grossly negligent families was very high (386), giving an average of 7.4 children per family. Thirteen families had ten or more children. The conditions in which many of the children lived are apparent from the following typical reports:

'Case 38 . . . whole property in disgraceful condition, walls badly soiled, furniture a very poor standard . . . Bedding very dirty, walls verminous. On opening the children's bedroom I found it impossible to enter owing to the revolting smell . . . Two single beds with filthy bedding, and the floor covered in excreta. Children in neglected and dirty condition. Case 37 . . . I learned that no provision had been made for the coming child despite the fact that the pre-maternity grant had been received and spent . . . I found that four of the chairs and one double bed had been chopped up and used for firewood. I also found that the top of a brand-new washing board had been chopped up and that floor boards had been taken up and used for the fire . . . When the midwife came to the house the mother was in labour and she was in bed with the other three children. The three children had to be bundled upstairs and laid on a cold bed with no coverings to get them out of the way. The midwife had to get coal from next door to have a fire to get hot water. (Probation Officer's report)[23]

The amount of delinquency was enormous. Among the boys, it was eight times higher for the 8—13 age group than the average for the city, and in the 14—17 age group, seven times higher. The girls' rate of delinquency was one-third of the boys' (the national average for female delinquency was one-tenth of male delinquency). Even when compared with control groups from two highly delinquent areas in the city, the research group came off worse. Larceny was the commonest offence, and breaking and entering followed.

Wilson found that in her sample only one boy had spent a period in a children's home when under five: he became delinquent, but so did his two brothers, who had remained at home. Many of the delinquents were certainly 'without shame or sense of responsibility':

> Case 51 . . . James appears to have no sense of guilt, but he feels it is his right to have money for the cinema. He goes every night . . . James's creed is now 'I see, I want, I take.' If he remains in this environment there is little one can do. (Probation Officer's report)[24]

However, this shamelessness was easily combined with the capacity for affection in the children, as the capacity of the parent to produce a delinquent child was easily combined with indulgent affection for it. Many of the mothers were very affectionate to their children and the children in turn liked them. But in addition to being delinquent, the children frequently found relationships with other adults and children outside the family an impossibility. In school they were either aggressive, or frightened and subdued, hardly able to make themselves understood by the teachers or the other children. Yet, in contrast to this failure in social relationships outside the home, they had very close ties with their sibs as well as their parents, using forms of communication that had grown up in that household and were limited to it.

An adult who interacts with a child certainly might, knowingly or not, shape that child's behaviour and expectations. He will reinforce and elicit certain modes of behaviour in the child and discourage others. A pattern of mutually sustained behaviour can thus grow up between the child and those to whom he is attached which further elaborates, extends and differentiates this tie in comparison with other peripheral contacts. But the interpersonal behaviour built up in this initial relationship (or relationships) may be more or less idiosyncratic to the relationship or household concerned, having little tendency to impart to the young child behaviour applicable to the building of other ties. In addition, the physical isolation of the child may militate against him gaining the necessary learning to make the initial personal approaches to others. He may thus be poorly equipped to establish alternative or supplementary relationships. I suggest that an early relationship simply in itself, no matter how intense and mutually satisfactory, confers on the participants no particular ability for other personal or social relationships. It will not do so unless some behaviour applicable to a wider variety of relationships is learnt in the context of this. The children in Stacey's study,[25] who had very close relationships with their mothers, rarely being separated (so that extra-familial experience was denied), and treated according to a permissive regime that was unlikely to have taught many specific rules for social intercourse, were socially less skilful than those with extra-familial experience and more explicit teaching.

Of course, the situation (described in the discussion of institutions, chapters 8 & 9) can also exist where nobody or scarcely anyone has reciprocated the child's attentions and thus allowed no learnt social behaviours to emerge, whether idiosyncratic or generalisable. This would happen with rejecting parents, who want little or no contact with the child.

In Wilson's study[26] the factors most strongly associated with the children's anti-social conduct and inadequacies were the lack of supervision exercised by parents whose control was lax or erratic. Then there was the isolation of the problem family from the larger kin group and the community at large. The children did not have the opportunity to learn from a variety of people sharing and enforcing the same norms of conduct, and dull parents had no familiar people to copy and emulate — people who in a more traditional community might if necessary interfere in a family if the parents were obviously failing to cope and conform to some standards.

The Manu child is also taught no generalised social skills, no concern, responsibility or altruism for others in the context of its strong attachment to its father. That a Manu adult will spend so much time amusing an infant in a society where friendliness between adults is an aberration, is indicative of the fact that he can only communicate with someone else on an elementary level. With other adults he would not know where to start and would undoubtedly be misunderstood. Mead comments that, unlike other societies she has studied, Manu children can play all the time: 'The only convention of the child's world is a play convention'; to expect a child to undertake a small task or mind a sibling is felt to be a 'terrible intrusion upon the children's leisure [which] must be avoided at all cost'.[27] Children do not have to defer to the wishes of adults if they do not want to, which is usual. Instead adults have to comply with a child's demands as and when they are made. Growing up is bitterly resented and the children possess an 'habitual contempt for grown-up life.'[28] To all questions about commerce, the children answer furiously: "How should we know—who's grown up here anyway, we or you? What do you think you are to bother us about such things! It's your business, not ours." '[29] Yet the environment in which Manu children grow up is virtually the ideal 'child-centred' one advocated by Western educationalists, a world where 'The whole adult scheme is phased in terms of children's claims upon it.'[30] There is this striking appreciation of children's 'needs', and few children are given such a stimulating environment for play:

Here in Manus are a group of children, some forty in all with nothing to do but have a good time all day long. The physical surroundings are ideal, a safe shallow lagoon, its monotony broken by the change of tide ... They are free to play in every house in the village, indeed the reception section of the house is often hung with children's swings. They have plenty of materials at hand, palm leaves, raffia, bark, seeds, ... red hibiscus flowers, coconut shells, pandanus leaves, aromatic herbs, pliant reeds and rushes.

> They have material in plenty with which they could imitate any province of adult life . . .[31]

But they didn't. Instead, 'Their play was the most matter of fact, rough and tumble, non-imaginative activity imaginable',[32] they had no dances, no guessing games, no riddles, no puzzles, no stories, no legends, no folklore, no clubs or societies, no use for art, nothing but a few incredibly monotonous chants and a limited language, deplete of imagery. As Mead says, this was no comment on their minds, but on the way in which they were brought up.

Useful social skills have to be taught; so also does a rich and varied linguistic expression and the accumulated heritage of any culture, its traditions, literature, arts, crafts, history, in any form, on any level. A child's needs of the moment have little future, and an education determined by these is a contradiction in terms. Cultural accomplishments and knowledge, and particularly the adult state itself, if they are to be handed on, must be seen as something worthy of emulation. This in turn means that they cannot logically have a status inferior or equal to childish wants and expressions.

A most vital part of the deliberate transmission of a civilised human culture is the teaching of rules of social morality. In Manus the doting father continually gives all sorts of exciting and varied experiences at the child's slightest whim, withholding little. Wants are instantly gratified and denied only for the single purpose of protecting property: thus it is not surprising that this is the only thing ever accorded deference and respect.

Small-scale societies, where individuals dwell openly in close proximity to each other, obviously provide easy opportunity for a child to acquire the behaviour necessary for his adequate functioning in that society or parts of it. But even in such societies we find quite detailed specialisation occurring in political, military, legal and ritual spheres. (The tendency is increasingly more pronounced where geographical and population size are greater.) These are tasks, far more than the economic division of labour, which require quite sophisticated abilities in order to understand, manipulate and control the affairs of men. Skill and confidence in handling human relationships are at a premium, and the people who have them, or can acquire them readily, will be at an advantage in competing for position. Ruling groups pass on their status to their descendants not only by buttressing their positions with wealth, force, ritual and religious blessing, but also by insisting that their children acquire wide and subtle social skills, and the confidence and experience to use them in widely different contexts.

In human societies, primitive and historical, insistence on a complex socialisation by ruling groups is too widespread to list. Almost everywhere there are attempts to exploit human cultural ability by copying the innovations and skills of others. Thus, the princes of the Near East sent their sons to the courts of Pharaoh to acquire the manners, diplomatic and political skills and literate communication to which they ascribed their rival's ascendancy. Perhaps the most striking example of formal child-exchange (which demonstrates a clear awareness of the social and cultural benefits of shared socialisation), is the giving of children as hostages following kin feuds in Saxon and Norse times in British history. Indeed it was common to possess a foster father (as well as natural parents) with whom much of childhood would be spent. In addition to constructively healing conflicts, the placement of children in households of greater status and educational accomplishment was eagerly sought by parents since it provided almost the only way to acquire socially advantageous manners, skills and experience. The large, open households of chieftains provided a similar learning environment to all the children of the various social strata who lived under their roofs. As an example, the great Icelandic scholar, historian, politician and lawyer, Snorri Sturluson — the 'Norse Leonardo' — was fostered as a favour to his parents by the most powerful, highborn chieftain in Iceland, Jón Loptsson. Sturluson probably acquired much of his knowledge of the classics, Norwegian history and law, as well as sharpening his remarkable talents for political intrigue in Loptsson's household.)

All over Africa there are traditions of sending children away to live with relatives,[33] often so that they can learn specialised skills. Sons of chiefs may be reared in the households of officials who will teach them their duties. Some tribes have a complex web of ties built up over vast distances due to the practice of rearing another's child.[34] Such placements are cultivated because they increase alliances and prevent potentially dangerous culture divisions and misunderstandings.

In medieval towns the guilds developed as organisations concerned with a variety of social, religious, legal, artistic and economic functions, besides skilled manufacturing. The form of child exchange which transmitted the urban culture of the guild life was the institution of apprenticeship. Here a child or adolescent left his parents to live with a fully qualified adult member of the guild, (the master-craftsman), who taught him not merely the 'mysteries' of the particular skill, but who was also to supervise and discipline the rest of his social development so that he would later be able to participate conscientiously in guild and civic life.

Long after the decline of the medieval guild system it was still the custom in pre-industrial Britain in both rural and urban districts for parents to 'apprentice' their children in an informal manner in a household of slightly more wealth, higher social status and educational level than their own. This happened all the way up the social hierarchy. Children would thus have the opportunity to acquire manners and skills wider than those their parents had to offer. This would also supply the important cement of mutually understood and shared values and norms, both geographically and throughout the different social strata.[35]

The end of these arrangements for child exchange, caused by the disruption and growth of population in the nineteenth century, saw the spread of private family life in the middle classes, which was eventually to evolve into the distinctive nuclear family of the twentieth century. But this brought with it problems of socialisation. Indeed, the undermining of ascribed status and the ending of purchase of public and professional office, made high-level capacities and skills crucial for achievement in a competitive world. More expertise was being asked while the opportunities to acquire it were being severely diminished. The middle-class answer was a salvaging and drastic overhaul of the old public school system. In the absence of the open household, guild or community of the past, formal institutions for socialisation and cultural transmission had to fill the void. These ceased simply to issue tickets for ancient universities to the aristocracy, and became places that taught moral and social duties, norms and values (built a 'character') as well as broadening their academic syllabuses. Boarding was an important aspect of the public school and its arrangements were to be extended rapidly to cover young children (the prep school).

The nineteenth-century working classes had also lost the cultural framework provided by their rural villages. Exploited and cowed during their long hours of work, their recreation was often a chaotic search for crude gratification. Personal relationships were frequently brutal and irresponsible. But although the ruling class regarded the working class as irresponsible, irreligious, drunken and violent, for the most part it opposed any widespread plan to socialise working-class children by a formal school system, as it had done for its own offspring, out of an astute self-interest. The a-cultural and almost a-social mob was preferable to an educated and responsibly organised proletariat. And for the very same reason, from the opposite viewpoint, reformers, radicals and trade union leaders pinned the greatest hopes of working-class advance on a formal education system. It was the gradual achievement of this that largely enabled the working class to become effective as a serious and organised social force. It began, as all such efforts at self-improvement must, with a copying of the values of the class above — respectability, thrift, piety and temperance. But the attainment of stable socialisation brought individual and collective benefits which long outlasted and outweighed these achievements.

This brief review of some historical arrangements for teaching and socialising children demonstrates that something far more vital than individual advantage depends on interaction with many individuals other than the biological mother, and that is the transmission of the intricate structure of behaviour that constitutes any human culture. Cultural accumulation and evolution have been vital and unique to man: yet each human being starts life as untutored as the first hominid millions of years ago in the processess of his culture. These have to be transmitted afresh to each individual by lengthy and complex teaching of the culture's life, work, ideas, skills, values and normative rules, by exposure to a variety of learning environments and a diversity of older individuals. They will take the young through the necessary steps for competent interaction with people and participation in the society's procedures and institutions. The more complex the culture, the more such effective transmission requires a great diversity of people and situations. The heart of the cultural process lies in relating and coordinating many individuals with each other, thus enabling them to participate in a lasting form of life far richer and broader than the confined span of their own isolated, direct personal experiences.

I have stressed how recent and how unusual is the modern nuclear family as a primary situation of socialisation. In the past in Britain privacy in the modern sense was virtually unknown: households, if not large, were still open and most relaxation was necessarily communal. In many other societies people have been born and reared, they have eaten, slept, worked, amused themselves and died practically in public. Because of this, children were provided with ample contact with a large number of adults and other children, often of different social levels. Where communal living declined historically, more formal and deliberate arrangements were, as we have seen, set up for child-exchange to accomplish what had previously happened as a feature of everyday life.

So, the process of cultural transmission depends in essence on some form of child exchange: exchange for the child of people, situations, learning environments. A 'socialisation' that provides only a basis of idiosyncratic interaction with one biological parent is no foundation at all for human participation in a cultural process: no common ground for communication, let alone any mutually coordinated and beneficial intercourse with others, could result from this.

It is often asserted, with obvious reference to man, that the more developed the species, the more it is dependent on lengthy learning processes and therefore, the longer is the requirement for maternal dependence. Such an argument could scarcely be more totally and disastrously false.

The tendency not to associate standardised cultural learning with human relationships is frequently due either to an assumption that somehow the term 'relationships' refers only to those within the family, or that there is a complete difference in essence between 'superficial' social intercourse and 'deep' personal relationships and that it is these that really matter.

But the most personal of relationships is dependent upon a vast amount of learnt expectations, assumptions, interests, attitudes, modes of conduct and techniques of communication (not least language). Romantic love, for example, is a comparatively recent cultural phenomenon, originating in literary invention. This is not to doubt the role of innate, particular factors in personal compatibility, but these are only given expression through acquired knowledge and conduct. The housewife who feels she has little to contribute in her personal relationships because she can bring no extra-domestic experience to these, is a case in point. One may think that the mysticism of the hermit who turns aside from institutional religion is the ultimate in individualism; but religion in any form, including the visions of the mystic, is a social manifestation *par excellence,* and this determines its form and content.

No relationship is purely formal or individualised. The relationship with an official or employer may be contractual or obligatory but his personal characteristics still partly determine how we behave towards him. A fellow guildsman or merchant can be both a companion and a business associate; a retainer may love the lord whom he is bound to obey, and so forth. We all recognise that there are people whom we only wish to acknowledge on a formal basis, those we might have an occasional drink or chat with, those we spend an evening with, and so on.

The existence of formal codes of behaviour establishes and regulates contact between people so that more particularized associations can grow. The absence of a radical split between personal relationships and everyday social interactions (including those with strangers), is illustrated by the success of behaviour therapy with people who cope poorly with interpersonal situations. Instructions and practice on how to handle encounters at work, in shops, restaurants, etc., also bring about an improvement in more intimate relationships. This improvement is seen, too, in the often dramatic changes in people from a background that deprived them of much in

the way of social skills when they enter the rather formal
environments of army, college, apprenticeship, etc. Appeals
of orthodox psychotherapy to 'change emotional
orientations' are likely to be singularly useless when faced
with the same problem. Prompting people to 'show
affection', 'love', 'make friends', etc., is not helpful advice
when these are just what the person desperately wants to do,
but does not know how to begin. Society regulates all kinds
of complex and necessary relationships between its members,
not just by providing opportunities for the emergence of
personalised ties, but also by setting appropriate limits to
these ties.

The idea that human relationships are basically
'monotropic' is absurd for a number of reasons. In envisaging
the pattern of our relationships as a kind of hopscotch from
child—parent to husband—wife to parent—child it fails
completely to explain how individuals can possibly live as
part of any society which must by its nature demand a
complex arrangement of interpersonal ties. The assumption
that these three relationships are somehow primeval, basic
and natural — an original archetypal family — does not bear
close examination. If, for example, it was 'natural' to have a
life-long monogamous association with a member of the
opposite sex, then there would scarcely have been the need
for the institution of marriage. Indeed, in many societies
marriage has been one of the most role-bound and formal of
relationships, enmeshed with elaborate kin regulations, with
obligations for the support of the young and old, with
patterns of stable inheritance, with the performance of ritual
and religious duties, economic tasks and so forth. The form
which marriage takes, and the rights and duties of the spouses
are set by morality, custom and law—not vice versa. It is
frequently seen as too important for even the choice of
partner to be left to the potential spouse. Polygamy has been
very common, as has concubinage, restrictions on them in
many societies being due more to limited wealth then
'monotropy'. It is not usual for parties to be allowed to
separate at will, as friends might do in a more personalised
informal relationship. In many societies it is outside marriage
that affectionate, personalised relationships occur: little
interest is shown in regulating these since they serve no other

predominant function beyond the individual happiness and companionship of the people concerned. Even where the wife is considered as an individual there are still times, even in our society, when she will be simply wife *qua* wife, and as such interchangeable in this role with others. A man may be liked as a friend, but labelled a 'bad husband'.

Again, there are plenty of societies in which the most important relationships, formal and informal, are considered to have virtually nothing to do with the home. In the Greek *polis,* public life was everything and the home little more than a breeding place (certainly not a place for personal attachment). Aristotle, indeed, defined man as a 'political creature'.[36]

Due to a variety of social changes, the relationship between husband and wife in the modern West is moving towards that of a voluntary friendly association with few formal components. But it is doubtful whether the relationship between parents and children could, or should, become as informal as this. Children are not chosen, although genetic inheritance frequently gives some compatibility. Children are dependent and require extensive physical care and protection. A child must be controlled by someone or some others until he can behave responsibly without supervision. He must learn a variety of skills and behaviours for which guardians will be responsible to a greater or lesser extent. The care of children must therefore involve some obligatory undertaking on the part of parents and/or other specific adults to provide some or all of these things. And furthermore, the ability to do this must involve passing on quite detailed child-care procedures, even for elementary tasks, to these adults, which will in turn enable them to care for and socialise the child.

It is no coincidence that we find that parents of battered and neglected children are likely to be on average much younger than others and socially more isolated.[37] [38] In other cultures where teenage (or child) marriage is practised, the couple live under the strictest supervision of elders who make sure that the infant is reared in the prescribed manner. Where there have been nuclear households (for example, in pre-industrial Britain),[39] these were open to the wider community and, furthermore, later marriage was the norm.

Expecting young, relatively unsocialised humans to rear their own young in isolation is simply asking for the same parental behaviour as Harlow found in his isolated monkey mothers.

But, unfortunately, bad parental behaviour and other deviance is accounted for almost wholly in terms of acquired emotional deficiencies, rather than in terms of non-acquired learning (as are most failures to learn social skills).

It is frequently maintained that bad parents had bad parents (in the sense of being cruel and neglectful), and one should therefore not really be surprised at their behaving as they do. Whether this is so or not,[40] the causal connection postulated is the same erroneous one used to account for the maternal failings of Harlow's monkeys. The mother, monkey or human, was not 'mothered' herself when young, and so she cannot pass this 'mothering' to her offspring. This presupposes an accumulated store of 'mothering' experiences, largely unremembered, but nonetheless kept somewhere (in the unconscious?), exerting an automatic effect on a mother's responses to her infant. But as we have already seen, the isolated monkey was a bad mother because she had no opportunity to interact with other monkeys and learn from them how to look after an infant.

In human beings, child-care is a culturally acquired skill like any other, yet we persist in believing in a maternal instinct, maturing in a correct emotional atmosphere during the mother's babyhood. Child-care varies enormously from society to society, and does not come naturally, even to apes and monkeys who even have to learn how to hold an infant.[41] Expecting good child-care from untaught, isolated parents is something no other society has ever demanded.

The answer does not lie in psychotherapy to replace the mother's missing mothering, or even in attempts to evoke more love, more empathy between mother and baby. Given that there are people low in sociability, aggressive and retarded, who ideally should not be in unsupervised contact with children in the first place, positive emotions, even if they can be evoked, are still not enough. More good might come from teaching a practical, basic regime of child-care which, if consistently applied, would replace chaos with predictability, and frustration and ignorance with an ability to cope. Mother and child might then get on more smoothly together and comprehend each other better.

19   Love and Goodness

... anyone who is to listen intelligently to lectures about
what is noble and just and, generally, about the subjects of
political science must have been brought up in good habits.
For the fact is the starting-point, and if this is sufficiently
plain to him, he will not at the start need the reason as well;
and the man who has been well brought up has or can easily
get starting-points.

Aristotle, Nichomachean Ethics

We have discussed the operation of social norms on
individuals, and we must now consider the closely related
question of how moral norms come to be acquired and
adhered to. This is all the more important because the
tradition of psychoanalysis has badly distorted much of our
moral vocabulary. Words such as 'guilt' 'shame' and
'conscience' have come to seem closely connected with
psychological reactions to particular individuals or incidents,
and hardly anything to do with moral rules in themselves.

But first it must be reiterated that before a child is able to
acquire complex ideas of any sort, moral or factual, a vast
amount of behavioural learning (of the stimulus—response—
reinforcement kind) must already have taken place. There is
an elementary groundwork of regular behaviour, compliance,
expectation and interaction with adults which must be laid
before a child can benefit from more developed teaching.

Many popular theories attempting to explain how some
people grow up to be morally good whereas others become
immoral or delinquent, frequently take the form of a
stockpiling hypothesis. If the growing person imbibes an
appropriate quantity of something, he will correspondingly
give it out in later life. The materialistic version of this is that
an unspecified level of affluence, particularly during
childhood, will produce people who are generous in their

turn. But by far the most widespread version of the stockpiling hypothesis is the love version: that social morality and responsibility in a person come more or less directly from having been loved as a child. Those who took in sufficient quantities of love at the critical early stages, will have a lot to give out later. Bowlby refers to 'spiritual nourishment' and elsewhere other writers continually talk of love being as necessary as food. Furthermore, if this 'need' for love goes unsatisfied, it is envisaged as growing in urgency and strength, and actually accumulating inside the child, who will later have almost insatiable requirements for love, so that he may hoard this commodity (if it is then available). On the other hand, those who have been able to hoard love early in life, can distribute it later (like food parcels). The infant who did not receive enough love from his mother will have little to distribute later, whereas the one who was well stocked will be able to be generous. This generosity with love is what is supposed to constitute social morality. The miserly end up in prison or the reformatory.

This kind of quantitative account, whereby love is almost like a physical fuel, has been very popular and influential in one version or another. It seems related to the notion of libido, and shares the defects of that concept.

Metaphors like hunger-drive are only useful in describing the effects on behaviour of environmental conditions operating through rather short time spans, after which the behaviour index returns rapidly to base level after the drive conditions are removed, and there are no residual effects that could accumulate over time.

It must be repeated that for young children, the only environmental process known to influence behaviour over long time spans is behavioural learning — the systematic modification of responses by reinforcers. If those environmental stimuli loosely called 'love' and 'mothering' — caressing, cuddling, etc. — do not enter into learning sequences as elicitors or reinforcers of behaviour, they will simply have no future effects, however intensely communicated. There is simply no mystical, hidden process whereby, for example, cuddling at six months is somehow transformed into a tendency to trust and responsiveness towards humanity at twenty years.

I have perhaps represented a particularly crass example of what I call the stockpiling hypothesis, dealing only with young infants. But it is reflected also in much literature concerning slightly older children who have come to use language and to form distinct relations with adults. The effective, positive reinforcers for infants are relatively simple pleasures, such as coloured moving object, pleasing combinations of shapes and sounds,cuddling and stroking etc. In the same way affection, praise, attention and a host of other things come to serve as generalised reinforcers for the older child. It is scarcely necessary to repeat that all manner of things can act as effective reinforcers depending on the capacities of the child, its past learning, its personality and so on.

Now, some variant of the theory that a loving early environment produces a good adult, has often seemed to be borne out by innumerable cases where, in fact, such a person did enjoy a happy, loved early childhood. But it is crucial that the way this happens be correctly understood. In such a home the positive reinforcers of attention and approval (as opposed to merely negative ones of avoidance of punishment) will have been employed at an early stage to instil conformity with, and adherence to, moral norms that are generally praiseworthy. But what is really central to the process is not that the reinforcers are loving ones, but that it is that particular behaviour, those particular values, which they are being used to reinforce. From this it follows that love could equally well be used to reinforce all kinds of other behaviour. Its effectiveness is not intrinsically connected with the kinds of ends it is employed to achieve. These ends are determined by the parents or educators, and their cultural norms. If the parents are criminals, or fierce anti-Semites or admirers of violence, the most likely effects of their love will be to reinforce and reproduce their criminality, anti-Semitism or taste for violence — unless their child is fortunate enough to come under some counteracting influence outside the parental home. Very many of the most appalling criminals have had happy and loving childhoods. They loved their parents in return, often most devotedly, but did not care in the least for anyone else.

Many people would like, understandably, to believe that if

a child has a loving relationship in his home, this will naturally generalise to other people, by a kind of association. Having trusted, loved and been loved in his relation with his parents, he will naturally be trusting and loving towards people in the outside world. But if this happens it will be because he has learnt such behaviour towards outsiders, by emulating his parents and receiving encouragement for it. He could perfectly equally be taught mistrust and hostility to all outsiders, who are completely distinguished in his mind from his own loving parents. The point is that the extent to which love and trust towards parents is allowed to generalise, the size of the group who are eligible to be loved and trusted, is set entirely by what lessons the parents impart about the outside society.

But surely, people feel, love is the very stuff of human goodness and worth, the central part of Christian and humanist ethics. How can it be unconnected with the development of morally good people?

Our ethical values place a very high priority on individual happiness and fulfilment; and for most people an important part of such happiness and fulfilment is to love and be loved by other particular people. But this does not mean that the good person is one who loves everybody. That would be logically impossible, for to love everybody means to love nobody in particular, except in the very extended sense in which someone is said to 'love' truth, beauty, mankind and so forth. The good person would be one who tried to bring about a world where everyone does enjoy the love of someone. That is, he has come to see the happiness of each individual as equally important, regardless of whether he personally likes or dislikes them, or even knows them.

The previous consideration about the part played by love in learning, served to demonstrate that, while children being loved and happy is a good end in itself, there is no necessary reason why it should create morally good and responsible adults. Love is personal and particular, while morality is essentially impersonal and general. Indeed, there is something disturbing in the suggestion that love for children should somehow have to depend for its *raison d'être* on psychological considerations of mental and social health — as if we were puzzled as to why children should be made happy,.

and needed the great therapeutic benefits pointed out to us, in case we might cease to care about the matter. If it is not obvious to anyone why it is better for a child to have affection and companionship rather than unkindness and loneliness, then no psychological discoveries are going to convince them.

Making a child happy need not necessarily be combined with effective moral teaching and upbringing, but is an independent end, desirable in itself. Nor need it be equated with the kind of love so strenuously urged by the child-care textbooks, namely continuous attention and protection by one or at most two parents with whom the child is supposed to form a completely monopolistic attachment. It is equally possible for siblings, grandparents or other children or adults in the immediate circle to provide the early personal relationships that are usually part of a happy childhood. And it is quite possible for some parents, who might be considered cold and unresponsive towards their children, to produce far more considerate, socially competent and responsible individuals, than those who provide their children with plentiful attention, interest and indulgence. The sparing attentions of the former enter into the child's behaviour to shape it to some constructive end; while all the warmth, security and love so indiscriminately given by the latter could be either quite ineffective, or else could accidently reinforce various patterns of behaviour that may later be harmful to others as well as unhelpful to the child. In this sense it is quite possible for a child to have 'too much love' — a possibility that modern child-care theorists vigorously deny. In many other societies and often in our own past parents tended to be rather formal educators of their children and mixed little with them on a more personal, relaxed level. Closer personal relationships existed instead with grandparents, siblings, nannies, etc.

Confusion over the function which elementary reinforcement serves in the learning and adaptations of a young child has led to many of the agonising dilemmas of parents about the very simple training of young children. Parents realise intuitively that some behaviour should be rewarded and other behaviour discouraged. But the traditional ways in which the latter has always been done — involving smacking or deliberate withdrawal of affection — are unacceptable today since they consist of a kind of punishment, which is felt to be wrong. It is seen as estranging the child, choking his sources of love, approval, reassurance and security. By being itself negative and rejecting to the child, it seems it can only produce hostility and rejection in its turn, and progressively alienate the child from the parents and everything they seem to stand for.

Punishment, then, is felt to be both acutely hurtful and disturbing to the child and obnoxious to any loving parent to have to administer. For this reason it is felt that there must be some way to encourage and bring out the right kind of response in a quite painless fashion, without the child realising it is being stealthily guided towards what is desirable. One cannot very well withhold affection (rejection) or categorically forbid the child certain things (threat of punishment); so one has somehow to distract its attention away from undesirable or anti-social behaviour and show it even more love or affection than usual. Some recent child-care books do manage to tiptoe towards recognising the need to check and punish some child behaviour, but even they have to represent it not as something undertaken for the sake of the wider society of other people, but as giving the child something he really wants ('children like a structured environment'; 'Getting angry with a child makes it feel wanted', etc.) Almost any version will do, but what cannot be faced is the simple idea that some basic training is needed because society, not the child's ego, demands it. The following quotation is typical:

> Children really like knowing there are limits on their behaviour. The existence of limits relieves them of making decisions: it also lessens their guilt. You can tell them that feeling ugly feelings and kicking a tree to relieve those feelings are all allowed. But you add that actually kicking the person they have the ugly feelings about is not allowed. You save them the guilt they would feel if they gave in to their impulses and kicked the person.[1]

(Such are the lengths to which writers on child upbringing will go to avoid calling things by their proper names. Just how a child could ever acquire the capacity to be guilty about hurting other people if the limits on its behaviour are established in such a roundabout way, is never explained.)

The woolly but deep-seated conviction that punishment and painful experience are not merely unpleasant in themselves, but must also cause undesirable traits in later life, and conversely, that a loved and happy childhood must produce a morally good adult, stems perhaps from what I call the 'like produces like' fallacy.

This reasoning has also served to bolster up what are really value-judgements disguised as facts about the way things are. The confusion is between the moral conviction that good ends should not be bought at the price of bad means, and the factual belief that bad means are actually counter-productive. Thus, from acknowledging (as we supposedly do) that it is a bad thing taken simply in itself for a child to be smacked (i.e. it would be preferable to achieve the same end by gentler methods), it is easy to slide into the quite different, and probably false belief that as a matter of psychological fact, smacks do not produce their intended result anyway.

Now many people have been encouraged in this last belief by observations of children from homes where they are heavily punished and yet delinquent. But, in fact, children in such homes are often unwanted and disliked, and punishment is applied by the parents purely to assuage their own violent and vindictive emotions, and not to shape the child's behaviour. The only effect is therefore to provoke a general avoidance and hostility. Not much learning can take place in an atmosphere of rejection since learning involves lengthy interaction with a child and this must in time imply acceptance in place of arbitrariness. But it happens to be a reality of the world that at the level of basic behavioural learning, noxious stimuli diminish the behaviour that they follow and that pleasurable stimuli reinforce it. Evidence shows that, contrary to popular sentiment, the countering of violence with the granting of staisfaction, or replying to selfish behaviour with continued acceptance, approval or love will only intensify this behaviour in the individual—who has made a successful adaptation in his own terms.

This is certainly not to deny that in some circumstances generous behaviour, repaying injury with kindness, etc, can dispel aggression and elicit better behaviour. But what is of the utmost importance is that where such responses work it is only because they appeal to implicit moral values which both parties already share. They involve such things as shaming a person, or bringing forth their admiration despite themselves. And these moves depend entirely on that person's having acquired a moral consciousness.

But before a moral consciousness can possibly be acquired, indeed before a child can learn any of the discriminatory competence necessary for it to act coherently and follow any objective beyond immediate gratification, it must simply be trained in elementary social cooperation. It is not enough that it simply be exposed indiscriminately to lots of 'stimulation'. There are plenty of sources of stimulation, such as the amusement to be had from tormenting animals or other children, or manipulating boiling saucepans, which have to be very definitely denied the child, if it is to go on to the next stage at all.

For the young child, this rudimentary inculcation of social rule-following is of a straightforward stimulus—response— reward kind. It does not involve understanding the rules; this can only come later. At this stage attempting to reason with a child, or to appeal to its conscience, is premature. Only consistent learning can shape its behaviour so that it can interact with others systematically enough to come within reach of reasoned explanation.

The young child is not yet a moral being. But this does not imply, as is so easily concluded, that it is therefore immoral. It is amoral simply because it is still comparatively formless. This is what is misunderstood by those who believe that any kind of compulsion in teaching a child is wrong or regrettable, that the child already has its own 'values' and for adults to train it in norms of behaviour is to impose their own values on it. Children simply do not come into the world with values — even incoherent ones — because values are social in origin and context. If some children arrive at school with distinct values, they have learnt these from other people.

The intellectual distrust of socialisation is the heir of a long tradition. Unthwarted growth, nourished by mother's milk and above all protected from artifical distortion (especially in the shape of education) would bring forth a happy, innocent, loving man as surely as a well-nurtured tree puts forth buds. The notion was in vigorous reaction to the opposite tradition, Judaeo—Christian in inspiration, which by and large saw elemental man as selfish, destructive and evil. Like most rival traditions, these two have existed mainly by taking in each other's washing. The most glaring fault shared by both in an absurdly exaggerated emphasis on the pure a-social individual and a corresponding neglect of learning and culture. It was supposed that one could quite sensibly ask whether natural man was benevolent or malevolent before he came into society. Natural man was envisaged as a lone, self-sufficient creature, like Robinson Crusoe or the Noble Savage, who at some time chose to associate in compact with his fellows.[2]

All such arguments are ridiculous. We can no more speculate about the moral qualities of pre-social man than ask what fish would have been like without water. And this applies to the moral character of infants prior to learning from other humans.

This simple truth is easily obscured by an almost irresistible tendency to project our own adult moral concepts on to infants, just as many people project human concepts on to animals. It is said, for example, that a newborn baby is essentially selfish or, alternatively, essentially trusting. But these notions cannot possibly apply to newborn babies. For a baby to be selfish as we understand the term, it must be in a position to choose between its own interests and those of other people, and this means it must already have learnt from them and be interacting with them. What should correctly be said is that a baby has yet no clear concepts of the interests of others, nor of its own interests contrasted with them: it just seeks simple kinds of gratifications in a more or less automatic way.

The most striking examples of the projection of adult concepts on to infants derive from the background of psychoanalysis, which I have already discussed. Young babies, even newborn ones, are supposed to be capable of aggression, hate, fear, guilt: and to make quite logical conjectures about things, distinguishing the Good and the Bad breast and later the Good and the Bad mother, fearing the world as threatening because the nipple has been taken away for ever, then deliberately trying to annihilate the world and afterwards feeling guilt when this is believed to have been done. But this is nonsense. How can one tell that what is going on is hate, as opposed to activity; fear, as opposed to simple aversion; guilt, as opposed to simple anxiety? Hatred involves some idea of other people as objects of hate; in order to fear, one must have beliefs about objective dangers; guilt implies a concept of a norm or rule which has been broken. If these concepts are not acquired through learning from other humans, then how on earth does the child come by them? Freudians have no explanation: the child is supposed to be equipped with them in a rudimentary way at birth. The picture they offer of a child coming into the world is rather like that of an explorer entering a very strange country. He is intelligent and coherent, but everything round him is so new to him that he makes some wrong guesses about it. It is certainly not a picture of how an embryonic individual acquires these human capacities in the first place.

What, then, is moral responsibility, and how is it acquired?

20   Learning Morality

'Now by self-sufficient we do not mean that which is
sufficient for a man by himself, for one who lives a solitary
life, but also for parents, children, wife, and in general for his
friends and fellow citizens, since man is born for citizenship.'
                                Aristotle, *Nichomachean Ethics*

Many people who do not necessarily accept crude stockpiling
theories about love nonetheless believe that moral
responsibility originates in the relationship between members
of a family. There is a sense in which this may be right, but it
is not the sense that is usually meant. What is generally
believed is that the family is in some way a kind of
microcosm of a larger society, and that love and trust among
its members is therefore the essential core of later moral
goodness and responsibility towards others.

This can hardly be true. Morality, as I have stressed earlier,
involves an extended sympathy beyond one's own group, a
disinterested concern and respect for the claims of all other
people, regardless of whether one personally likes or loves
them. Being considerate to those we love is natural enough,
but it is not at all to be equated with morality. It is precisely
because we do not and cannot love everybody that morality
becomes so necessary.

One of the essential things that distinguishes moral
principles from simply likes and dislikes, is that they are
universal, not particular, in character. If a moral principle is
sincerely and consistently held, it necessarily applies equally
to everyone in the relevant circumstances, and not just to
oneself and one's immediate circle. The only difference
between having a genuine moral objection to poverty or
violence, as opposed to merely a personal objection to being
poor or injured oneself, is surely that in the first case one is
equally concerned with all poverty or violence, whoever is

suffering it. In other words, the formal character of morality is strongly akin to concepts of justice and fairness, in that a central feature is the non-privileged status of the moral subject: if I demand this right myself, I thereby demand it for others too.

It should be clear why moral values cannot consist only of generous and wholesome emotions, or the disposition to feel such emotions. They must be such as to give a person a reason for acting in certain ways whether his feelings are tending that way or not. Of course, there are moral feelings — which promote morally good and important actions, and the cultivation of them is of obvious importance. But what gives them moral significance is the moral value of the action. For a person to hold to a certain moral value does not just mean that he experiences certain emotions frequently.[1]

'Extended sympathy', to which I have referred, does not denote an emotion, but a capacity for moral imagination, an ability to see how the consideration we show people in familiar circumstances can apply equally to others in very different surroundings. It is manifested, for example, in the ability to see the injustice of racial or sexual discrimination, even in a social situation where more of the dominant group take it entirely for granted.

Now, whether or not something like extended sympathy arises from within a family or not, depends crucially on what sort of behaviour and attitudes towards outsiders are practised and taught. A child might well learn sympathy, reciprocity and concern for his parents and sibs as a result of a loving relationship in the home but, as I have argued, there is no reason why he should generalise this into an impersonal concern for outsiders unless he is taught to.

Indeed, there are obvious obstacles to this generalisation. Families, involving biological ties, are closed institutions — unlike communities, which anyone can join who voluntarily conforms to the required conditions. They involve special, exclusive attachments and obligations to a few other people, and they do not naturally foster a sense of responsibility towards a larger surrounding community (today there is often no such community). I shall return to this later. At the moment, suffice it to say that, in many respects, love within a family is in competition with outside loyalties and commitments. (A standard excuse for moral or political cowardice is concern that wife and children may suffer.)

Where the family does produce morally responsible adults this is because it has been a suitable learning situation, and because positive moral norms have been explicitly taught, practised and emulated. These norms, and the family's adherence to them, originate not in the Oedipal triangle or as an extrapolation of the child's warmth and security, but solely because the parents have acquired them from the outside culture, and succeeded in transmitting them effectively.

The sense in which it may be true that moral responsibility originates in the family is simply this: in our type of society the nuclear family happens to be the primary institution for socialising the young, handing on the skills and norms of the society. There is not the slightest reason to suppose that it is the only institution that could fulfil this function. Indeed, in Britain today, it is not even a good one for this purpose.

Morality is not, of course, simply to be lumped with social norms, for it contains the possibility of questioning and rejecting social norms. Any convincing account of how children are educated into morally responsible adults must do justice to this distinction.

The earliest learning must be of the simply behavioural kind, which alone imparts coherent skills and competence to interact with others. The process obviously becomes more pervasive and elaborate as the child extends its activities, learns to speak, walk and so on. At this stage it is largely conditioned by appropriate reinforcers simply to comply with basic social and moral requirements. The mechanisms involved are, crudely, punishment, reward and imitation, although even these do not operate in an entirely simple way – for example, the behaviour of others and its consequences, is assimilated readily by the child onlooker, even though he himself is not being rewarded or punished.

Imitation, familiar to every parent, has been studied in experiments intended to show the ease with which children copy aggressive behaviour – which is, after all, one of the simplest and most direct responses to any problem. Imitation of aggression appears to be rapid, particularly where the subject is actually rewarded. Such imitation follows whether children see actual aggression or a representation of it, but does not follow when the actors are seen to be punished for the aggressive action. It also appears that the spontaneous aggression occurring in the children's play is encouraged and extended by the presence not only of a rewarding adult, but of a merely non-punishing one as well. The child treating neutrality as support for his current behaviour.

Now this kind of behavioural learning, if applied consistently, serves to create compliance with basic social rules, cooperation with adults and peers, and the use of a primitive moral vocabulary; and unless this is achieved there is little to build on. But although the child knows and obeys some moral rules, it cannot be said to understand them. It has no grasp of the reasons that justify them. It feels powerful inhibitory anxiety over some action or even the thought of it; or it calculates that punishment will follow if it is caught; or at the most it accepts that an action is to be done or not done because adults say so.

Indispensably necessary though behavioural learning is, it obviously could not provide a complete explanation of the acquisition of moral concepts and the adoption of moral principles. Among moral adults, it is never a justification for one's moral beliefs or behaviour simply that one was conditioned or brought up that way. There is still the question to be faced, whether the belief or behaviour is right or not. And if the person asking the question is rationally persuaded that it is not, the only thing for them to do is to escape their upbringing, as others have done before them — by seeking countervailing forms of support and reinforcement for alternatives.[2]

There is some evidence to suggest that, in our society at least, children take fairly easily to a rigid and absolute idea of moral rules. They are seen as simple, clear commandments emanating from some unquestionable authority, deviation from which must always be punished whoever the culprit and whatever the particular circumstances. Although a clear distinction is not made between the source of authority and the source of punishment, this kind of attitude is already very different from the simple hedonistic desire to bring about pleasant consequences and avoid painful ones. The rule does not consist in doing what will avoid punishment — rather, punishment is for the sake of the rule. It is just as disturbing to the child that someone suffer punishment inappropriately, as that someone trangress the rule without being punished. The core idea here is consistency, though not necessarily justice or fairness. Whether there need to be definite authority figures, and whether these are parents, older children or later, God, seems largely a matter of the particular cultural situation. The point is that the compelling nature of the rules is understood as emanating from some objective, external authority that is simply to be obeyed. This state is still not one of moral understanding. The child does not necessarily see the point of the rules, nor does it distinguish different kinds of rules — for example, not to steal, from not to cross the road without looking both ways. Nor does it see that rules apply very differently to situations, that some rules override others, and that authority itself may need some kind of justification. As far as the child is concerned, rules of morality are to be followed in basically the same way as elementary rules of arithmetic.

There are, of course, very fundamental differences between the two, which come to be grasped only through far more informal kinds of education. Although there is broad agreement over general moral principles, there can be no correct textbook answers to what is right in a particular situation, because there can be no textbooks. Nor can there be professional experts in moral goodness, nor is it enough just to do what everyone else does and approves of, either. No logical proof can be given why it is wrong to cause people pain, and nobody can take a holiday from morality as they can from mathematics.

If someone genuinely asked how to live their life in the most valuable and worthwhile way, then probably the most useful answer that could be given would be to select the best, most admirable person they could find and try and be like them.[3] It would not be providing them with a code of precepts, but it would be a more valuable help to them to understand what morality really is. Now it is quite possible for a child (or for that matter an adult) to be taught mathematics effectively by someone he hates, fears or distrusts. But it is scarcely possible for him to learn such things as fairness, sympathy, respect or integrity from such a person, because a necessary basis for understanding what these are (as opposed to simply obeying rigid rules), is a developed sense of reciprocity, an ability to visualise the situation of others and see oneself as subject to the same considerations. These things are more moral capacities than explicit lessons. But without them he will be unable to understand the point of moral principles, and make them his own instead of merely conforming to them.

Now there is no particular reason why the people from whom he learns these capacities have to be parents, and certainly no necessity for a special, exclusive attachment to one or two people (which if anything would hinder his grasping the universal character of moral obligation). Nor need the relationship be one of 'love'. What is indispensable is that it involve relations of mutual recognition, trust, help and interest, so that he can see himself as a person among others with the same kind of wants, sensibilities, demands and obligations. Again, there is no reason to believe that if a bad environment prevented someone from forming these relationships in childhood, he is incapable of making this good in later life.

A person acquires moral principles not as an isolated lesson but as part of learning the way of life of the group into which they have entered. This is not to say that right and wrong behaviour do not need to be explicitly emphasised and explained, but rather that the kinds of principles a person holds become refined, modified and made applicable only through social experience, by acting according to moral rules and appreciating the consequences. Two necessary aspects to this maturation are, coming to value a principle in and for itself, rather than because it is held by the other people one trusts and respects; and actually coming to discover what one's own principles and values really are. And this demands experience of moral conflicts where there are compelling claims on a person, where people who have mutual trust and respect are obliged to oppose one another, and where an individual is forced to make choices and be responsible for them — forced not by any coercion or pressure, but by the logic of the situation and the values they hold. In this way a person comes to distinguish genuine guilt from embarrassment, agreement about moral principles from personal liking, and the rational acceptance of obligation from the external imposition of duties.

In the last paragraph I stopped referring to the child and talked instead of 'the person'. The fact is that very many adults think and behave in ways which correspond to the child's more primitive moral stages. To them, moral rules are not really different from rules of etiquette or fashion or tradition: one observes them because it is the Done Thing, it is what Respectable People do. It is important to understand that such people are not hypocritical: they simply have no real moral understanding. They have social standards, which they derive entirely from what others do, but no moral standards. To understand morality depends on actually holding some kind of moral principle, and this in turn depends on being able to defend some action whether or not this coincides with what most people think. Such people are the backbone of silent majorities. They are not objectively harmful, provided the moral norms of the society are good. But they would never be the ones to try and prevent society from getting worse.

There is a final point to be made about the development of moral responsibility, one which is easily overlooked by those who think there is just one true code of morality and that moral disputes could in principle be settled if people were all taught this. I have talked about how, from merely conforming to moral principles, a person comes to understand them and eventually adopt them as his own. It is tempting to view this as a quite straightforward transition, but it is not so. Adopting moral principles is not just the routine internalization of society's rules, and conscience is not just a self-policing faculty that does the job previously done by external authority. For a person freely and knowingly to adopt a moral principle entails the possibility that he can likewise reject it. Any view of moral standards which baulks at this, simply misunderstands what moral principles are.

The fact that underlying moral values tend to persist in society, that most morally responsible people do not, in fact, reject large parts of the moral tradition in which they are

educated, does not detract at all from the above point. It is
precisely because moral rules are those which are of greatest
importance and concern the ultimate ends of human life and
action, that they only change slowly. It is because moral rules
are the most fundamental kind of obligation, capable if need
be of overriding all other considerations, that the real values
an individual sincerely holds will tend, in their most general
aspects, to overlap those of others.[4]

The fact that a morally educated person must be in a
position to reject some moral principle, should give no
encouragement whatever to those misguided people who talk
glibly about schoolchildren 'rejecting' the values of the
school, or rebel students 'rejecting' all the values of their
society. While it is the individual who has moral
commitments and is answerable for them, the values to which
he is committed are not something private, not a matter of
taste or fashion. Nor is morality a game one can get bored
with and contract out of. It is logically absurd for someone
to think they could consistently reject all moral principles,
for that would leave nothing in favour of which they are
rejected. The only way in which moral principles can be
genuinely rejected — the only grounds on which 'rejection'
can have meaning — is by appeal to some other, contrary
moral principles. And commitment to these similarly requires
the social background of education and understanding of
moral life.

21 Conclusions

'Wise men will apply their remedies to vices, not to names . . . Otherwise you will be wise historically, a fool in practice . . . You are terrifying yourself with ghosts and apparitions, whilst your house is the haunt of robbers.'

Edmund Burke

What I have said in the rest of the book has centred round accumulated evidence of various kinds, and where I have interpreted this evidence I have tried to follow the simplest and least fanciful readings of the situations. The views which I offer about the causes and consequences of the whole current child-rearing ideology are, of course, more directly controversial. But disagreement with them is not sufficient to dismiss the accumulation of evidence, and those who dislike my interpretation of it must supply another, unless they can challenge the evidence itself. I say this because the responsible, thinking part of our society has been radically misled on some very important subjects for a considerable time. Of course, for those confirmed in adherence to one or another sect of psychoanalysis (or those to whom any experimental science is suspect), there is no problem: evidence carries no authority if it clashes with their deepest convictions. But for others, the re-examination of a lot of accepted beliefs cannot be avoided for much longer.

The Maternal Deprivation Theory has been the pivot of my argument. But we have not simply found that one unbroken attachment to mother is not so vital after all, so that we can proceed to rummage elsewhere in the child's early experience for the foundations of its adult character. What is mistaken is our whole assumption that people's important human qualities must be formed by unconscious, quasi-biological processes in the isolated, individual child at some critical period before it even goes to school. It is to be emphatically asserted that, apart from initial genetic predispositions, these qualities are created almost entirely by cultural transmission, by socialisation and learning from the wider community of human beings. The hope that by continued research we shall discover the true 'needs' of the child, and by shaping our child-care policies around them, produce healthy,considerate, cooperating beings, is a complete will-o-the-wisp. There is simply no natural a-cultural way in which to bring up children.

It is therefore obvious why a comprehensive answer cannot be given to the question: 'If the child-care experts are wrong, if love and indulgence and continual presence are not quite what is needed, then how do I bring up my child to be a good, loving responsible adult?' Not because there is no answer but because the question itself is wrongly put: it presupposes the continuation of just the same individual agencies and circumstances – the nuclear family, the child's close possessive attachment to one or two adults, and so on. What can be said very readily is that making a child (or anyone else) happy is a good thing in itself, but producing desired behaviour is achieved not by strictness or indulgence, but by consistent reinforcement, the sophistication of which depends on the child's maturity. But as for the much greater business of rearing good, morally responsible citizens, the answer does not lie in the individual family's choice of which behaviour will be reinforced simply because the modern private family, even at its best, is inherently unsuitable as the main instrument of social and cultural transmission. Socially good qualities – competence, cooperation, responsibility, moral understanding – can only be created through practice and participation in public, communal life, not by any process of individual nurture, determined by the child's 'needs'. *A child-centred society is a cultureless society* – for human beings a contradiction in terms.

It might seem odd that I maintain that the modern intellectual climate is wedded to the notion of natural child-care, when there is today a strong tendency to explain human characteristics in terms of a cultural environment, a tendency which emphatically repudiates genetic and organic explanation. But this concern is not so much an attempt to understand the influence of culture, as to track down a conspiratorial enemy. The difference in talents, intelligence, health and performance we perceive in our fellows is represented as so many veils of delusion created by society, arbitrary labels attached to people who then act them out in life's puppet show. It is presupposed that somewhere behind all this there is a real world where, if it were attained, no individual's rich potential would be thwarted.

Very ancient literary and philosophical traditions exist about long-lost states of near paradisial simplicity and wholeness. A dominant theme is that men once lived in a natural harmony with each other in economic abundance — a world without scarcity, or conflict, achieved without cultural regulation or design. Central to these notions is the idea that culture is articifical, the result of some primeval mistake or sin but whose rule is regrettably necessary as long as human nature retains a disastrous flaw or is under the sway of evil powers. Many have made the lost past into a realisable future Utopia, and many more, while not subscribing to a specific lost paradise myth, believe that there is somewhere a state in which man was intended to live, a natural environment where the ills, evils and limitations of his present predicament will be shaken off. Such beliefs have increased their hold tremendously in the last century, and now affect all sections of society and levels of sophistication. That the environment we now inhabit is not the proper one for mankind is what lies behind the continual assertion that the mental and physical diseases we suffer from are the result of the 'unnatural' strains of 'modern living'. In a similar way, intellectuals have been preoccupied with the alien, harmful effects which cultural impositions have on creativity and generous dispositions.

Given these assumptions, there will continue to be an intensive search for the key to harmony and wholeness, or some remedy that will rid us of the flaw which bedevils us and blights our chances. Apocalyptic solutions are still put forward (mainly in Marxist form), and so are more mundane and pragmatic ones, such as yet more economic growth. The type of solution I have been concerned with in this book sees our basic flaw in some fault in child-rearing, repeated by each parent, each generation, on each child.

That there might be genetic boundaries to what any

individual can become and achieve is a highly unpopular notion. It is obviously anathema to the reforming Left and its intellectual advisers. Having traded the aim of radical structural change in the social system for that of equality of opportunity in a fundamentally unchanged system, it would make cruel nonsense of the bargain if, after all, people are inherently unequal in intelligence and other desirable personal assets, and if even the most meritorious application cannot redress the balance. Far better that it be due to something environmental and therefore alterable – if not at school, then in the home, in early childhood. If you accept a society of unabashed individual achievement and mobility, then high IQ and various talents must become enormously important competitive weapons. Indeed the more social mobility that occurs, the more frequently it is denied that there are any opportunities at all for working-class children, who labour under acute 'disadvantages', while those in professional families are the products of 'privilege'. This blandly ignores the fact that the expansion of the middle classes is due to recruitment from below, not to the fertility of a socio-economic bourgeois caste.

This mobility is increasingly saddling reformers with the problem of why so many groups are left behind, why so many children are 'under-achievers'. The cause is looked for in some hitherto unnoticed form of unequal opportunity, providing the *raison d'être* for the long, laborious and ever-expanding effort of research, in which the crucial 'deprivation' period of a child comes to be sought progressively further and further back into infancy.

Although genetic theories hurt the social democrat most, emphasis on environment has been extraordinarily congenial to the middle class. It has not been unwelcome (or accidental), to find that educational potential is formed in the delicate pre-school years, and that it involves a rich, elaborate and above all expensive environment, and an acquaintance with a somewhat involved tradition of amateur psychology. And there exists in modern child-care a justification of eminent respectability for the grossest familial selfishness. If the first five years really is the determining period, in which neglect cannot be made good later, if children need so much attention that no adult can be expected to concentrate on more than one or two (three at the most), then the over-riding dedication of parents to the competitive life-chances of their offspring appears not as any kind of social selfishness, but actually as a positive duty towards the next generation.

The acknowledgement of biological limitations operating in human society is felt to deny the possibility of improving the human condition and enriching human experience. This is, however, likely to be advanced by piecemeal policies more in touch with the exigencies of everyday life than much of modern education and welfare, being a little more realistically aware of what can and cannot be altered. But to be effective, we need not merely to understand the role of biology in human development, but, more important, the role of cultural transmission. A detailed examination of the present vogue for a-cultural Rousseauesque schemes of childrearing is outside the scope of this book, but it can be said quite definitely that their popularity is intimately connected with the role of women and family, and with our increasing moral confusion. (The Maternal Deprivation Theory, of course, makes much of the natural importance of motherhood particularly for social morality, which arises in an instinctual fashion from maternal care.)

As many writers have recently pointed out, this century has exhibited pronounced tension over the role of women. They have achieved a certain level of legal and physical emancipation which it would be difficult to rescind: on the other hand, there has been a stubborn refusal to admit them into the mainstream of social and economic life, a refusal involving endless attempts at justifying the fundamentally nineteenth-century, secluded wife-mother ideal. It would appear that the more external restrictions are removed, the more imperative do internalised controls become. In this century such controls have had to be based on a more dignified concept of 'separate but equal', rather than the clear and traditional 'separate because inferior' explanation. Domesticity, wifedom, motherhood have somehow had to be accorded a status equal to (and as interesting as) a life in the wider society. Traditions of pseudo-psychology, deriving from psychoanalysis, have promised extravagant biological fulfilment to women who have the courage and maturity to

Child Care: Sense and Fable

accept 'femininity', and an extensive range of mental and physical ills to those who do not. Transcendental orgasms (a particularly American aspect) and the ineffable, mystical creativity of giving birth, into which the whole meaning and purpose of life can somehow be telescoped, have garnished segregation. But even more effective have been the infantile libidinal foundations of personality. Breast-feeding, toilet-training, cuddles and play – all the apparently mundane and innocent details of the nursery – have been moved by the heirs of Freud to the very centre of civilisation's hopes and aspirations. A mother must have the incalculably delicate skills of a psychological surgeon whose smallest slip could have untold consequences; by comparison with the awful responsibilities falling to a mother of children in their First Five Years, those of directors or cabinet ministers can be regarded as small beer.

This nurturing of the embryo personality has been represented as so bound up with the mother's biological presence and processes, that it cannot be delegated. Nor is it an explicit skill requiring technical training, being basically instinctual (what every good mother knows), requiring her to 'arrange' her natural responses to her child in such a way that the unconscious processes can do their mysterious work unhindered.

This involves a complicated problem of combining the riskiness and delicacy of the whole process with a surprising lack of any specialised training. The recipe for correct child-rearing contains amazingly little to be learnt, but plenty of occasion for fretful fear that the unconscious processes might be going wrong, a fear which can only be allayed by constant vigilance and protective attention. It contains, in fact, in nicely adjustable proportions, both the carrot and the stick. By devoted, scrupulous attention to the precious First Five Years, one can rear a child with high intelligence and creativity, generous, loving, psychologically healthy – perhaps even a genius. But neglect of the infant's vital needs, failure to supply enough love and attention, even perhaps putting one's own fulfilments and ambitions first, could cause his personality irreparable damage. That women are (or should be) outside much of the cultural and social process is highly relevant to the way in which the doctrines of critical formative periods consistently represent the operative mechanisms as biological, instinctual, unconscious, subliminal — anything but deliberate and contrived.

In the approval given to the strengthening of family life in the decades of the welfare state, praise has not simply gone, rightly, to the greater consideration shown to children and the rise of the responsible working-class husband: but also to the family's greater privacy, its self-sufficiency and inward-looking orientation at the expense of external links. The planning of new estates and urban re-development has largely proceeded on the assumption that the only relationships in a person's life are two-generational nuclear family ones, and a blind, senseless destruction of community has been one of the results.

A tremendous weight of sentiment has seen in private family life a cradle of all the virtues. The various churches long ago forgot about the Christian community as a serious social entity, and threw their moral authority decisively behind the family ethic. The important moral problems to them are almost exclusively familial and personal, pertaining to the private lives of individuals: sexual indulgence and information, pornography, divorce and contraception, drinking, gambling, and so on. The 'moral fibre of society' means, by definition, private (especially sexual) morality, whose ideal is always that of wholesome family life. The suspicion or outright antagonism of Christianity to family and marriage in the past, because they militated against either spiritual preoccupations (the Catholic emphasis), or civic virtues (the Protestant emphasis), have today been completely reversed. The obsessive interest in sexual sin has swallowed the broader concerns of the past century, and now represents the decrepit rump of a virtually defunct religion. For many decades a tenacious view of social morality, propagated by many eminent leaders of public opinion, has connected public failings closely with private morality. If there is crime and violence, it is thought natural to look at the figures for divorce, VD, and so forth. (We are all familiar with the common explanation for the fall of the Roman Empire, in Cinemascope and Technicolor.) On superficial scrutiny Freudian theory might appear at odds with traditional conservative attitudes, but in fact it has an uncanny similarity with them. Both attitudes see moral capacities as something exuded by the interpersonal interactions of the nuclear patriarchal family — not imparted explicitly, and not imparted by any other social entity.

It is, of course, a highly popular national pastime to ridicule all attitudes going under the heading of 'middle class': but enthusiasm for the game should not be allowed to cloud the fact that nearly all the radical opponents are carrying on the same crucial defects of the middle-class tradition — privacy, family, individualism — too often elevated by bad theory into revolutionary virtues and deliberately stripped of even the minimal middle-class commitment to basic socialisation of the young. As a consequence, it is, for example, proposed in all seriousness, that in the name of 'preventing the imposition of middle-class values on children', we should refrain from teaching children any values, and rather let them individually 'discover their own'. Both conservative and radical share all the assumptions of an extraordinary individualistic tradition which sees man as formed outside society, living his life and pursuing his goals independently of it and even in opposition to it. All the conflicts of ideals, explanations, and values are fought out within these unnoticed confines.

Extreme individualism has permitted a fundamental reversal of some older left-wing positions. It used to be believed that knowledge, education, training and organisation were what gave people power and liberty; now, following Rousseau, these things are what enslave us. For the first time in a very long period, there has appeared, not just qualms about severe or lenient, formal or informal methods of teaching, but a widespread repudiation of socialisation on principle. Human freedom is now equated with minimising and even abolishing the handing on of a culture.

Many of those who are in effect pursuing this end would hotly reject this description of it. Much of it springs, not from political radicalism or from reading Rousseau, but from the pseudo-disciplines of the social sciences, that proliferate particularly in colleges of education. But only the implicit acceptance of this position could lead so many intellectuals to argue seriously that we have no right to teach a child anything it does not agree to be taught, or to train it in anything whose purpose it does not immediately comprehend and 'accept'.

This position is made up essentially of two main (and frequently conflated) views of the individual child: one moral, one psychological. First is that it is plainly and simply wrong to coerce a child (or anyone) for any end. And the second — an independent proposition — is that refraining from such coercion will in fact produce a socially good, intellectually creative and psychologically healthy individual by a process of spontaneous natural development.

The moral viewpoint considers the child a free and sovereign individual very strictly and completely. He has full and inalienable rights vis-à-vis interference by society and a set of values, ideas, and opinions which are his own making and enjoy equal validity with all others. Socialisation — the deliberate inculcation of the appropriate skills and values of the surrounding society, the initiation of the child into an existing human culture — is a repressive tyranny and furthermore is the very thing that forms the cement of all political tyranny. Some, like the idealist coming to terms with unavoidable violence, have regretfully accepted that there is just no alternative in some circumstances to applying at least some degree of repression. But the premise is nonetheless very widely accepted that compulsory training or teaching is at bottom indefensible.

The full and literal implementation of the no-compulsion ethic would of course lead to the most appalling results, with individuals as socially and personally inept, incoherent and helpless as any Cromagnon orphan: a social and cultural heritage, except of a very primitive elemental kind, would virtually cease to exist.

Fortunately, few are moral purists, although vague guiltiness about compulsion is general. More subscribe to what I call the psychological view of the individual child. To them, both compulsion and social breakdown are wrong and distasteful, but the solution to the dilemma happily involves no dichotomy. A tolerant, voluntary child environment, will, if properly managed, allow those social and creative qualities we value so much to unfold and grow in each individual. Compulsory teaching or training must (by *a priori* commonsense), produce outward conformity but inward boredom and resentment; whereas toleration, freedom and discovery must likewise encourage the flowering of tolerant, freedom-loving and creative qualities. The results of applying these principles over a wide area of social and educational policy have at best, not come up to expectation, and at worst, have been a failure of possibly disastrous proportions. But faith is still strong and there has been, if anything, an intensification of misguided research into the identification and understanding of the 'true needs' of the individual child. When we can eventually winkle these out, we shall have achieved the synthesis of an upbringing which is both perfect freedom and the requisite educational nurture for the regeneration of society. In such a climate psychoanalytical ideas about the natural growth of the conscience (or superego), from emotional interchange between parent and child in the earliest years are highly serviceable to a generation that wishes to evade responsibility for both the choice and transmission of norms and values. Prescriptions for more mothering, 'better family life', and the rest, simply serve to wash everyone's hands of the moral responsibility that should fall to all mature members of human groups.

In our time, due to the unprecedented effects of economic growth, individual mobility, mass communication and continual technological revolution, there has been a marked erosion of all enduring, wider social entities between the individual and the anonymous agencies of the state. This situation, the result of so many unintended by-products of social and physical changes, aided and abetted by certain dominant beliefs and values, is resulting in growing numbers of people who have scarcely acquired the rudiments of a human culture — a growth of Feral Man.

The most alarming aspect is probably the sharp increase in crime, violence and aimless destruction of all kinds, with larger proportionate increases as one goes down the age scale. Also much crime, often of a highly dangerous and serious nature, is committed by those well under the age of criminal responsibility. Vandalism, once an uncommon occurence, is now automatically accepted as an inevitable fact of the urban environment, even gross cases are hardly worth reporting. Actually, to use the expression 'crime' for much modern anti-social behaviour is rather misleading, since it has no end beyond the most transitory titillation. The delinquent is frequently far too unsocialised to control his pursuit of instant excitement for rational gain.

The high rates of maladjustment reported for schoolchildren (who are usually excessively aggressive or withdrawn and frightened) is not entirely accountable for in terms of the survival of the weak. (Even these will do better in some environments than others.) Many more children enter school with very limited means of communication and largely devoid of any grounding in any cultural heritage of songs, stories, rhymes, etc., beyond random, meaningless snippets picked up from the commercial media. There are complaints that some children don't even know 'how to play'. As destruction and violence spreads into schools, the educational drawbacks of the home are made more difficult to compensate for. Any instruction demands at least a minimum of attention and concentration on the task in hand. Somebody with little control, whose behaviour is chaotic much of the time, is in no position to acquire any skills. The amount of school violence and truancy has not yet reached American proportions, but there is no reason to suppose it cannot.

The situation is not explicable simply by resort to a 'cycle of deprivation' argument, which seems to presuppose an iron law of environmental determinism, affecting a set number of families generation after generation. Certainly 'problem families' show the faults and inadequacies I have discussed and more, and other things being equal, these problems are likely to be handed on. But indices of deprivation and anti-social conduct are now appearing in families that simply cannot be equated with this group. The backgrounds of many of these suggest that the two ways usually proposed to break the cycle — economic improvement and/or attention to individual emotional needs of children, are misguided.

Delinquents, for example, frequently come from families who by any standard are well-housed, well-fed, well-dressed and physically healthy[1,2] and are a reflection of the fact that the overwhelming majority of families now enjoy a standard of living higher than even the recent past and in most other countries today. Schools are better equipped and more attractive than they have ever been, and children have a wide freedom of choice to do what they are interested in. There are more leisure facilities for the older child, more medical care, more psychotherapy and counselling, more sympathetic and less punitive ways of dealing with transgressions.

In general, children in present-day society have a very favoured and protected emotional environment, compared with the none-too-distant past. Families are smaller and domestic work lighter for the mother. Few parents are now lost to children through death and loss of siblings is rare. Much emphasis is placed upon children being 'wanted' and their right to affection and attention, including from the father, is always being emphasised. In contrast to their very subordinate position in the family of the past, where children were required to 'help' the parents in and out of the home, the ethic in homes of all classes is now commonly that 'It's all for the kiddies'[3] and the children accordingly are given priority.

It is certainly true that as conditions improved at the end of the nineteenth century and beginning of the twentieth (for example, the extension of education to all, the clearance of the worst slums of the Industrial Revolution, the implementation of Factory legislation and the Public Health Acts, the improvement in the legal position of married women and the decline in drunkenness), there came about also a decline in criminal behaviour and both public and private life became safer, stabler, and pleasanter for its participants. This welcome trend has not managed to survive the post-war years despite the continuation of the improvement in conditions of life, particularly as they affect children and which are supposed to be so beneficial to them and their conduct. If these favourable circumstances of today are felt to be inadequate for the new generation, then most people in the recent past, all in the distant past, plus the vast majority in the world today, must be the most hopeless, retarded mental and social cripples.

Unless there are deep counteracting forces of which we know nothing, and unless the elementary empirical canon of concomitant variation is somehow at fault (that is, unless our world is close to that of Alice's Wonderland), we can confidently predict that the high level of crime will not be lowered or many of the deprivations of children reversed by providing the child with more familial love and maternal company – however desirable these things may be for their own sakes.

It is little use saying automatically that an inarticulate, destructive child is not really loved, for this is just what many parents (often in confusion), have tried to do. The public usually understand the demand that they must give as much love as possible to their child as meaning that they must show it physical affection, protect it, defend it, place it above others, approve its actions and comply with its wishes whenever possible, shielding it from stress and upset. It is of little use to parents to add the casual rider to this child-care advice that good parents will transmit social skills and moral responsibility anyway, and that this is all part of the 'right kind of love'. The typical result is that the parent given in even more to the child's demands, pleads, cajoles and sometimes abandons any hope of control or influence in mystification – 'I've done the best for him.' And it is becoming near impossible for many children to acquire any social competence or standards if they did not obtain them from their biological parents.

Present child-care theory cannot help us to solve the problems which it has helped to engender. To do so, its whole approach would have to shift, like the deprived child, from the biological to the cultural, from the individual to the social, from the particular to the general and from stimulation to learning. At present it is atavistically set on tracking down our instincts, finding out what makes us feral rather than human. In one respect my use of the adjective feral is disanalogous with the case of animals. Domesticated species who 'go feral' are able to survive by falling back on a complex and developed system of instinctual mechanisms transmitted to them more or less intact by heredity. Man has been a social, cultural creature for so long that his genetic pool contains few such instinctive resources. For the human individual the feral condition is unlikely to be that of the savage but self-sufficient life of the cunning and resourceful urban hunter or scavenger: rather it is the hapless inability to cope of the maladjusted member of a multiple problem

family, or the motiveless self-indulgence of the delinquent
which turns the cities into depleted wastelands for all. Indeed
man's disposition to be attracted to stimuli of all kinds
depends upon cultural training to channel this gift into
worthwhile, coordinated pursuits, restricting it in some
ways, developing it in others. Left to itself, it is dangerous to
the individual, other people and destructive of the
environment.

Present leaders, forced to take notice of the growing
phenomena of 'cultural deprivation' and 'impoverished
environments' are at least right in believing that the solution
lies partly in investment in education. But the ends of
education should not be seen as merely boosting the
competitive life chances of the working class, so that
education is shrugged off as useless if it cannot end
inequality. And investment should not be viewed as making
schools so intrinsically stimulating that the pupils will find it
less tempting to smash them. It is, on the contrary, the
establishment of the school as one of the agencies for
teaching children cooperative social behaviour and imparting
civic and communal values. The elementary foundations of
this should start in the nursery school and provide a basis for
later schooling to teach (and permit the practice of), more
sophisticated   techniques   of   civilised   living,   ethical
deliberation, democratic organisation and decision making.
This could, among other things, constitute an apprenticeship
in participation and basic politics which might help people in
later life. This is not to instil 'obedience to the system', as
some would have it, but to give the best means for the
individual to cope with it.

The fear of being (or being thought) authoritarian, has
frequently blurred hopelessly the essential distinctions
between teaching standards of behaviour and imposing mere
conformity: and second, the distinction between teaching a
particular (perhaps bad) set of values and teaching any values
at all. As I explained in the last chapter, one is only able to
question the values one is taught by reference to some other
values, and these in turn must come from somewhere.
Without first acquiring some moral standards, taking them
seriously and coming to understand the point of them, a
person literally cannot know what values are, and cannot

possibly be in a position to question or modify what he has been taught. If we really want to develop in people critical attitudes towards given values, it is indispensable that we start by inculcating the fundamental moral principles which we ourselves take seriously, and making the reasons for these understood.

Parallel with a broadening of the role of the school, there is a crying need for a general widening of the guardianship and upbringing of children. One of the most undeniable of children's rights, as it is everybody's, regardless of age, is the right not to be assaulted, and if one cannot fend for oneself, the right not to be neglected. The present atomisation of family life, aided by a reluctance of authorities to interfere (sanctioned for far too long by erroneous theory), has created a situation where far too many children are condemned to a wretched existence without hope of escape or redress. Parents should be seen as having a child in trust, and not as a chattel. It should therefore be axiomatic, and not a matter of parental choice, that the child's development be periodically assessed by persons outside the family.

There is a need for both creches and nursery schools to be created as an integral part of housing units. Ideally some of the staff should be well known and resident in the area. The emphasis must be on an opening up of the nuclear family, a sharing of parental functions by people who become involved with children not biologically theirs. There should always be people available in any area for advice and emergency child-minding. But what is crucial is that the deliberate professionalisation of child-care be avoided. To be shunned like the plague is an emphasis on qualifications and certificates, surrogates for degree courses, one year, two years, three years, filled with the speculations of frustrated intellectuals whose only idea of extending parental responsibility would involve extension of their own pseudo-expertise. The eager transmission of vast amounts of socio-psychological theory in the name of the professionalisation of social work and teaching, has frequently left the unfortunate practitioners with little or no actual skills with which to do their job (some colleges of education do not even teach such mundane matters as how to teach reading), but plenty of misleading, half-digested ideas with which to sow additional confusion. The continuity of culture involves people socialising the young into their own experiences and practices. It cannot be completely delegated, as can other things, to 'experts' with procedures and aims set apart from a communal form of life. And the skills involved in child-care, like all other skills, are best transmitted by some form of apprenticeship, by learning from those in the immediate community who do it well. If the skills of child-care are being poorly handed on by many of the population now, better transmission will not be helped, but decidedly hindered, by making child-care a closed speciality which the layman does not understand without the requisite theoretical background.

What must be investigated are ways of introducing (or re-introducing – always remembering the traditional role of the grandmother), certain skills and facilities into urban areas, which are then adopted and function automatically and informally.

Those who emphasise the importance of some continuity in human relationships (particularly for children), should appreciate that both senses of this continuity, continuity of people, and the continuity given by learnt behaviour (which enable the individual to establish new relationships) would be greatly advanced by both shared child-care arrangements and imparting the skills of considerate social interaction to children.

It is said that parents who ill-treat their children sometimes expect a sophisticated love and deference from children that is more properly asked for from other adults, and that they are accordingly infuriated and betrayed when the little child simply cannot give this. But it must be realised that, in the light of the only images of child-rearing which many a teenage girl is exposed to, this does not seem an unreasonable demand. The suggestion of a dreamy love relationship with baby, is found not only in the child-care books, but in every woman's magazine and babyfood advertisement. Children represent endless fun and playful joy – like cuddly kittens. Reality is different: harder, dirtier, noisier and thus, mystifying and incomprehensible. We need to be a little cooler and more formal, and to emphasise to prospective parents the necessity for a serious committment to the care and future of a child: obligations that cannot always rely on emotion for their support. If there is a clear acceptance of the duty to care for a child in a responsible manner, then, as the child is cared for, a closer, affectionate relationship has a stabler, calmer basis on which to grow. If there is any incompatibility, bitterness and abandonment are less likely.

A great deal of emotion is invested in parent–child relationships in modern society: both parent and child have the expectation that the relationship will answer all their requirements for the perfect, mutually satisfying personal relationship. Yet the parties, unlike friends, cannot and do not choose each other. At a time of life when she is physically and mentally at her most agile and receptive, a woman is often expected to fulfil herself entirely in child-care. All her requirements, for human company, sympathy, support and stimulation are to be largely found in the presence of an infant. The other side of the coin is that angry adolescents and young adults often attempt to force parents into being people they cannot hope to become (in fact, their ideal adult), interpreting their failure as a lack of love and concern.

As if there were not enough obstacles in the way of the modern couple learning the skills of child-rearing, there has been also the unfortunate attitude that young parenthood is a sign of maturity and responsibility: a highly praiseworthy occupation in contrast to the life style of young people who get involved in political and social life. But many are now coming to regret the results of a trend so enthusiastically encouraged. The young parent is all too frequently unskilled in child-care, to a greater or lesser extent unsocialised, with the result that she (or he) either cannot control her temper in dealings with children or obtains a vicarious delight and excitement from encouraging their delinquencies. At the age when people are most emotionally and intellectually changeable and receptive, their energies might be better spent in the wider world, learning and exploring the possibilities of their own personality than in dealing with the problems of the next generation. The sentimentality of the notion that it is nice 'to grow up with one's children' to be 'young with them' is a dangerous doctrine. Children require level-headed parents; they can find their own playmates. Although many adolescents do now mature earlier and may be able to cope

with children, it is forgotten that those who take far longer
to control their impulses and learn from others (because of
organic defects, low IQ, deficiencies in their background,
etc.) also have the democratic right to reproduce early and
are equally entitled to the privacy of a nuclear home. An
improvement in the over-all care and socialisation of children
could probably be partly obtained by encouraging the raising
of the age of parenthood. This involves more consideration of
the place of young adults in a society which thinks almost
exclusively in terms of parents and children and makes slight
provision, particularly in housing, for those who are neither.
There need to be alternatives to the young person remaining
in the parental home with all its restrictions, starting a
family, or 'dropping out'. And part of this alternative must
be the right to a sex life without the price of
children – something which is still not being properly faced,
particularly in connection with women and particularly in
the working class.

The discovery that the first five years are not so crucial
after all does not automatically lighten the burden of
child-care. In fact, the doctrine of monotropy has long
absolved most of us from any task beyond blaming mothers.
That child-care is not a biological process connected in some
instinctual way with femaleness, means that men as well as
women, can and should participate in it. Furthermore,
women's demands to share the rights which men
automatically have to both career and children, should cease
being treated as a call for some form of wicked neglect of
children and be regarded as perfectly justified.

Perhaps we may feel slightly guilty over the fact that if
child-care becomes more explicit its scope becomes more
finite. There is an end to what one can and cannot do for
children, to things one can and cannot achieve. By contrast,
the psychoanalytic tradition led us to worry continually that
the child was not getting enough of vaguely defined
attentions, that things may be going wrong inside without
any way of really telling, that one could always do more, that
one should never cease looking for crucial experiences which
could make all the difference depending on how they are
handled.

Unless we become more rational over this whole question,

there is the danger that fashion will swing as violently in one direction as it already has in another. Already there is a certain groundswell of hostility, of adults giving vent to long-suppressed feelings about the selfish, rude, aggressive, over-indulged and ever-demanding drag of the modern child. Problems which are not plumbed to the bottom have a habit of generating pendulum swings, in which each side defines itself by its opponent and nothing new is learnt. There is a genuine alternative between personal renunciation to the next generation and barricaded isolation. If we could cease being so 'child-oriented', recognise our rights to relationships with other adults and to pursue things we enjoy and value in themselves instead of always being inhibited by the desire to do well by the children, then at last we might not feel quite so trapped and angry, and at the same time make growing up more attractive to children that it is now.

To argue the need to strengthen and re-establish community and cultural transmission, as I have done, does not, of course, mean an endorsement of any find of folk tradition or a slavish obedience to parochial norms. We all know of enduring cultural traditions, many of whose elements are bigoted, violent, chauvinistic or criminal; and of communities so poor, ignorant and narrowly conformist that the young ask nothing but to escape from them to the more anonymous freedom of the big city. It is a familiar (and commercially very lucrative) phenomenon that far more people want to romanticise folk communities than to live in them. And while this pretentiousness may be ridiculous rather than harmful, it undoubtedly has its dangerous possibilities: witness the conscious elevation of pseudo-folk traditions (in theory by D.H. Lawrence and in practice by the Nazis) as a vehicle for authoritarianism and a cult of the irrational and instinctual.

The viable way of escape from the narrowness of one's background is not into atomistic individualism but rather into a different and more congenial community, as so many youth discover who enter student communities rather than simply marry and set up a nuclear household somewhere else. And communities whose traditions and norms are undesirable should not simply be broken up, especially if, as is common, there is no alternative community of any kind. Rather they should be exposed as far as possible to alternatives, and their members put in a position to make piecemeal choices about the styles of life they follow. This would argue, for example, the important function of the school as an institution separate from the parental home and practices, which teaches a wider culture and presents alternatives not met with in the home and immediate neighbourhood.

Gradual changes of this kind – the cultural mobility of individuals and the cultural modification of communities – are possible, because our total culture is an open one, containing very many different traditions and values which people can appeal to and build on. An important thread running throughout it is that of diversity, toleration and pluralism, and this allows individuals or groups, in effect to use one tradition in their culture to criticise another, without general communication breaking down so radically that it is no longer correct to speak of a culture.

A culture is not something that can be abandoned at will or created to order ('pop culture' and similar phenomena, artificial fabrications serving manipulative ends). One cannot stand outside one's whole culture and criticise it (by what standards, and where did one get them from?). But what can be done is to reject, abandon or change elements from inside the culture, moving within the diverse and often conflicting alternative traditions it offers. It is only because our over-all culture includes these alternatives that critical judgements about specific cultures can make sense, and conscious cultural change is possible at all.

Yet there is no avoiding the conclusion that these recommendations to halt the growing malaise of social impoverishment and cultural breakdown are measures that run contrary to some of the fundamentals of present social policy. Solutions at present being canvassed in high places not only fail to recognise the problem but include accelerating those very social developments that have created it. More economic growth, we are assured, will allow greater material and hence educational redistribution, which will give the unskilled working class equal opportunity to rise in the world. But it has been the very fact that people from the unskilled working class have risen which has so helped to cause the greater impoverishment of those left behind. Even if tomorrow's university entrants and subsequent professional classes contain a strictly proportionate sample of today's unskilled working-class children, how will that greater upward movement of individuals do anything at all to help the remaining unskilled working class? Or is it supposed that all are going to be upwardly mobile and migrate to semi-detached houses in the suburbs.

The re-establishment of urban communities as self-sustaining carriers of a culture rather than clusters of atomised dependents on social welfare agencies, requires some form of brake on social and geographical movement. For only in this way will a town or neighbourhood be populated by a reasonable cross-section of ability, personality types and age-groups, who expect to live there a large portion of their lives and will therefore tend both to cooperate with others and to locate their aspirations in the improvement of the area rather than escape from it. The need to retain the intelligent and gifted proportion of the population, who are now being lost, is absolutely crucial if people are to have models to copy, enabling them to improve and enhance the quality of their lives. It is also crucial if an urban community is to have the leaders to enable it to organise and fight its battles effectively. If this is élitist and authoritarian, then it is at least a policy of anchoring a genetic élite (which exists whether we like it or not) into the interests and purposes of the whole society rather than their own easy advancement. And it is also a policy of creating kinds of authority other than those whose existence depends upon a clause in an Act: authorities who will be obeyed because they are known and chosen, who can provide for urban inhabitants what shop-stewards provide for industrial workers.

To counteract nearly all the present tendencies and create the minimum conditions in which the renewal and improvement of communities could occur, would require deliberate planning for a mixture of income groups, of types of housing and of occupations within the same fairly small areas. More difficult still, it would require every possible incentive that a non-coercive administration can provide, to shift the goals of personal economic ambition and the popular definition of living standards, away from the mirage of endless private acquisition towards far wider and better public, shared amenities, with all the implications this would have for economic growth and manipulatable consumption in the modern Keynesian economy.

I have come a long way from the Maternal Deprivation Theory. I have tried to outline some of the reasons why the Theory, and its wider ideological background of early experience doctrines, should gain such universal acceptance and authority when it enjoys so little scientific support. These doctrines are part of an intellectual atmosphere which is in every sense bankrupt and which should now be consciously repudiated; a tradition which wilfully ignores the influences of human culture, society, learning and rationality in the life of an individual, because it has ceased to see individuals in a social context at all. For far too long this attitude has reflected, justified and perpetuated a social state of affairs in which the norm for the whole population is isolated, independent, child-centred nuclear families, whose values and aspirations are properly expected to be exclusively home-centred and individualist: a society without social entities.

I began by quoting Bowlby and will end the same way. Bowlby is surely right when he says, in *Attachment and Loss*:

> Man's capacity to use language and other symbols, his capacities to plan and build models, his capacities for long-lasting collaboration with others and for interminable strife, these make man what he is.

But what follows could not be more disastrously wrong:

> All these processes have their origin during the first three years of life, and all, moreover, are from their earliest days enlisted in the organisation of attachment behaviour ... [this is] the phase during which a child is acquiring all that makes him most distinctly human.

Chapter Notes

Acknowledgements

Chapter Notes

Introduction

1 D. W. Winnicott's *The Child, the Family and the Outside World* (Penguin Books, 1964) is a popular exposition of this belief about the damage which can be done by social and cultural attempts to interfere with the child's natural development process; this process includes the unfolding of the baby's innate morality.
2 John Bowlby, *Can I Leave my Baby?*, National Association for Mental Health, London, 1958, p. 6
3 ibid.
4 See, for example, the classic volume on the subject, *Britain in the Sixties: the Family and Marriage*, first published by Penguin Books as a Special in 1962 and subsequently revised and reissued as a Pelican in 1972.
5 Michael Rutter, *Maternal Deprivation Reassessed*, Penguin Books, 1972

1 Maternal Deprivation

1 John Bowlby, *Maternal Care and Mental Health*, 2nd ed., World Health Organisation, Monograph Series No. 2, Geneva, 1952
2 John Bowlby and Mary D. Salter-Ainsworth, *Child Care and the Growth of Love*, 2nd ed., abr. and ed. by Margery Fry, Penguin Books, 1965
3 ibid., pp. 13—14
4 ibid., p. 14
5 ibid., p. 14
6 ibid., p. 14
7 ibid., p. 14
8 ibid., p. 14
9 ibid., p. 21
10 ibid., p. 22
11 ibid., p. 22
12 ibid., p. 28
13 ibid., p. 28
14 ibid. pp. 65—6
15 D. Burlington and A. Freud, *Infants Without Families*, Allen & Unwin, 1944

16 Bowlby and Salter-Ainsworth, op. cit., p. 56
17 W. Goldfarb, 'Variations in adolescent adjustment of institutionally-reared children', *Amer. J. of Orthopsychiat.*, 17, p. 449, 1947
18 Bowlby and Salter-Ainsworth, op. cit., p. 62
19 ibid., p. 93
20 ibid., p. 94
21 ibid., p. 112
22 Benjamin Spock, *Problems of Parents*, p. 156, Bodley Head, 1963
23 Bowlby, *Can I Leave my Baby?*, National Association for Mental Health, London, 1958, p. 13
24 Bowlby and Salter-Ainsworth, op. cit., p. 108
25 John Bowlby interviewed in *The Times Educational Supplement*, 14 January 1972
26 'Nursery and Infant Schools', *The Times Educational Supplement*, 23 June 1972
27 'Playgroups for (non-working) Mothers', *The Times Educational Supplement*, 7 May 1971
28 Play schools 'no substitute for homes', *Evening Standard*, 29 December 1972
29 Expert Committee on Mental Health, WHO, 1951
30 See Report of the Platt Committee on the Welfare of Children in Hospitals, HMSO, 1959
31 Bowlby and Salter-Ainsworth, op. cit., p. 78
32 ibid., p. 80
33 Bowlby, *Maternal Care and Mental Health*, p. 46
34 Bowlby and Salter-Ainsworth, op. cit., p. 53
35 ibid., p. 201
36 ibid., p. 54
37 ibid., p. 78
38 ibid., p. 203
39 D. Burlington and A. Freud, op. cit.

2 Original Findings

1 Bowlby, *Forty-four Juvenile Thieves, their Characters and Home Life* p.2 Baillière, Tindall & Cox, 1946. (Part of this work was first published in the *International J. of Psycho-analysis*, vol XXV, pp. 19–53, 1944.)
2 ibid., p. 2
3 ibid., p. 31
4 ibid., p. 41
5 ibid., p. 49
6 ibid., p. 3
7 ibid., p. 3
8 ibid., p. 15
9 ibid., p. 5
10 ibid., p. 3
11 ibid., p. 5

12 ibid., p. 6
13 ibid., p. 5
14 ibid., p. 6
15 For example, the Minnesota Multiphasic Personality Inventory (MMPI). See S. R. Hathaway and J. C. Mckinley, *MMPI Manual*, Psychological Corporation, New York, 1943
16 For a test for maladjustment in children, see D. H. Stott, *The Social Adjustment of Children*, Manual to the Bristol Social Adjustment Guides, University of London Press, 2nd ed., 1962.
17 *Forty-four Juvenile Thieves . . .*, p. 7
18 Quite regardless of whether such maladjustment results from serious mental disturbance, which it often does not.
19 *Forty-four Juvenile Thieves . . .*, p. 16
20 ibid., p. 7
21 ibid., p. 7
22 ibid., p. 20
23 ibid., p. 26
24 ibid., p. 22
25 ibid., p. 24
26 ibid., p. 52
27 Cecil Woodham-Smith, *Florence Nightingale*, 4th imp., Fontana, 1970, pp. 14–15. First published by Constable, 1951.

3 Some Tests of the Hypothesis

1 N. O'Connor, 'Mother–Child Separation', *Acta Psychologica*, Vol. XII, pp. 174–91
2 *Forty-four Juvenile Thieves . . .*
3 Siri Naess, 'Mother–Child Separation and Delinquency', *Brit. J. Delinq.*, 10, 1959, pp. 22–35
4 ibid., p. 31
5 J. Cowie, V. Cowie and E. Slater, *Delinquency in Girls*, Heinemann, 1968
6 James J. Cockburn and Inga Maclay, 'Sex Differentials in Juvenile Delinquents', *Brit. J. Crim.*, vol. 5, 1965, pp. 289–308
7 F. I. Nye, *Family Relationships and Delinquent Behaviour*, 1958
8 J. H. Bagot, *Juvenile Delinquency*, Cape, 1941
9 J. G. Field, 'Two Types of Recidivist and Maternal Deprivation', *Brit. J. Crim.*, vol. 2, 1962, p. 377
10 In *Causes of Crime*, ed. Lord Pakenham, Weidenfeld & Nicolson, 1958, p. 51
11 J. G. Field, op. cit., p. 379
12 J. M. B. Douglas and J. M. Blomfield, *Children Under Five*, Allen & Unwin, 1958
13 J. M. B. Douglas, 'Broken Families and Child Behaviour', *J. Royal Coll. Phycns Lond.*, 4, pp.203–10
14 Alan Little, 'Parental Deprivation, Separation and Crime: A Test on Adolescent Recidivists', *Brit. J. Crim.*, vol. 5, p. 419, October 1965. pp. 419–30

15   ibid., p. 424
16   Bowlby and Salter-Ainsworth, op. cit.
17   Alan Little, op. cit., p 427

4   Crime: Learning and Personality

1   D. A. Grant, 'Classical and Operant Conditioning' in A. W. Melton
    (ed.), *Categories of Human Learning*, Academic Press, New York,
    1964
2   One of the most interesting questions at present is that of the
    acquisition of the grammatical structures of language. There are
    some persuasive arguments that this cannot be accounted for in
    learning theory terms. See the famous Skinner–Chomsky dispute.
    (For a brief outline of this, refer to 'A Symposium on Innate Ideas'
    by N. Chomsky, N. Goodman and H. Putnam in *The Philosophy of
    Language*, ed. by J. R. Feale, Oxford University Press, 1971.)
3   R. B. Cattell, *The Scientific Analysis of Personality*, Penguin
    Books, 1965
4   H. J. Eysenck and S. Rachman, *The Causes and Cures of Neurosis*,
    Routledge & Kegan Paul, 1965
5   P. E. Vernon, *Personality Assessment: A Critical Survey*, Methuen,
    1964
6   W. H. Sheldon and S. S. Stevens, *The Varieties of Temperament :
    A Psychology of Constitutional Differences*. Harper, New York,
    1942

5   Criminological Research

1   S. Glueck and E. T. Glueck, *One Thousand Juvenile Delinquents*,
    Harvard University Press, 1934
2   *Juvenile Delinquents Grown Up*, Commonwealth Fund, New York,
    1940
3   *Unravelling Juvenile Delinquency*, Commonwealth Fund, New
    York, 1950
4   *Family Environment and Delinquency*, Routledge & Kegan Paul,
    1962
5   *Delinquents and Non-Delinquents in Perspective*, Oxford
    University Press, 1968
6   *Predicting Delinquency and Crime*, Harvard University Press, 1959
7   By delinquency the Gluecks mean such crimes as theft, burglary,
    assault, sexual attacks and so on. Their definition for selecting the
    five hundred boys was the committing of repeated acts which, if
    the agent is over the statutory court age of sixteen, are punishable
    as crimes (that is, felonies or misdemeanours). The Gluecks
    excluded such trivial misbehaviour as truancy or stealing once or
    twice as a child: such 'misconduct or maladaptation cannot be
    deemed either habitual or symptomatic of deep-rooted causes'

(*Unravelling Juvenile Delinquency*, p. 14). The reader is also encouraged to refer to Appendix A in *Family Environment and Delinquency*. This gives the case of Henry W. as an example of the method of constructing the social histories of five hundred delinquents and non-delinquents.

8 *Unravelling Juvenile Delinquency*, p. 274
9 ibid., p. 278
10 Report of the work of the Institute of Criminology to the NUT Conference, *The Times Educational Supplement*, 5 January 1973
11 J. Shields, *Monozygotic Twins*, Oxford University Press, New York, 1962
12 H. J. Eysenck, 'The Inheritance of Introversion–Extroversion', *Acta Psychologica*, vol. XII, 1956
13 H. J. Eysenck and D. Prell, 'The Inheritance of Neuroticism: an Experimental Study', *J. Men. Sci.*, 97, pp. 441–6
14 T. C. N. Gibbens, *Psychiatric Studies of Borstal Lads*, Oxford University Press, New York, 1963
15 W. H. Sheldon, E. M. Hart and G. McDermot, *Varieties of Delinquent Youths*, Harper & Bros, New York, 1949
16 W. Healy and A. Bronner, *New Light on Delinquency and its Treatment*, Yale University Press, 1937
17 W. E. Roper, 'Comparative Study of the Wakefield Prison Population', *Brit. J. Delinq.*, July 1950 and April 1951, vol. 1, pp. 15–28 and 243–70
18 F. W. Warburton, 'Observations on a Sample of Psychopathic American Criminals', *Behaviour Research and Therapy*, 3, p. 129
19 R. G. Andry, *The Short-Term Prisoner – A Study in Forensic Psychology*, Stevens & Sons, 1963
20 Sir Cyril Burt, *The Young Delinquent*, University of London Press, 1925; rev. 4th edn 1957
21 W. Healy and A. Bronner, op. cit.
22 Sir Cyril Burt, op. cit., p. 101
23 ibid., p.98. Similar findings have also been made by W. McCord and J. McCord, *The Psychopath: An Essay on the Criminal Mind*, Van Nostrand, 1964, and by Lee N. Robins, *Deviant Children Grown Up*, Williams & Wilkins, Baltimore, 1966
24 Mary D. Ainsworth,* *The Effects of Maternal Deprivation: A Review of Findings and Controversy in the context of Research Strategy*, WHO, Geneva, 1962
25 R. G. Andry, *Delinquency and Parental Pathology*, Methuen, 1960.
26 Bowlby and Salter-Ainsworth, op. cit., p. 229
27 G. Rowntree, 'Early Childhood in Broken Families', *Population Studies*, 8, 1955, p. 247
28 Mary D. Salter-Ainsworth, op. cit., pp. 115–16
29 S. Glueck and E. T. Glueck, *Unravelling Juvenile Delinquency*, p. 122

* Mary D. Salter-Ainsworth is also referred to simply as Mary D. Ainsworth in much of the literature.

30 ibid., p. 122
31 *The Times Educational Supplement*, 5 January 1973
32 Bowlby and Salter-Ainsworth, op. cit., p. 229
33 S. Glueck and E. T. Glueck, *Juvenile Delinquents Grown Up*
34 ibid., p. 108
35 S. Glueck and E. T. Glueck, *Five Hundred Criminal Careers*
36 *Later Criminal Careers*, Commonwealth Fund, New York, 1937
37 *Juvenile Delinquents Grown Up*, pp. 268—9
38 ibid., p. 268
39 S. Naess, 'Mother—Child Separation and Delinquency: Further Evidence', *Brit. J. Crim.* 2, 1962, p. 361
40 B. Wootton, *Social Science and Social Pathology*, Allen & Unwin, 1959
41 Michael Rutter, 'Parent—child separation: psychological effects on the children', *J. Child Psychol. Psychiat.*, vol. 12, 1971, pp. 233—60

6   Criminal Character

1   Mary D. Ainsworth, op. cit. p. 117
2   Bowlby, *Forty-four Juvenile Thieves*: 'I am doubtful, however, whether the law-abiding Affectionless Character exists.' Consequently, 'It is probably true to say that the Affectionless Character always steals and usually becomes a recidivist.'
3   Mary D. Ainsworth, op. cit., p. 116
4   Hilda Lewis, *Deprived Children: The Mershal Experiment*, Oxford University Press, 1954
5   L. E. Hewitt and R. L. Jenkins, *Fundamental Patterns of Maladjustment: The Dynamics of their Origins*, State of Illinois, Springfield, Illinois, 1946
6   D. H. Stott, op. cit.
7   Hilda Lewis, op. cit., p. 44
8   ibid., p. 75
9   ibid., p. 76
10 ibid., p. 77
11 ibid., p. 41. Lewis is referring to Bowlby's statement that 'It is true that they are sometimes sociable in a superficial sense, but if this is scrutinised we find that there are no feelings, no roots in these relationships.' (*Int. J. Psychol. Anal.*, 21, 1940, p. 158)
12 ibid., p. 41
13 D. H. Stott, 'The Effects of Separation from the Mother in Early Life', *The Lancet*, 1, 1956, p. 624
14 ibid., p. 626
15 ibid., p. 626
16 See the report in the *Guardian* (3 October 1973) on research on battered children and NSPCC treatment centres.

7 *Affectionlessness and Psychopathology*

1 Bowlby and Salter-Ainsworth, op. cit., pp. 32—3
2 W. McCord and J. McCord, op. cit.
3 Michael Craft, *Ten Studies in Psychopathic Personality*, John Wright, Bristol, 1965
4 H. G. Gough, 'A Sociological Theory of Psychology', *Amer. J. Sociol.*, 53, 1948, pp. 359—66
5 Michael Craft, *Psychopathic Disorders and their Assessment*, Pergamon Press, 1966. See the chapter 'The Meaning of the Term Psychopath' for a discussion of history and views. (See also R. D. Hare, *Psychopathy: Theory and Research*, John Wiley & Sons, 1970)
6 Craft, ibid.
7 Hare, op. cit., p. 17
8 H. J. Eysenck, *Crime and Personality*, Methuen, 1964
9 Roper, op. cit.
10 For example, J. R. Knott, E. B. Platt, M. C. Ashby and J. S. Gottlieb, 'A familial evaluation of the EEG of patients with primary behaviour disorder and psychopathic personality', *EEG and Clinical Neurophysiology*, 5, pp. 363—70
11 Margaret Mead, *Male and Female*, Penguin Books, 1950, p.69
12 Hare, op. cit.
13 ibid.
14 M. Rutter, *Maternal Deprivation Reassessed*, Penguin Books, 1972
15 Lewis, op. cit.
16 Stott, 'The Effects of Separation . . .', *The Lancet* 1, 1956
17 In *Causes of Crime*, ed. Lord Pakenham, Weidenfeld & Nicolson, 1958
18 Craft, op. cit.
19 J. Oltman and S. Friedman, 'Parental Deprivation in Psychiatric Conditions', *Diseases of the Nervous System*, 28, 1967, pp. 298—303
20 ibid., p. 157
21 Robins, op. cit.
22 Hare, op. cit., p. 97
23 Knott *et al.*, op. cit.
24 Shields, op. cit.
25 ibid., p. 104
26 Craft, op. cit.
27 ibid.
28 Craft, *Ten Studies in Psychopathic Personality* (John Wright, Bristol, 1965) discusses the literature.
29 M. Drillien, 'Physical and Mental Handicaps in the Prematurely Born', *J. Obstet. Gynaec. Brit. Empire*, 66, 1959, p. 721
30 D. H. Stott, *The Social Adjustment of Children*, 2nd ed., University of London Press, 1962
31 *Thirty-three Troublesome Children*, National Children's Home, 1964

32   'Why Maladjustment?', article in *New Society*, 10 December 1964
33   H. F. R. Prechtl, 'Mother–Child Interaction in Babies with Minimal
     Brain Damage', in *Determinants of Infant Behaviour*, ed.
     B. M. Foss, vol. 1, Methuen, 1963
34   D. Baird, 'Contribution of Obstetrical Factors to Serious Physical
     and Mental Handicaps in Children', *J. Obstet, Gynaec. Brit.
     Empire*, 66, 1959, p. 743
35   *Brit. Med. J.*, 'Suicide Risk in Teenage Pregnancy', June 1971
     p. 602
36   Shields, op. cit. Also the discussion in Eysenck, *Uses and Abuses of
     Psychology*, Penguin Books, 1953
37   Craft, *Psychopathic Disorders* . . ., Pergamon Press, 1966
38   S. Glueck and E. T. Glueck, *Family Environment and Delinquency*,
     Routledge & Kegan Paul, 1962
39   Prechtl, op. cit.
40   D. H. Stott, 'Why Maladjustment?' (see note 32)
41   H. Edelston, *The Earliest Stages of Delinquency, A Clinical Study
     from the Child Guidance Clinic*, E. S. Livingstone, 1952
42   ibid., p. 92
43   ibid., p. 93
44   ibid., p. 93
45   ibid., p. 94
46   ibid., p. 137
47   M. Rutter, *Maternal Deprivation Reassessed*, Penguin Books, 1972
48   Unless Rutter resorts to the extravagant theories of R. D. Laing,
     which I am sure he would be most reluctant to do.
49   Ronald Lloyd and Stanley Williamson, *Born to Trouble: Portrait of
     a Psychopath*, Cassirer, 1968. (The concluding chapter, from the
     psychiatrist's viewpoint, is by Michael Craft.)
50   Hare, op. cit., pp. 110–18
51   S. Glueck and E. T. Glueck, *Juvenile Delinquents Grown Up*
52   Roper, op. cit. p. 261. Also T. C. N. Gibbens, D. A. Pond and
     D. Stafford Clark, 'A Follow-up Study of Criminal Psychopaths',
     British Journal of Delinquency, 1955, p. 143
53   Bowlby, *Forty-four Juvenile Thieves* . . ., Baillière, Tindall & Cox,
     1946
54   Henry V. Dicks, 'The Predicament of the Family in the Modern
     World', *The Lancet*, 5 February 1955, p 295
55   Royal Medico-Psychological Association, 'Report to the LCC
     Committee on Juvenile Delinquency', Supplement of the *J. Men.
     Sciences*, July 1950
56   Craft, *Psychopathic Disorders and their Assessment*, op. cit.,
     pp. 11–13

8   *The Spitzian Scare*

1   Dr Eustace Chesser, 'Is the Family Dead?', *Daily Telegraph*
    Magazine, 24 September 1971

2 See, for example, Sheila Kitzinger, *The Experience of Childbirth*, rev. edn, Penguin Books, 1967, p. 222. She warns the new mother that her offspring's physical health and survival depend upon plentiful love.

3 See L. Casler, 'Perceptual Deprivation in Institutional Settings' in *Early Experience and Behaviour*, R. Newton and S. Levine (eds), Charles C. Thomas, Springfield, Illinois, 1968. She argues that institutionalised children are a highly selected and atypical group.

4 R. A. Spitz, 'Hospitalism' in *Psychoanalytic Study of the Child*, Vol. 1, International Universities Press, New York, 1945, p. 53

5 As the pseudonyms might suggest, Foundling Home is the 'bad' institution (without maternal presence) and Nursery the 'better' one, with the mothers present for at least a part of the time.

6 R. A. Spitz, 'Hospitalism: A Follow-up Report', *Psychoanalytic Study of the Child*, vol. 2, International Universities Press, New York, 1946, p. 113

7 R. A. Spitz and K. M. Wolf, 'Anaclitic Depression . . .', *Psychoanalytic Study of the Child*, vol. 2, International Universities Press, New York, 1946, p. 313

8 For example, Spitz and Wolf, 'Autoerotism. Some empirical findings and hypothesis on three of its manifestations in the first year of life', *Psychoanalytic Study of the Child*, vol. 3/4, 1949, pp. 85–120

9 Spitz, 'The Psychogenic Diseases in Infancy: An attempt at their Etiologic Classification', *Psychoanalytic Study of the Child*, vol. 6, 1951, pp. 255–75

10 Spitz, *The First Year of Life*, International Universities Press, New York, 1965

11 Samuel Pinneau, 'The Infantile Disorders of Hospitalism and Anaclitic Depression', *Psychological Bulletin*, vol. 52, No. 5

12 Spitz and Wolf, 'Anaclitic Depression', loc. cit.

13 Spitz, 'The Influences of the Mother–Child Relationship and its Disturbances in Mental Health and Infant Development', in *Mental Health and Infant Development*, ed. K. Soddy, Routledge & Kegan Paul, 1955

14 Spitz, 'The Psychogenic Diseases in Infancy . . .', loc. cit., p. 271

15 Spitz, *The First Year of Life* (see note 10)

16 Spitz and Wolf, 'Anaclitic Depression', loc. cit.

17 ibid. 'We have observed cases in which, after a period of two weeks, the developmental quotient dropped again. It did not drop to the previous low levels reached during the depression.'

18 Pinneau, op. cit.

19 Spitz. 'Hospitalism . . .', loc. cit. p. 66

20 Spitz and Wolf, 'Anaclitic Depression', loc. cit. p. 331

21 Pinneau, op. cit.

22 Spitz, 'Reply to Dr Pinneau', *Psychol. Bull.*, vol. 52, No. 5, 1955, p. 453

23 Spitz and Wolf, 'Anaclitic Depression', loc. cit. p. 33

24 Spitz, 'Hospitalism . . .', loc. cit.

25 Spitz, 'Hospitalism: A Follow-up Report', loc. cit.
26 Spitz and Wolf, 'Anaclitic Depression', loc. cit.
27 Spitz and Wolf, 'Autoerotism . . .', loc. cit.
28 Spitz, 'Hospitalism: A Follow-up Report', loc. cit.
29 Spitz, 'Reply to Dr Pinneau'. loc. cit., p. 455
30 Spitz, 'Hospitalism . . .', loc. cit., p. 60
31 See the following summaries: 'Child Care in OMNI Institutes', *The Times Educational Supplement*, 4 June 1971, for eleven of the most striking court cases since 1964; and 'Nursery children bitten, assaulted, infected, silenced', Anthony Johnson, *T.E.S.*, 5 March 1971.
32 Spitz and Wolf, 'Autoerotism', loc. cit.
33 Spitz, 'Hospitalism . . .', loc. cit., p. 60
34 Spitz and Wolf, 'Anaclitic Depression', loc. cit.
35 Spitz, 'Hospitalism . . .', loc. cit. p. 65
36 Spitz and Wolf, 'Autoerotism', loc. cit., p. 98
37 Pinneau, op. cit.
38 Spitz, 'Hospitalism . . .', loc. cit., p. 59
39 ibid., p. 62
40 Spitz, 'The Influences of the Mother–Child Relationship . . .' in *Mental Health and Infant Development*. ed. K. Soddy, Routledge & Kegan Paul, 1955
41 ibid.
42 Spitz, 'Hospitalism . . .', loc. cit., p. 68
43 Spitz, 'The Influence of the Mother–Child Relationship . . .', loc. cit. p. 107
44 Spitz, 'Hospitalism: A Follow-up Report', loc. cit., p. 117
45 William L. Langer, 'Europe's Intitial Population Explosion', *Amer. Hist. Rev.*, 69, pp. 1–17
46 C. F. Whitten, M. G. Pettitt and J. Fishoff, 'Evidence that Growth Failure from Maternal Deprivation is Secondary to Undereating', *J. Amer. Med. Assn*, vol. 209, 1969, pp. 1675–82
47 Spitz, 'Hospitalism . . .', loc. cit.
48 Spitz, 'Reply to Dr Pinneau', loc. cit.
49 See, for example: 'Disorganising Factors of Infant Personality', *Amer. J. Psychiat.*, 98, 1941; *The Rights of Infants*, Columbia University Press, New York, 1943
50 Spitz, 'Reply to Dr Pinneau', loc. cit., p. 453
51 W. Dennis and M. G. Dennis, 'The Effects of Cradling Practices upon the Onset of Walking in Hopi Children', *J. of Genetic Psychol.*, 56, 1940, p. 77; also W. Dennis, 'Infant Development under Conditions of Restricted Practice and Minimum Social Stimulation', *Genet. Psychol. Monograph* 23, 1941, p. 143; W. Dennis, Infant Development under Environmental Handicap', *Psychological Monographs* 71, 1957, No. 436
52 See Graham Chedd, 'Can the Mind Flourish Despite Neglect?', *New Scientist*, 11 January 1973
53 John Brierly, 'The Crucial Years of Life', *New Society*, 4 October 1973

54 See C. Blakemore and G. F. Cooper, 'Development of the Brain Depends on the Visual Environment', *Nature*, vol. 228, p. 1170

9   *Extra-familial Upbringing*

1 Frances Power Cobb, *Workhouse Sketches*, 1861, in British Museum collection
2 Report of the Care of Children Committee, 1946, Cmd. 6922
3 See mainly: W. Goldfarb, 'Effects of Early Institutional Care on Adolescent Personality', *J. Exp. Educ.*, 12, 1943; 'Infant Rearing as a Factor in Foster Home Replacement', *Amer. J. Orthopsychiat.*, 14, 1944, p. 162
4 L. Casler, 'Maternal Deprivation: A Critical Review of the Literature', *Monograph Soc. Rev. Child Dev.*, 26, 1961, No. 2
5 Goldfarb, 'Variations in Adolescent Adjustment of Instituionally Reared Children', *Amer. J. Orthopsychiat.*, 17 1947
6 L. Bender, 'Infants Reared in Institutions', *Bull, Child Welfare League of America*, 24, 1945, No. 7, pp. 1–4
7 L. G. Lowrey, 'Personality Disorder and Early Institutional Care', *Amer. J. Orthopsychiat.*, 10, 1940, pp. 576–85
8 Goldfarb, 'Effects of Early Institutional Care on Adolescent Personality', *Amer. J. Orthopsychiat.*, 14, 1944, p. 441
9 N. O'Connor, 'The Evidence for the Permanently Disturbing Effects of Mother–Infant Separation', *Acta Psychol.*, vol. 12, 1956, pp. 174–91
10 Goldfarb, 'Infant Rearing and Problem Behaviour', *Amer. J. Orthopsychiat.*, 13, 1943, p. 249
11 N. O'Connor, op. cit.
12 E. E. Levitt, 'Alleged Rorschach Anxiety Indices in Children', *J. Proj. Tech.*, 21, 1957, pp. 231–64
13 Bowlby and Salter-Ainsworth, op. cit., p. 44
14 William Sargent, *The Unquiet Mind*, Pan Books, 1971, p. 34
15 ibid., p. 24
16 Rutter, *Maternal Deprivation Reassessed*, Penguin Books, 1972
17 M. K. Mason, 'Learning to Speak after Six and a Half Years of Silence', *J. Speech and Hearing Disorders*, vol. 7, 1942, pp. 295–304
18 K. Davis, 'Final Note on a Case of Extreme Isolation', *Amer. J. Sociol.*, vol. 52, 1947, pp. 432–7
19 Mary D. Salter-Ainsworth, op. cit., p. 133
20 H. M. Skeels and H. B. Dye, 'A Study of the Effects of Differential Stimulation on Mentally Retarded Children', *Proc. Amer. Assn. Ment. Defect.*, vol. 44, 1939, pp. 114–36
21 S. A. Kirk, *Early Education of the Mentally Retarded: An Experimental Study*, University of Illinois Press, 1958; Z. A. Stein and M. Susser, 'Mutability of Intelligence and Epidemiology of Mild Mental Retardation', *Rev. Educ. Res.*, vol. 40, 1970
22 M. Berger, 'Early Experience and other Environmental Factors', in

Handbook of Abnormal Psychology, ed. H. J. Eysenck, 2nd edn, Pitman, 1973

23 J. B. Garvin and L. S. Sacks, 'Growth Potential of Pre-School Children in Institutional Care: a Positive Approach to a Negative Condition', *Amer. J. Orthopsychiat.*, vol. 33, 1963, pp. 399—408

24 H. L. Rheingold and N. Bayley, 'The Later Effects of an Experimental Modification of Mothering', *Child Dev.*, vol. 30, 1959, pp. 363—72

25 Hilda Lewis, op. cit..

26 A. Freud and S. Dann, 'An Experiment in Group Upbringing', *Psycho-Anal. Study Child*, 6, 1951, pp. 127—168; A. Freud and D. Burlington, *Young Children in Wartime*, Allen & Unwin, 1942; Burlington and Freud, *Infants Without Families*, Allen & Unwin, 1944

27 A. Freud, 'Young Children in Times of Social Disturbance', in *Mental Health and Infant Development*, ed. K. Soddy, Routledge & Kegan Paul, 1955

28 Michael Craft, *Psychopathic Disorders and their Assessment*, Pergamon Press, 1966

29 A. D. B. Clarke and A. M. Clarke, 'Cognitive Changes in the Feeble-minded', *Brit. J. Psychol.*, 45, 1957; A. D. B. Clarke, A. M. Clarke and S. Reiman, 'Cognitive Changes in the Feeble-minded: Three Further Studies', *Brit. J. Psychol.*, 49, 1958; A. D. B. Clarke and A. M. Clarke, 'Recovery from the Effects of Deprivation', *Acta Psychol.*, 16, 1959

30 'Animals in this state undergo physiological changes such as impaired tissue replacement, reduced resistance to infection, etc.

31 L. L. Heston, D. D. Denney and I. B. Pauly, 'The Adult Adjustment of Persons Institutionalised as Children', *Brit. J. Psychiat.*, 112, 1966, pp. 1103—10

32 ibid., p. 1108

33 ibid., p. 1108

34 ibid., pp. 1108—9

35 ibid., pp. 1108—9

36 See, for example, the remarks of Dr Eustace Chesser, *Love Without Fear*, rev. edn, Arrow Books, 1966, p. 187

37 See J. W. Eaton, *Culture and Mental Disorders*, Free Press, Glencoe, 1955

38 M. Spiro, *Children of the Kibbutz*, Harvard University Press, 1958; B. Bettelheim, 'Does Communal Education Work?', *Commentary*, February 1962; *The Family and the Sexual Revolution*, ed. Edwin M. Schur, Unwin, 1964; R. Kohen-Raz, 'Mental and Motor Developments of Kibbutz Institutionalised and Home-Reared Infants in Israel', *Child Devel.*, vol. 34, 1968, pp. 489—504; L. Miller, 'Child Rearing in the Kibbutz', in *Modern Perspectives in International Child Psychiatry*, ed. J. G. Howells, Oliver & Boyd, 1969

39 Bowlby and Salter-Ainsworth, op. cit., p. 209

40 ibid., p. 49

10 Bowlby's Sanatorium Study

1 John Bowlby, M. Ainsworth, M. Boston and D. Rosenbluth, 'The Effects of Mother–Child Separation: A Follow-up Study', *Brit. J. Medical Psychol.*, vol. 29, 1956, p. 211
2 ibid., p. 218
3 See, for example, F. Kräupl Taylor's letter in *The Lancet*, 22 March 1958 and Bowlby's reply, 17 May 1958
4 Bowlby *et al.*, op. cit., p. 218
5 ibid., pp. 216 and 219
6 ibid., p. 224
7 Kräupl Taylor (see note 3 above)
8 See also J. G. Howell's letter in *The Lancet*, 29 March 1958
9 Bowlby *et al.*, op. cit., p. 226
10 ibid., p. 213
11 ibid., p. 213
12 ibid., p. 228
13 ibid., p. 230
14 ibid., p. 231
15 ibid., p. 228
16 ibid., p. 231
17 ibid., p. 232
18 ibid., p. 227
19 ibid., p. 236
20 ibid., p. 235
21 ibid., p. 235
22 ibid., p. 236
23 ibid., p. 236
24 Bowlby, *Forty-four Juvenile Thieves* . . ., Ballière, Tindall & Cox, 1946, p. 40
25 D. H. Stott, 'The Effects of Separation from the Mother in Early Life', *The Lancet*, 1, 1956, p. 624
26 ibid., p. 626
27 ibid., p. 626
28 Bowlby *et al.*, op. cit., p. 233
29 ibid., p. 234
30 ibid., p. 234
31 ibid., p. 235
32 ibid., p. 240
33 Bowlby, 'A Note on Mother–Child Separation as a Mental Health Hazard', *Brit. J. Medical Psychol.*, vol. 31, 1958, p. 247. Also letter to *The Lancet*, 1 March 1958, p. 480
34 Bowlby, 'Childhood Mourning and Psychiatric Illness' in *The Predicament of the Family*, ed. P. Lomas, Hogarth Press, 1967, p. 167
35 Salter-Ainsworth in *Child Care and the Growth of Love*, Penguin Books, 1965
36 Ainsworth, *The Effects of Maternal Deprivation* . . ., WHO, Geneva, 1962, pp. 108–112
37 Bowlby *et al.*, op. cit., p. 240

38 Bowlby, letter to *The Lancet*, 1 March 1958, p. 480
39 Bowlby, *Can I Leave my Baby?* National Association for Mental Health, London, 1958
40 H. Edelston, letter to *The Lancet*, 12 April 1958, p. 797
41 This is certainly not outside the limits of feasibility. Very large-scale surveys have been accomplished, dealing with far more complex variables. There have been surveys of the prevalence of separation in the general population, but these are usually dismissed because they do not involve a 'thorough clinical appraisal of personality' (Ainsworth and Bowlby, 'Research Strategy in the Study of Mother–Child Separation', *Courrier* (French Publication), 4, No. 3, 1954, p. 116).
42 Bowlby, *Attachment and Loss*, vol. 1, Hogarth Press, 1969; both volumes published by Penguin Books: see p. 25 of paperback edn.
43 B. Wootton, 'A Social Scientist's Approach to Maternal Deprivation' in *Deprivation of Maternal Care: A Reassessment of its Effects*, WHO, Geneva, 1962, p. 71
44 Bowlby, 'Childhood Mourning and Psychiatric Illness', loc. cit., p. 143

11   The Emotional Sell

1 Something approximating to this may be true for someone institutionalised for many years – because the institution does not allow for human relationships, not because the person is really incapable of them.
2 Bowlby, 'Separation Anxiety', *Int. J. Psycho. Anal.* 41, 89–113, 1960, p. 90
3 Albert J. Solnit and Morris Green, 'Psychological Considerations in the Management of Death in Pediatric Hospital Services', *Pediatrics*, vol. 24, 1959, p. 110
4 Bowlby, *Child Care and the Growth of Love*, Penguin Books, 1965, p. 55
5 Ainsworth, *The Effects of Maternal Deprivation: Review of Findings and Controversy*, WHO, Geneva, 1962, p. 99
6 'Are We Doing Enough to Make Children Happy in Hospital?', report by Paula Davies, *Daily Telegraph*, October 1969. The Platt Committee (Report on the Welfare of Children in Hospitals, HMSO, 1959) claimed to have been strongly influenced by Robertson's films.
7 'John, aged seventeen months, in a residential nursery for nine days', Film No. 3, 1969a. Selections from the press reviews are available from the Tavistock Clinic, London.
8 'John: Little Boy Lost, who may cause a Revolution in Child Care', article on the film by James and Joyce Robertson by Judith Simmons in *Nova* July 1970
9 ibid.

12 A Look at Short Separation

1 A. Myrdal and Viola Klein, *Woman's Two Roles*, rev. edn, Routledge & Kegan Paul, 1968, p. 124
2 ibid., p. 127
3 J. G. Howells and J. Layng, 'Separation Experiences and Mental Health', *The Lancet*, 2, 1955, p. 285
4 M. Stacey, Rosemary Dearden, Roisin Pill and Daniel Robinson, *Hospitals, Children and Their Families*, Routledge & Kegan Paul, 1970
5 R. S. Illingworth's 'Children in Hospital', *The Lancet*, 17 December 1955
6 Bowlby, interview in *The Times Educational Supplement*, 14 January 1972
7 Hilda Lewis, *Deprived Children*, Oxford University Press, 1954
8 C. Heinicke and I. Westheimer, *Brief Separations*, Longmans Green, 1966
9 H. R. Schaffer, 'Activity Level as a Determinant of Infantile Reaction to Deprivation', *Child Devel.*, 37, 1966, pp. 595–602
10 Heinicke and Westheimer, op. cit.
11 ibid. Summary of French study.
12 Hilda Lewis, op. cit.
13 Howells and Layng, op. cit.
14 J. Robertson, 'Young Children in Brief Separation', *Psychol. Anal. Study Child*, vol. 26, 1967, pp. 264–315. (Later published as a booklet by Quadrangle Books, New York, 1971; available from the Tavistock Child Development Research Unit of the Tavistock Clinic in London.)
15 ibid., p. 283
16 ibid., p. 273
17 ibid., p. 297
18 ibid., p. 284
19 ibid., p. 286
20 ibid., p. 313
21 ibid., p. 313
22 ibid., p. 306
23 J. W. B. Douglas and J. M. Blomfield, *Children Under Five*, Allen & Unwin, 1958
24 Howells and Layng, op. cit.
25 Douglas and Blomfield, op. cit.
26 Stacey *et. al.*, op. cit.
27 ibid., p. 92
28 ibid., p. 59
29 Prechtl, 'Mother–Child Interaction in Babies with Minimal Brain Damage', in *Determinants of Infant Behaviour*, ed. B. M. Foss, Methuen, 1963
30 D. H. Stott, 'Why Maladjustment?', article in *New Society*, 10 December 1964; *Thirty-Three Troublesome Children*, National Children's Home, 1964

31   M. Drillien, 'Physical and Mental Handicaps in the Prematurely
     Born', *J. Obstet. Gynaec. Brit. Empire*, 66, 1959
32   Harriette Wilson, *Delinquency and Child Neglect*, Allen & Unwin,
     1962
33   Stacey *et. al.*, op. cit., p. 148
34   ibid., p. 148
35   ibid., p. 116

13   Fantasies of Infant Thieves (and Adult Theorists)

1   Spitz, 'Reply to Dr Pinneau', *Psychol. Bull.*, vol. 52, No. 5, 1955,
     p. 453
2   Robertson, 'Young Children in Brief Separation', loc. cit., p. 309
3   Bowlby *et al.*, 'The Effects of Mother–Child Separation: A
     Follow-up Study', *Brit. J. Medical Psychol.*, vol. 29, 1956, p. 211
4   For a simplified and accurate synopsis, see Ernest Jones, *What is
     Psychoanalysis?*, Allen & Unwin, 1959; another useful account is
     David Stafford-Clark's *What Freud Really Said*, Macdonald, 1965
5   Spitz, *The First Year of Life*, International Universities Press, New
     York, 1965, p. 285
6   Albert J. Solnit on Spitz's infants in 'A Study of Object Loss in
     Infancy', *Psychol. Anal. Study Child*, vol. XXV, 1970, p. 264
7   Spitz, 'Hospitalism', *Psychol. Anal. Study Child*, vol. 1,
     International Universities Press, New York, 1945, pp. 67–8
8   ibid., p. 68
9   Bowlby, *Child Care and the Growth of Love*, Penguin Books, 1965
10   ibid., p. 62
11   ibid., p. 64
12   Juliette Farez-Bontonier, 'Group Influence on Personality
     Development' in *Mental Health and Infant Development*, ed.
     K. Soddy, Routledge & Kegan Paul, 1955
13   Anna Freud, 'Young Children in Times of Social Disturbance' in
     Mental Health and Infant Development (See Note 12)
14   Melanie Klein, *Our Adult World and its Roots in Infancy*,
     Tavistock Pamphlet No. 2, 1959, p. 4
15   ibid.
16   ibid.
17   Klein, *The Psychoanalysis of Children*. Hogarth Press: first
     published 1932; 3rd edn reprinted 1969; p. 185
18   Klein, *Our Adult World* . . ., loc. cit. p. 6
19   Klein, 'Weaning' in *On the Bringing Up of Children*, ed.
     J. Rickman, Kegan Paul, 1936, p. 41
20   Klein, *The Psychoanalysis of Children* (see Note 17) p. 336
21   ibid., p. 337
22   Klein, *Our Adult World* . . . (see Note 14), p. 12
23   Bowlby, *Forty-four Juvenile Thieves* . . ., Baillière, Tindall & Cox,
     1946, p. 51
24   ibid., p. 51

25 ibid., p. 51
26 Margaret Mead, 'A Cultural Anthropologist's Approach to Maternal Deprivation', *Deprivation of Maternal Care*, WHO, Geneva, 1962
27 In an article on care orders: 'Everyone seems to agree that children should not be taken into care . . .' – Angela Phillips, *Spare Rib*, No. 31
28 ibid.
29 S. Smith and S. Noble, 'Battered Children and their Parents', *New Society*, 15 November 1973
30 *Forty-four Juvenile Thieves* . . . (see Note 23), p. 51
31 Bowlby, 'Processes of Mourning', *Int. J. Psycho. Anal.*, 42, 317–40, 1961, p. 332
32 Bowlby *et. al.*, (see Note 3)
33 Bowlby, *Child Care and the Growth of Love*, p. 18
34 Bowlby, 'Childhood Mourning and Psychiatric Illness' in *The Predicament of the Family*, ed. P. Lomas, Hogarth Press, 1967, p. 145
35 Bowlby, 'Processes of Mourning', loc. cit., p. 333
36 ibid., p. 336
37 ibid., p. 336
38 Bowlby, 'Childhood Mourning . . .' (see Note 34), p. 149
39 ibid.
40 Bowlby, 'Processes of Mourning', loc. cit.
41 Bowlby, 'Childhood Mourning . . .' (see Note 34), p. 141

14 The Status of Kleinian Theory

1 Bowlby, *Maternal Care and Mental Health*, 2nd edn WHO, Monograph Series No. 2, Geneva, 1952
2 Bowlby, *Forty-four Juvenile Thieves* . . ., Baillière, Tindall & Cox, 1946, p. 50
3 ibid., p. 50
4 Klein, 'Weaning', in *On the Upbringing of Children*, ed. J. Rickman, Kegan Paul, 1936, p. 32
5 Klein, *The Psychoanalysis of Children*, Hogarth Press, 1932; 3rd edn reprinted 1969; p. 29
6 ibid., p. 25
7 ibid., p. 25
8 Klein, *Our Adult World and its Roots in Infancy*, Tavistock Pamphlet No. 2, 1959, p. 4
9 H. V. Dicks, 'How the Emotions Grow', *New Society*, 2 December 1965
10 D. W. Winnicott, *The Child, the Family and the Outside World*, Penguin Books, 1964. Originally published in 2 vols, *The Child the Family* and *The Child and the Outside World*, Tavistock Publications, 1957
11 Klein, *The Psychoanalysis of Children* (see Note 5)
12 Sigmund Freud, *Collected Papers* vol. 3, Hogarth Press, 1950

13 See W. A. Marshall, *Development of the Brain* for a summary of brain growth in infancy: Oliver & Boyd, 1968

14 See P. H. Wolff, 'The Natural History of Crying and other Vocalisations in Early Infancy' in *Determinants of Infant Behaviour*, ed. B. M. Foss, vol. IV, Methuen, 1965

15 Dicks, op. cit.

16 Or, more correctly, *alarm*. Fear in its normal use presupposes beliefs — true or otherwise — about danger. Such beliefs are not assumed in the research I am discussing.

17 Wolff, op. cit.

18 ibid.

19 George A. Morgan and H. N. Ricciuti, 'Infants' Responses to Strangers during the First Year' in *Determinants of Infant Behaviour* (see Note 14)

20 See the detailed exposition of his recent position in *Attachment and Loss* (Hogarth Press, 1969).

21 Freud, *The Question of Lay-Analysis*, in *Two Short Accounts of Psychoanalysis*, trans. James Strachey, Hogarth Press, 1959; Penguin Books, 1962, p. 127

22 ibid., p. 127

23 Freud, Collected Papers, vol. 3 (see Note 12)

24 Ernest Jones, *Sigmund Freud: Life and Work*, vol. 2, Hogarth Press, 1953

25 E. Glover, *On the Early Development of the Mind*, International Universities Press, New York, 1956, p. 76

26 A far more intensive study and criticism of this analysis is provided in J. Wolfe and S. Rachman, 'Psychoanalytic Evidence: A Critique based on Freud's Case of Little Hans', *J. Nerv. & Ment. Disease*, 131, 1960

27 Freud, *Collected Papers*, vol. 3 (see Note 12)

15 The Scientific Credentials of Psychoanalysis

1 For example, some theory about the surface of Pluto is in principle testable, even though a test is practically impossible. But the claim that astral influences are stronger in person A than in person B is not even testable in principle.

2 Freud, 'Five Lectures on Psychoanalysis' in *Two Short Accounts of Psychoanalysis*, trans. James Strachey, Penguin Books, 1957, p. 55

3 See the analytical case: Carney Landis, 'Psychoanalytic Phenomena' in *Critical Essays on Psychoanalysis*, ed. S. Rachman, Pergamon Press, 1963

4 Freud, *New Elementary Lectures on Psychoanalysis*, Norton, New York, 1933

5 S. Rachman, *The Effects of Psychotherapy*, Pergamon Press, 1971

6 J. Wolfe and A. Lazarus, *Behaviour Therapy Techniques*, and Carney Landis and Professor Boring in *Critical Essays on*

Psychoanalysis, ed. S. Rachman, Pergamon Press, 1963

7 Jones, *The Life and Work of Sigmund Freud*, Hogarth Press, 1953

8 P. Bailey, 'The Great Psychiatric Revolution' in *Critical Essays on Psychoanalysis*, op. cit.

9 The teachings of psychoanalysis are based upon an incalculable number of observations and experiences, and no one who has not repeated these observations upon himself or upon others is in a position to arrive at an independent judgement of it' — Freud, *An Outline of Psychoanalysis*, Norton, New York, 1949, p. 12

10 Freud, 'Five Lectures on Psychoanalysis', loc. cit.

11 Freud, 'Fragment of an analysis of a case of hysteria' in *Complete Works*, Hogarth Press, 1953, pp. 58—9

12 Freud, 'Five Lectures on Psychoanalysis', loc. cit., p. 67

13 Jones, op. cit., p. 351

14 David Stafford-Clark, *What Freud Really Said*, Macdonald, 1965. The only evidence Stafford-Clark appears to have mustered for the validity of Freud's theories is that Freud was a 'genius'. Jones (op. cit., p. 360) refers to his mater's 'flawless integrity' and says that the 'application of Freud's ideas could only exert a beneficial effect' (ibid., p. 464).

16   Motherhood and Monkeys

1 The interpretations put upon this research are those of popularizers who have fastened on aspects in it that seem to fit their requirements. Harlow himself has been open-minded, although unfortunately he obviously began with some unexamined assumptions that have coloured his terminology.

2 Harlow, 'The Maternal Affectional System' in *Determinants of Infant Behaviour*, ed. B. M. Foss, vol. II, Methuen, 1963

3 ibid., p. 24

4 H. F. and M. K. Harlow, 'Effects on various Mother—Infant Relationships on Rhesus Monkey Behaviours' in *Determinants of Infant Behaviour*, vol. III, Metheun, 1965, p. 24

5 ibid.

6 H. F. Harlow, S. Suomi and C. J. Domek, 'Effect of Repetitive Infant—Infant Separation in Young Monkeys', in *J. Abnor. Psychol*, vol. 76 (2), 1970, pp. 161—72

7 R. A. Hinde, Y. Spencer-Booth and M. Bruce, 'Effects of Six-Day Maternal Deprivation on Rhesus Monkey Infants', *Nature*, vol. 210, 1966

8 Harlow and Harlow, op. cit. (see Note 4)

9 Harlow, 'The Maternal Affectional System' (see Note 2)

10 Harlow and Suomi, Report to the National Academy of Sciences Meeting in Washington, 1970; also discussed in *New Scientist*, 14 May 1970. See also 'Social Recovery by Isolation-Reared Monkeys', *Proc. Nat. Acad. Sci.*, vol. 68, 1971, pp. 1534—8

11 C. H. Turner, R. K. Davenport and C. M. Rogers, 'The Effect of

Early Deprivation on the Social Behaviour of Adolescent Chimpanzees', *Amer. J. Psychiat.*, vol. 125, 1969

12 W. A. Mason, R. K. Davenport and E. W. Menzel, 'Early Experience and the Social Development of Monkeys and Chimpanzees' in *Early Experience and Behaviour*, R. Newton & S. Levine (eds), Charles C. Thomas, Springfield, Illinois, 1968

17 Instinct and Human Attachment

1 Bowlby, *Attachment and Loss*, Hogarth Press, 1969; Penguin Books, 1971, p. 365
2 ibid., vol. 1, p.85 (Penguin Books)
3 Due to its size and muscular strength, the gorilla is something of an exception. He is not, of course, a plains-dweller and normally has the protection of trees, although it has been observed that some older gorillas, too massive to climb easily, will remain on the ground, where their very bulk stands them in fairly good stead. See George Schaller, *The Year of the Gorilla*, Collins, 1965
4 M. R. A. Chance and C. J. Jolly, *Social Groups of Monkeys, Apes and Men*, Cape, 1970; I. de Vore (ed.), *Primate Behaviour: Field Studies of Monkeys and Apes*, Holt, Rinehart & Winston, 1965; A. M. Schreier, H. F. Harlow and F. Stollmitz (eds), *Behaviour of Non-Human Primates*, vol. 2, Academic Press, 1965
5 R. A. Hinde, 'Rhesus Monkey Aunts' in *Determinants of Infant Behaviour* ed. B. M. Foss, vol. III, Methuem, 1965
6 See M. Chance, 'Mother Monkeys and their Infants' in *Science Journal*, January 1971, for a good summary of the material available on infant-care in wild monkey groups.
7 Bowlby, 'Mother–Child Separation' in *Mental Health and Infant Development* ed. K. Soddy, Routledge & Kegan Paul, 1955. We cannot be interpreted as meaning clan or kin relationships where everyone is interrelated, which might be co-extensive with social ones, if societies are small. He explicitly limits 'family' to 'child-parent', 'husband-wife' and 'parent-child'.
8 Bowlby, *Attachment and Loss*, vol. 1 p. 221 (in the Penguin edition)
9 ibid., p. 357
10 P. H. Wolff, 'The Development of Attention in Young Infants', *Ann. New York Acad. Sci.*, vol. 118, p. 815–30
11 Margaret Mead, *Growing Up in New Guinea*, first published 1930; published in Penguin Books 1963; pp. 60–61 (Penguin edn)
12 Mead, 'A Cultural Anthropologist's Approach to Maternal Deprivation' in *Deprivation of Maternal Care: A Reassessment of its Effects*, WHO, Geneva, 1962
13 Mead, *Coming of Age in Samoa* first published 1928; published in Penguin Books, 1961
14 Wolff, 'Natural History of Crying . . .' in *Determinants of Infant Behaviour*, ed. B. M. Foss, vol. IV, Methuen, 1965

15   H. F. Harlow, 'The Maternal Affectional System', in *Determinants of Infants Behaviour*, vol. II, Metheun, 1963

16   H. Orlansby, 'Infant Care and Personality', *Psychol. Bull.*, 46, 1949

17   W. A. Mason Motivational Aspects of Social Responsiveness in Young Chimpanzees', in *Early Behaviour*, H. W. Stevenson, E. H. Hess and H. W. Rhinegold (eds), John Wiley

18   W. A. Mason, 'Determinants of Social Behaviour in Young Chimpanzees' in Schreier, Harlow and Stollmitz (eds), *Behaviour of Non-Human Primates* (see Note 4)

19   Harlow, op. cit.

20   Chance (see Note 6)

21   Harlow, 'The Development of Affectional Patterns in Infant Monkeys' in *Determinants of Infant Behaviour* (see Note 14), vol. I, p. 87

22   Harlow, *The Maternal Affectional System* (see Note 15)

23   ibid., p. 8

24   Bowlby, 'Mother–Child Separation' (see Note 7)

25   M. D. Salter-Ainsworth, 'The Development of Infant–Mother Interaction among the Garda' in *Determinants of Infant Behaviour*, vol. II, p. 103

18   Early Relationships

1   R. L. Frantz, 'Pattern Vision in Newborn Infants', *Science*, vol. 140, 1963, pp. 295–7

2   B. M. Wilcox and F. L. Clayton 'Infant Visual Fixation on Motion Pictures of the Human Face', *J. Exp. Child Psychol.*, vol. 6, 1968, pp. 22–32

3   Frantz, 'Pattern Discrimination and Selective Attention as Determinants of Perceptual Development from Birth' in A. H. Kidd and J. L. Rivoire (eds), *Perceptual Development in Children*, International ities Press, New York, 1966

4   Frantz 'Visual Perception from Birth as Shown by Pattern Selectivity', *Ann. New York Acad. Sci.*, vol. 118, 1965, pp. 793–814

5   Frantz, 'Pattern Discrimination . . .' (see Note 3)

6   M. Lewis, 'A Developmental Study of Information Processing within the First Three Years of Life: Response Decrement to a Redundant Signal', *Monogr. Soc. Res. Child Devel.*, vol. 34, no. 9, 1969

7   Frantz, 'Visual Experience in Infants: Decreased Attention to Familiar Patterns Relative to Novel Ones', *Science*, vol. 146, 1964, pp. 668–70

8   H. R. Schaffer, 'The Onset of Fear of Strangers and the Incongruity Hypothesis', *J. Child Psychol. Psychiat.*, vol. 7, 1966a, pp. 95–106

9   R. G. Wahler, 'Infant Social Attachments: a Reinforcement Theory Interpretation and Investigation', *Child Devel.*, vol. 38, 1967,

pp. 1079–88

10   Schaffer, op. cit.

11   F. Bodman, 'Constitutional Factors in Institution Children', *J. Men. Sci.*, vol. XCVI, January 1950, p. 252

12   R. S. Illingworth, 'Children in Hospital', *The Lancet* 17 December 1955

13   H. R. Schaffer, 'Some Issues for Research in the Study of Attachment Behaviour', in *Determinants of Infant Behaviour*, ed. B. M. Foss, vol. II, Methuen, 1963

14   ibid., p. 187

15   ibid., p. 187

16   Leon J. Yarrow, 'Research in Dimensions of Early Maternal Care' in *Perspectives in Child Psychology*, (eds), T. D. Spencer and N. Kars (eds), McGraw-Hill, 1970

17   D. A. Freedman, 'Hereditary Control of Early Social Behaviour' in *Determinants of Infant Behaviour*, vol. III

18   S. Scarr, 'Social Introversion-Extraversion as a Heritable Response', *Child Devel.*, vol. 40, 1969, pp. 823–32

19   H. R. Schaffer and P. Emerson, 'The Development of Social Attachments in Infancy', *Monogr. Soc. Res. Child. Devel.*, vol. 29, No. 3, 1964a

20   ibid.

21   Margaret Mead, *Growing Up in New Guinea*, first published 1930; published in Penguin Books, 1963

22   Harriette Wilson, *Delinquency and Child Neglect*, Allen & Unwin, 1962

23   ibid., pp. 98 and 99–100

24   ibid., p. 140

25   Stacey *et al.*, *Hospitals, Children and their Families*, Routledge & Kegan Paul, 1970

26   Harriette Wilson, op. cit.

27   Margaret Mead, op. cit., p. 87

28   ibid. p. 94

29   ibid., p. 71

30   ibid., p. 76

31   ibid., p. 94

32   ibid., p. 96

33   Esther N. Goody, 'The Varieties of Fostering', *New Society*, 5 August 1971

34   Goody, *Contexts of Kinship*, Cambridge University Press, 1973

35   See Peter Laslett's *The World We Have Lost*, Methuen, 1965, for a full discussion of child placement in pre-industrial society.

36   *Nichomachean Ethics*, Book IX, 9

37   S. Smith and S. Noble, 'Battered Children and their Parents', *New Society*, 15 November 1973

38   A sample of teenage parents showed them to be 'impatient and irritable towards their children – with unrealistic expectations'; they easily resorted to heavy punishments. Teenage parents 'show greater intolerance'. Article in *The Times Educational Supplement*,

21 September 1973
39 Laslett, op. cit.
40 At the time of writing this has not, in fact, been conclusively demonstrated, but is based largely on hearsay and anecdote. Since bad parents are predominantly young, one wonders about the experience of older parents who, in their turn, had bad parents.
41 George Schaller, *The Year of the Gorilla*, Collins, 1965

19 Love and Goodness

1 Priscilla Chapman, *Families Today*, Fontana, 1969, p. 86
2 An experiment was alledgedly once proposed to keep a child in isolation until the age of about ten, to find out whether the natural language of man was Hebrew or Greek!

20 Learning Morality

1 A particularly grotesque example of the error of equating morality with the emotion of love arose in the Sharon Tate murder trial. One of the girls who, while drugged, had stabbed the victim repeatedly, was asked at her trial whether she had realised that what she was doing was wrong. She asked, how could it be wrong when it was done with love? This kind of answer strains meaning to the utmost, but the only kind of sense it seems to have is the idea that the test for whether anything is wrong is simply the presence or absence of a certain sensation at that moment. This sensation the girl on trial was somehow able to identify as 'love'.
2 It would, perhaps, seem possible to represent rational moral conviction as itself a reinforcer, so that conflicts of this kind are really decided by which reinforcer is stronger. But this would be an extension of the concept of reinforcement to cover virtually every kind of human motivation and would empty it of all distinct scientific content.
3 P. H. Nowell-Smith, *Ethics*, Penguin Books, 1954
4 This is not to say that there cannot be conflicts, even irreconcilable ones, but rather that very widespread and general conflict over fundamentals would take away the conditions for our being the social species we are.

21 Conclusions

1 The sons of men in professional, semi-professional and managerial occupations are now well represented in investigations of delinquent behaviour — *The Teacher*, June 1970.
2 *Probationers in their Social Environment*, HMSO. This document drew attention to the high standards of material conditions in the

homes of most probationers and to the presence of boys with fathers in the high income bracket.

3 Michael Young and Peter Wilmott, *Family and Kinship in East London*, first published 1957, rev. edn, Penguin Books, 1962

Acknowledgements

Acknowledgement is made to the following for their kind permission to reprint material from copyright sources: University of London Press Ltd (Sir Cyril Burt, *The Young Delinquent*); Oxford University Press (J. Shields, *Monozygotic Twins*); Penguin Books (John Bowlby, *Child Care and the Growth of Love*); *The Lancet* (letter from John Bowlby of 1 March 1958; D. H. Stott, 'Effects of Separation from the Mother in Early Life'); *New Society* (D. H. Stott, 'Why Maladjustment?'); Allen & Unwin (Harriette Wilson, *Delinquency and Child Neglect*); The Nuffield Foundation (*Deprived Children: the Mershal Experiment* published by Oxford University Press); The Institute for the Study and Treatment of Delinquency (S. Naess, 'Mother–Child Separation and Delinquency'; J. G. Field, 'Two Types of Recidivist and Maternal Deprivation'; J. Cockburn and I. Maclay, 'Sex Differentials in Juvenile Delinquents': all published in the *British Journal of Criminology*, formerly the *British Journal of Delinquency*); Dr William Sargent, William Heinemann Ltd and Little, Brown & Co. (*The Unquiet Mind*), also published by Pan Books; Michael Craft and the Pergamon Press (*Psychopathic Disorders and their Assessment*); The World Health Organisation (John Bowlby, *Maternal Care and Mental Health*, Monograph Series No. 2, 1952; Mary D. Ainsworth *et al.*, *Deprivation of Maternal Care: a Reassessment of its Effects*, Public Health Papers No. 14, 1962); William Morrow and Company Inc. (Margaret Mead, *Growing Up in New Guinea*, also published in Britain by Penguin Books; *Male and Female*, also published in Britain in hardback by Victor Gollancz Ltd and in paperback by Penguin Books); The Hogarth Press Ltd (*The Complete Psychological Works of Sigmund Freud*, Standard Edition, vols X, XI and XX, *The Predicament of the Family*, ed. Peter Lomas); The Hogarth Press and the Melanie Klein Trustees

(Melanie Klein, *The Psychoanalysis of Children*); Basic Books Inc., New York (John Bowlby, *Attachment and Loss; Collected Papers of Sigmund Freud,* ed. Ernest Jones, vol. III, trans. Alix and James Strachey, published by arrangement with The Hogarth Press Ltd and the Institute of Psychoanalysis); W. W. Norton & Company Inc., New York (Sigmund Freud, *The Question of Lay Analysis,* also published in Britain by Penguin Books); Routledge & Kegan Paul Ltd (*Mental Health and Infant Development,* ed. K. Soddy; M. Stacey *et al., Hospitals, Children and their Families; On the Bringing Up of Children,* ed. J. Rickman); James Robertson and the Tavistock Clinic (*Young Children in Brief Separations* reprinted from *The Psychoanalytic Study of the Child*); The British Psychological Society (John Bowlby, Mary D. Ainsworth, M. Boston and D. Rosenbluth, 'The Effects of Mother–Child Separation: A Follow-up Study', *British Journal of Medical Psychology*); The Institute of Psychoanalysis and John Bowlby (*Forty-four Juvenile Thieves,* first published in the *International Journal of Psychoanalysis* and issued as a separate volume by Baillière, Tindall & Cox); Liveright Publishing Corporation (*Five Lectures on Psychoanalysis* in *General Selection from the Works of Sigmund Freud,* ed. J. Rickman, also published in Britain by Penguin Books); *British Journal of Psychiatry* and Professor L. L. Heston (L. L. Heston, D. D. Denney and I. B. Pauly, 'The Adult Adjustment of Persons Institutionalised as Children', in vol. 112 of the *British Journal of Psychiatry,* pp. 1103–10)

In addition I have to thank Professor H. J. Eysenck for his encouraging support for this book. I am also greatly indebted to Stephen Williams, who has read and discussed the work at every stage, making many important suggestions and criticisms and helping particularly with the sections on scientific methodology and moral education. My gratitude, too, to Mike and Ruth Garrod, who assessed the book from the standpoint of the educated lay reader and suggested a number of basic alterations, nearly all of which I have incorporated. And finally my ⁹thanks to Susan Mason, who typed the manuscript and showed such an interest in the material — a friend in need.